Raceform describes the going for the  on the round course and soft in the s ... the 2½ miles race, the probable favou ... form on soft ground, and over the ext ... the Paradise Stakes at Ascot over 2 m ... finished 3 lengths second to Ramsin ... Du Cadran on soft going in May. The ... admittedly beating Rock Roi by 4 len ... ous year's St Leger had never encountered anything softer than "dead" ground, or tackled a trip any further than 2 miles. So that it looked at the time, as it still does today on re-reading the form, that given the conditions, the consistent Rock Roi was near-enough "home-and-hosed".

I can remember arguing as much when discussing the race with Bert*, a colleague from work, in the pub that lunchtime. And I seem to have convinced him, because knowing I was intent on slipping out to the betting shop that afternoon, he asked me to put on a bet for him as well. And of the two of us sitting at that table, it certainly wasn't Bert who nearly fell off his stool when he produced the £50 - which was the equivalent of almost two weeks' salary at that time.

In the race itself, Rock Roi took the lead from over two furlongs out and went on to win as expected; 4 lengths ahead of Random Shot, with Charlton finishing 18 lengths further back behind Orioso in 4th. Opening at 3/1, Rock Roi started at 2's, and my records show my "paltry" £5 going on at 11/4, presumably accompanied by Bert's impressive £50.

If Rock Roi had been disqualified, as he was to be in 1972, then clearly things might have been different. But he wasn't**. And so it was at that point that I first came to realise two things. One, that while there was sometimes good money to be made, it was always more likely to go to people such as Bert, with his seeming indifference towards the value of money; rather than to someone more inclined to go weak at the knees at the very thought of risking £50. And two, recounting this story to other people at the time, simply brought home the fact that 99% of the population would probably have never even heard of Rock Roi in the first place. So that while racing might always provide an interest, as it was unlikely to ever fund any sort of extravagant lifestyle, it might be an idea to try and keep things in perspective. And to occasionally stand back from the daily preoccupation with form and results, so as to find time for other things. Such as for instance, producing a book about, er...

* Readers can rest assured that if I were making any of this up, "Bert" isn't exactly the first name I'd choose. So sorry Bert if you're still around. And now about that drink...

Secrets of Successful Betting
Michael Adams

Published in 2002 by Raceform Ltd
Compton, Newbury, Berkshire, RG20 6NL
Raceform Ltd is a wholly owned subsidiary of MGN Ltd.

A catalogue record for this book is available from the British Library.

ISBN 1-901100-09-X

Set in 10pt ITC Bookman Light.
Typesetting and layout by the author.

Printed by Bookcraft, Midsomer Norton.

Contents

Contents

Introduction

Scope and Objectives

What's often lacking in books about betting is any really satisfactory account of book-makers and the betting market. And yet these areas can be important, because whatever approach is taken to form and selection, it's the betting market alone that allows those without access to specialised or inside information, to occasionally bet at favourable prices. And so these are the topics which are considered first.

Attention then turns to a number of other equally neglected aspects of betting, including hedging bets and coupling prices, a novel way of appraising each-way bets, the real problem with all multiple bets, and a critical look at the most commonly suggested alternatives to level staking.

And while there may seem to be quite a few tables, these are solely concerned with fairly routine aspects of the betting market and staking, and have nothing to do with any "rocket science" concerning the selection process itself; which instead concentrates mainly on those aspects of form, whose significance seems most often to be overlooked by the market in general,

And so to this end, the book is divided into three main parts. The first is concerned with betting and staking; the second with form and selection; while the final reference section contains all the longer tables - some of which provide information which seems to be largely unavailable elsewhere - together with any other material whose inclusion earlier on would have badly interrupted the overall flow.

General Approach

Many people back horses for much the same reason they and others may also buy lottery tickets - for entertainment, and the excitement which stems from the uncertainty of the outcome. And for the possibility however remote, of a big return. Which are things that they can't necessarily find anywhere else. So that while it may be thought useful for books supposedly aimed at the so-called "serious punter", which are anyway often riddled with errors themselves, to try and distance themselves from the majority who bet mainly for pleasure and interest, often by just simply referring to them all as "mugs", there'll be none of that nonsense here.

But whether it's directed at "serious punters" or not, the fact remains that the subject matter of much of this book makes fairly heavy going. And so by way of relief, a more whimsical note has been struck on occasion, relying mainly on short extracts from the work of Robert Lynd, and a poem by R.B. Paterson; further details of whom can be found on page 194.

It's maybe no coincidence, that the front-page splash chosen for the first issue of the re-launched tabloid "Sun" in Nov.1969, was "HORSE DOPE SENSATION"; as race fixing and doping stories can always be relied on to provide good sensational copy. And in the same way, hardly a year goes by without yet another exposé in the Press or on TV, high-lighting all the latest injustices being meted out to the hapless punters; whether they concern fraudulent tipsters, bookies who've made a run for it, horses which quite clearly didn't, or maybe more seriously, manipu-lated s.p's Here though, its been decided to stay firmly on the sidelines, for three main reasons. First, because whatever the merits of their case, aggrieved parties in such dis-putes are often talking out of their pockets anyway; second, because many of these things tend to even themselves out in the long run; and third, because the airing of such griev-ances, however well justified, simply isn't the intended purpose of this book.

Terminology

While the term "punter" has an impeccable sporting pedigree, nowadays it seems it can be applied to the customers and clients of almost any kind of business; although not necessarily by the customers themselves. And so for these reasons, the word "backer" has been used throughout instead, to refer to anyone who speculates, however unwisely, on the outcome of horse races. While for much the same reasons, all bogus over-reliance on bookmakers' slang has also been avoided.

Although in their time women have pioneered mathematical racing systems - as did Byron's daughter Lady Ada Lovelace, while losing the family fortune in the process; have represented Ladbrokes on the rails, as did Mrs Helen Vernet; and have bet as fear-lessly as did the Hon Dorothy Paget and Mrs Pat Rank; although in the latter case using her husband's money, which is probably the best system of all, unless otherwise stated, all participants in this book whether human or equine are assumed to be male.

And Finally

The horses whose stirring names were used for some of the examples, originally ran in the Waterloo Handicap Hurdle which took place at Haydock Park on Feb 2nd 1967, and which was won incidentally by Josh Gifford on Ross Clan at 9/4.

Part One:
Betting

Bookmakers

But if ever there was a body of men who deserve to prosper it's the bookmakers. They are respectable, indefatigable, charitable men. They are charitable, not in the niggling fashion of Organised Charities but with the gracious fairy-tale and Father Christmas charity. They give you money without asking you to work for it.

No employer I ever knew offered me a five-pound note for guessing the name of a horse. Yet that is what every bookmaker, even the humblest of them, does daily. If I guessed West Countryman the fault cannot be imputed to the bookmakers. They were perfectly willing to pay out if I guessed Grandcourt.

Robert Lynd

1:Bookmakers

This chapter tries to give a realistic account of how bookmakers operate, and in the process explains what's meant by such terms as overround prices, field money, and takeouts. And possibly the simplest way to do this, is to follow the way these ideas have developed from the earliest days.

Bookmaking in the modern sense only emerged during the latter half of the 18th century, as most betting before then was between private individuals. However these early bookmakers probably did most of their business in the cockpits; as until they were finally outlawed in the mid 19th century, cockfights were among the most popular sporting events of their time, attracting considerable betting from partisan crowds drawn from all sections of society.

While at the races, up until the 1840's both the bookmakers and backers could be found gathered around a betting-post situated alongside the course. * Because in the days before purpose-built enclosures and grandstands, many of the spectators would either be mounted on horseback themselves or riding in carriages, from where they would follow the races. The bookmakers however usually remained on foot, which is believed to account for one of their earliest nicknames of "legs".

---

* Much of the off-course and ante (betting) post betting at the time was conducted in the Betting Rooms, the most famous of which was attached to Richard Tattersall's Auction Rooms at Hyde Park Corner; itself close to another favoured haunt of the racing fraternity, the Turf Tavern. However, only the more established bookmakers were admitted into the Room itself, while the others had to conduct all their business outside. Then, when the betting enclosures were set up on the racecourses, the name and the custom were preserved. So that even 200 years later, all the most important business is conducted by the bookmakers who operate **inside** Tattersall's Enclosure or **Tatts**, either along the rails or on the boards; whereas all the bookmakers with pitches in the cheaper enclosures, are said to be betting **outside**.

Match Betting

Horse races at that time took various forms, ranging from matches to events run in long series of heats. But maybe the single biggest difference from today was in the distances run, as races of five miles and over were not that uncommon. And there was a significant difference in the betting as well. Because no matter how many runners there were in any race, the bookmakers would only ever offer two prices, one for the favourite and another for the rest of the field.

Overround Prices

One advantage in only having to offer two prices, was that it was virtually impossible for the bookmakers to make a mistake. As they would for example if they were to offer 11/10 against both runners in a two horse race; as anyone who backed both horses for the same amount would then be assured of a profit. And any set of prices which would allow such a possibility are described as being **overbroke**, whereas prices which prevent it are said to be **overround**. And finally in theory at least, it's also possible for a set of prices to be **fair**, so that they favour neither backers nor bookmakers.

In the early days therefore, it was quite easy for the bookmakers to ensure that their prices were always overround; because with the favourite inevitably quoted at odds-on, all that was needed was for the other price to be smaller than the equivalent price at odds against. So that if for instance the favourite was 4/6, the price of the other runner would need to be smaller than 6/4 against. And while overround prices in

themselves couldn't guarantee the bookmakers a profit on every race, they at least helped them to avoid the inevitable losses which would have resulted from their betting overbroke.

Field Money and Takeouts

Before looking at some actual examples, it's first necessary to define two other technical terms. The first of these is the **field money**, which refers to the total amount staked on all the runners in any particular race - the bookmaker's total receipts in other words. The second is the **takeout**, which refers to the total amount including returned stakes which he would have to pay out on any one particular horse in the event of it winning; so that every runner in a race has its own separate takeout. And it's by constantly comparing the field money with his biggest takeouts, that the bookmaker can keep track of his liabilities, and his overall position, during the course of betting on a race.

Betting to Figures

Field money, takeouts, and overround prices all form part of what's known as **betting to figures**, which became widespread, once the bookmakers came to realise that they didn't have to rely on superior knowledge of form in order to outwit backers. But that instead, all they needed to do to stay ahead of the game, was ensure that their prices were always overround, and that by the start of the race, their field money always exceeded their biggest takeouts. And some of the general principles can be seen in the simplified match book opposite.

This table shows the stakes, field money, and takeouts for a match in which all the bets have been struck at the same two prices - at some time prior to the off.

stake	price		takeout
£300	1 / 3	New Liskeard	£400
£50	2 / 1	Pinewood	£150

field money

£350

With only £350 field money and a takeout of £400 on the favourite, the book stands to lose £50 if it wins; although with only £150 to pay out on Pinewood it stands to win £200 if it loses.

Beside standing the £50 loss, the bookmaker has two other options. Firstly he could try and attract more support for Pinewood, which in reality might mean having to ease the price to say 9/4. However to keep things simple for the moment, assuming he managed to take a further £75 at the same price of 2/1, then the situation would be as follows -

stake	price		takeout
£300	1 / 3	New Liskeard	£400
£125	2 / 1	Pinewood	£375

field money

£425

Which now gives the book a profit of £25 if the favourite wins, and £50 if it loses.

Another option, would be to lay off some of the liabilities on New Liskeard. If for instance £180 of the field money was staked on the favourite with another bookmaker at 1/3, then this would cancel out £240's worth of liabilities on the horse, while still leaving the field money bigger than either of the takeouts.

stake	price		takeout
£120	1 / 3	New Liskeard	£160
(£300-£180)			(£400-£240)
£50	2 / 1	Pinewood	£150

field money

£170
(£350-£180)

Which again gives a profit whichever horse wins.

The Growth in Sweepstakes

While betting was mainly confined to the cockpits and competitive matches, there was still always a chance for bookmakers to balance their books in one way or another.

However towards the end of the 18th. century, the number of matches started to decline in the face of the growing popularity of sweepstakes; five of which survive as the Classics of today. At first though, because the bookmakers hadn't yet found a way of framing overround prices for large fields, match betting of a kind still prevailed in every race. So that all the bookmakers present usually offered just two prices, one for an agreed favourite, and another for the rest of the field - presumably because bets laid against any other runners would have been impossible to lay off elsewhere. Although accounts differ, as to whether anyone who wanted to bet against the favourite by backing the field, was actually required to make a selection and name a particular horse.

But the likely effect of this change can be seen in the following table, which uses the same two prices as the previous match.

stake	price		takeout
£33.33	2 / 1	Nomme De Guerre	£100
£75	1 / 3	Vittorio Senechio Marquita Tamorn Charlemagne	£100
field money £108.33			

Because the field has the shortest price it's now technically the favourite. However what would normally be considered to be the favourite - the horse which appears to have the best chance, and so is thought likely to attract the most support, is in fact Nomme De Guerre.

The problem now though, as can clearly be seen from the figures, was that anyone who wanted to back one particular horse, rather than simply the whole field against the favourite, would have had to accept a much shorter price for their selection than was available for the favourite itself, which supposedly had the better chance.

And so, as many such backers probably chose not to bet at all, the bookmakers no longer had any realistic chance of balancing their books, as they still could do in the cockpits, and had previously done with matches. And the growth in the popularity of sweepstakes and handicaps meant these problems could only get worse; at least until a solution of some sort could be found.

Ogden

According to most accounts, it was a Lancashire bookmaker called Ogden who was the first to offer a separate price for every runner in a race: and this is said to have occurred at Newmarket in 1790, ten years after the first running of the Derby. Quite how he managed it isn't known, but it may have been connected with takeouts.

In all the examples used so far where it was already known that the two prices were overround, it was fairly easy to calculate a stake for each runner which would produce a takeout which was smaller than the field money - and therefore guarantee a profit whichever horse won. And so possibly Ogden was the first to recognise, that if stakes could be calculated for a full set of prices, which again all produced takeouts which were smaller than the field money, then those prices would be overround as well. Which is easiest to work out, if each of the runners is staked to take out £100.

The first table shows a possible set of prices for the six runners in the last race. With field money of only £95.80, to us these prices are clearly overbroke, giving a profit of £4.20 to anyone who backed every runner to take out £100. Which is exactly what the bookmakers at the time were all afraid of.

stake	price		takeout
£33.33	2 / 1	Nomme De Guerre	£100
£20	4 / 1	Vittorio	£100
£16.66	5 / 1	Senechal	£100
£11.11	8 / 1	Marquita	£100
£10	9 / 1	Tamorn	£100
£4.70	20 / 1	Charlemagne	£100
Field Money	£95.80		

However, as Ogden may have been the first to realise, all that was needed was to keep cutting prices until the field money finally came to more than £100. As here, where shortening the second, third, and fourth favourites, turns a guaranteed loss of £4.20 into a potential profit of £8.33.

stake	price		takeout
£33.33	2 / 1	Nomme De Guerre	£100
£25	3 / 1	Vittorio	£100
£20	4 / 1	Senechal	£100
£15.30	11 / 2	Marquita	£100
£10	9 / 1	Tamorn	£100
£4.70	20 / 1	Charlemagne	£100
Field Money	£108.33		

The Ideal State

Any such arrangement of stakes and prices that yields the same profit, no matter which horse wins, is sometimes referred to as the **ideal state**. And it appears in many popular accounts of the subject, by way of explaining how the bookmakers can apparently guarantee themselves a profit in every race. However there's often a big difference between what's supposed to happen in theory and what actually happens in practice, a point which is usually overlooked.

Because in fact, from a bookmaker's point of view, there can be four possible outcomes when making a book. First, there's the ideal state just referred to; which is rarely if ever achieved in practice, because of problems in attracting sufficient support for outsiders. Second, there's betting overround and ensuring some sort of a profit on every horse; which is possible in competitive races where all the runners are seen to have some sort of a chance. Thirdly, and probably the most common, are races where despite offering overround prices, the bookmaker is unable to cover all his liabilities especially on the favourite, and so stands to lose money if it

wins. And lastly there's the possibility of the bookmakers betting overbroke, either individually, or collectively - in terms of their best available prices at the same or at different times. And while such a possibility seems to exercise the imagination of many backers - and sets of overbroke starting prices do in fact crop up from time to time, how often this actually occurs in the course of betting can only be guessed at.

The £100 Takeout

As already noted, the most useful form of the ideal state is the **£100 takeout**. And because the stake needed to take out £100 at any particular price turns out to be the same as the corresponding chance percentage, it also offers a fairly straightforward method of calculating overrounds.

So that for instance, in a race between five evenly matched runners, the chance of any one of them winning is one in five or 20%, and a fair price for picking the winner would be 4/1 against. And likewise when staking £20 at 4/1, as the stake is returned with winning bets, the total return on a winner would again be £100, as shown below.

	equivalent stake			price/chance percentage		takeout
	£20	4 / 1		20%	Nomme De Guerre	£100
	£20	4 / 1		20%	Vittorio	£100
	£20	4 / 1		20%	Senechal	£100
	£20	4 / 1		20%	Marquita	£100
	£20	4 / 1		20%	Tamorn	£100
Field Money	£100			100%		

By shortening these prices to 3/1, the same race can also be used to illustrate the overround.

	equivalent stake		price/chance percentage		takeout
	£25	3 / 1	25%	Nomme De Guerre	£100
	£25	3 / 1	25%	Vittorio	£100
	£25	3 / 1	25%	Senechal	£100
	£25	3 / 1	25%	Marquita	£100
	£25	3 / 1	25%	Tamorn	£100
Field Money	£125		125%		

So that now, with prices representing a total chance percentage of 125%, and the field money therefore standing at £125, with a £100 takeout the bookmaker is assured of a £25 profit whichever horse wins.

The Totality of Prices

In effect, by offering all five horses in this last race at 3/1, the bookmaker is attempting to sell 25% or one quarter shares in the outcome of the race to five different people. What makes this possible, is that backers tend to overestimate the chances of their own selections anyway. So that in this case it's not inconceivable, that the backers of all the five runners could sincerely believe that their own selection had a better than 25% chance. And while this example may appear somewhat exaggerated, it's still likely that if the collective judgements of the backers of the various runners in any really competitive race were expressed in percentage terms, they'd add up to more than 100% anyway. And without the need for any prompting from the bookmakers.

In technical terms, bookmakers are said to be concerned with the **totality of prices,** whereas backers are normally only interested in one, that of their own selection.

And even among backers who are aware that prices overall are stacked against them, the majority will naturally tend to assume that this will always be at the expense of other less knowledgeable backers, rather than at their own.

Percentages and Rates of Return

By using percentages it's a fairly simple matter to calculate overrounds, and the bookmaker's theoretical rate of return. So that in the last example the overround was 25 percent. This is 1/5th or 20 percent of the total 125 percent and so gives the bookmaker a 20 percent rate of return - rather than 25 percent as it might at first appear.

It's important not to make the mistake of assuming, that because the overround for the race as a whole is 25 percent, the overround for each runner will only be 5 percent. The point is that this 5 percent still represents 1/5th of the horse's price percentage. And so in any race, on average the overround and the rate of return on each runner will be the same as for the race overall, after allowance is made for the bias in prices described in chapter 2.

Further information about prices and percentages, including full sets of tables, and alternative methods of working them out, can be found on page 120.

Conclusion

It might seem as though bookmaking has progressed a long way in the last 200 years; and that this has only been made possible through mathematics, and advances in bookmaking theory.

And yet throughout all that time, the bookmakers' biggest stand-by has still always been their ability to lay horses, most especially favourites, at prices which turn out to have been marginally too short. Because while they can expect to lose overall whenever the favourite wins, the point is that this only occurs in around 33% of races, and then at an average price of 7/4.

But then this is only possible anyway, because backers, in their enthusiasm and their willingness to risk their money on horses at all, can often be inclined to overestimate their actual chances. And exactly the same holds true, whether the backers in question were acting on an overheard remark in the Turf Tavern of 200 years ago, or are following a leading ratings service of the present day.

Because no matter how much information is made available, and whatever form it takes, the bookmakers can always rely on two things. Firstly, as information increases so does the potential for confusion among backers. And secondly, a sizeable majority of those backers can always be relied on to read rather more into any information that they do consider relevant, than may be strictly warranted by the facts; certainly when judging by results.

This is why bookmakers have been able to survive the introduction of home video recorders, which in theory have the potential to revolutionise race-reading; and why in reality, backers have very little to gain overall, from proposals such as the compulsory declaration of horses' racing weights.

Bookmakers' Badges

Some of the bookmakers wore horseshoes in their buttonholes with their names printed on them. They wore them, I noticed, the wrong way up. A horseshoe should be worn with the heels pointing upwards - cup shaped, so to speak - so as not to spill the luck out. Even so I am forced to admit that the bookmakers looked more prosperous than I do, with my five rusty horseshoes all in the right position above the mantelpiece.

R.L.

2:The Betting Market

This chapter describes various aspects of the on-course betting market, including the market mechanism itself, the scale of prices used, and the contrasting attitudes of bookmakers and backers to those prices; and also how backers can make use of this knowledge to secure the best prices.

It's the prices being offered in Tattersall's Ring, which determine both the screen or board prices relayed to the betting shops prior to the off, and the starting prices announced shortly afterwards. And those ring prices are themselves the product of two main factors; the level of opening prices, and the market mechanism which governs price changes once betting has begun.

Opening Prices

Opening prices may simply follow the forecast "tissue" prices which are circulated by the on-course bookmakers' organisations, or they could be the work of individual bookmakers and the specialist odds-compilers who may also be responsible for their early

and ante-post prices. And what's worth bearing in mind about all such prices, is that they're not necessarily intended to reflect the horse's actual chances; but rather how it's thought the betting public are likely to view the race, given the information they can be expected to have at their disposal.

And while in general, public opinion can sometimes turn out to be notoriously fickle, in the more limited area of racing with its recognised opinion formers such as the press and the various ratings services, it's still going be more predictable than are the actual results of races, which will always remain subject to far greater uncertainty.

Also, because of the way such prices are compiled, it's maybe not surprising if they can often show a fair degree of unanimity as well. All of which can only suit the bookmakers anyway; given that they're usually more concerned with betting to figures by making a balanced book, rather than running up substantial liabilities on just the one or two overpriced horses.

The Market Mechanism

The most important market mechanism on the racecourse, is the one by which the bookmakers quote cramped opening prices, which are deliberately set two or three points short of the prices at which they eventually expect to bet. And then, by gradually easing those prices in small steps, they're able to generate just enough support for each horse at the shortest possible price.

The bookmakers are also helped by the fact that among the supporters for any particular horse, there are always going to be those who are more enthusiastic about its chances than the rest. And it's these more optimistic backers who are going to be the first to take any price. Which can then present their more cautious, or maybe more realistic, fellow backers with something of a dilemma: which is to either settle for that price themselves or to wait, only to see it possibly shorten up again.

And so it could be said that it's these over-enthusiastic backers accepting what turn out to be unrealistically short prices who really drive the market; and so provide the bookmakers with most of their income.

The extent of this over-optimism can be seen in the following table, which gives the results for 13 sample starting prices taken from the data beginning on page 149. These show the minimum price at which it would have been possible to show a profit when backing those horses. The fifth column also shows the number of steps between this target price and the actual starting price.

actual price	runners	winners	target price	steps
1 / 3	55	40	2 / 5	2
1 / 2	137	88	4 / 7	2
10 / 11	357	182	1 / 1	2
11 / 8	606	248	6 / 4	2
6 / 4	744	259	15 / 8	3
2 / 1	1448	418	5 / 2	2
9 / 4	1567	425	11 / 4	2
3 / 1	2519	571	7 / 2	2
4 / 1	3491	593	5 / 1	2
5 / 1	4177	607	6 / 1	2
10 / 1	6483	508	12 / 1	2
20 / 1	8810	221	40 / 1	6
33 / 1	11141	123	100 / 1	7

So that for instance, there were 1448 runners starting at 2/1, and of these 418 won. However if the backers in question had only held off, even when the price first eased to 9/4, and had waited instead for the 5/2, then they would have made a profit on those races of £15 to a £1 stake.

What's also worth noting is that these figures are based solely on starting prices. And so because the shortest prices are quite likely to have been shortened up again before the off, in some cases it's quite possible that earlier on in the betting, some of these may have come closer to the target price than the final figure indicates.

Opening Prices II

Given what's already been said, clearly bookmakers have to be especially careful when setting their opening prices. So that if say they laid a horse directly off an opening price of 11/10, when possibly they could have laid it at evens or 10/11 instead, then this is simply throwing money away. So that book-makers don't normally expect their opening prices to be taken. Which is why backers would usually be best advised to keep their hands in their pockets as well.

The Scale of Prices Used

Confusion can often arise because of the undue significance which some backers, especially value enthusiasts, can place in bookmakers' prices. Because it's all too easy to run away with the idea that these prices, such as say evens, 11/10, and 5/4, must bear some relation to the runners' actual chances in the race.

However as has just been seen in relation to the opening show, the scale of prices used seems to be primarily designed to suit the bookmakers' own convenience. Because it clearly makes sense for them to ease their prices by the smallest possible steps which are compatible with the limited time there is available for betting on each race. So that if for instance, it's possible to generate just enough support for a horse by easing its price from even-money to 11/10, then it would clearly be foolish to instead ease the price straight to 5/4.

And in addition to this, every time the bookmakers ease the price of a horse they're taking the initiative; and so they're exerting psychological pressure of a kind on backers to respond in some way. And tightly grouped prices offer them much more scope for such changes, or "triggers", with which to spur the more reluctant backers into action.

Another factor governing prices was their close relationship to pre-decimal currency, which they show up to advantage. So that for instance with 8 half-crowns to the £1, 11/8 represented £1 7s 6d (£1.37½p) or 11 half-crowns to £1, 13/8 represented £1 12s 6d (£1.62½p) to £1, and so on. While with 20 shillings to the £1, 100 shillings was £5. So that 100/6 was equivalent to £5 to 6s (30p); 100/8 represented £5 to 8s (40p); and 100/30 was £5 to 30s (£1.50p). And one advantage of such prices may have been that they greatly simplified the calculation of returns. But while that may no longer apply, there's no doubt that they still seem to roll off the tongue rather more easily than do some of their suggested decimal replacements.

Contrasting Attitudes to Prices

While it may only seem to be stating the obvious, in fact there's more than one reason why bookmakers are always looking to lay the shortest possible prices.

Firstly, the shorter the price, the more field money it generates in relation to the takeout, or liabilities incurred. So that while at even-money every £200 of takeout represents £100 of field money, to generate that same amount of field money at 10/1 would mean taking on a liability of £1100.

Secondly and related to this, the shorter a price is, the bigger proportion of business it represents for the book. So that while an even-money chance could be expected to provide at least half if not more of the field money, the 10/1 chance would normally only ever produce a fifth as much, if that.

And thirdly, bookmakers can be naturally suspicious of anyone taking an unhealthy interest in outsiders with little apparent chance; as clearly such situations offer far greater scope to those in possession of inside or specialised information.

Backers on the other hand, whether they back favourites or outsiders, will naturally always want to bet at the biggest possible prices: even despite maybe knowing in the backs of their minds, that shorter prices do in fact generally produce the best returns.

All of which can create something of a problem, the consequences of which can be seen in the following table. This is based on the starting price bands table on page 150, and gives the backer's percentage return on turnover for 8 price-bands, which cover the entire range.

Price band			runners	winners	percent	capital	pcreturn
1 / 28	-	2 / 5	386	304	78.76	5.46	1.41
40 / 95	-	4 / 5	1490	839	56.31	-108.45	-7.28
5 / 6	-	6 / 4	3524	1479	41.97	-277.17	-7.87
13 / 8	-	3 / 1	10971	2975	27.12	-1111.00	-10.13
100 / 30	-	15 / 2	28865	4204	14.56	-3553.17	-12.31
8 / 1	-	16 / 1	39534	2442	6.18	-10066.50	-25.46
18 / 1	-	60 / 1	35557	540	1.52	-20434.00	-57.47
66 / 1	-	500 / 1	5883	17	0.29	-4456.00	-75.74
			126210	**12800**	**10.14**	**-40000.83**	**-31.69**

Taken overall therefore, rates of return for backers are inversely proportional to prices - i.e. the smaller the price the higher the rate of return is likely to be. Which is maybe only what's to be expected, given the

bookmakers' need to lay short prices for the biggest amounts and their general unpopularity with backers. And just as with the previous table, because the shortest prices are the most likely to be shortened up again before the off, figures such as these which are based solely on starting prices, may well tend to understate the disparity in returns, between long and short prices.

The Pattern of Betting

In terms of betting patterns, horse races cover a complete spectrum, with highly competitive handicaps with 10/1 joint-favourites at one end, and races featuring odds-on favourites at the other. And generally speaking, the shorter the price of the favourite in any race, the more clearly defined will be the pattern of the betting. And this can be confirmed in the betting ring itself, by following SIS or Teletext betting shows, or by studying the betting reports in the racing press.

In races with a clear favourite, every bookmaker will usually be trying to lay that favourite first, so as to get as much field money into his book ahead of the competition; all of whom needless to say, will be trying to do exactly the same thing. So that in general the prices of favourites can be expected to be eased first, by at least one or two points from the opening show, until they've generated enough support. Following which they may well be shortened up again, as the bookmakers ease other prices in an attempt to lay the rest of the field. However with the favourites safely in the book, they can become progressively less enthusiastic as they work their way down the card, and their prices may tend to reflect this.

There can though be two exceptions to this pattern, where instead of being eased up, opening prices are taken and shorten up straight away. The first, are horses which may have already featured heavily in early betting on the day of the race, while the second are long-odds-on favourites. Because in their desperation to lay really short prices, it seems that the bookmakers are sometimes prepared to do almost anything to avoid scaring the backers away entirely; even to the extent of occasionally offering favourable opening prices. So that paradoxically, the shorter an opening price is, the greater the chance of it being taken-up straight away.

Whereas in competitive handicaps with joint or co-favourites, there may often be no obvious pattern to the betting at all, as various bookmakers try to lay different horses at one and the same time. Which can then offer anyone betting on-course a big advantage, as there are likely to be much greater differences in the prices on offer, than are being reflected in any of the off-course betting shows.

Taking Prices

According to the account given earlier, it might seem as if the betting market is always going to find itself at the mercy of incurable optimists, jumping in and accepting what turn out to be unrealistically short prices. However the point is, that this mainly applies to the more popular types of horses on which the bookmakers take most of their money; rather than to the types of selection which, for that very reason, are singled out for attention in the second part of this book. And so it can still be worth following some general rules, so as to obtain the best price wherever possible.

Opening Prices III

For the reasons just given, and apart from the exceptions just mentioned, these should generally be avoided.

Cramped Starting Prices

When backing popular favourites, it can be equally important not to wait too long either; or even worse accept starting price. The reason for this is that office money for such horses is often placed on-course as late as possible. However this isn't being done to hedge liabilities as such, which would normally be done at the best possible prices; but rather to force down prices even further, after they've already been shortened up in preparation for the off.

Other Runners

Many runners in the middle order of the betting and outsiders, scarcely move in the betting at all, and so the rule against betting at opening prices hardly applies. However unless there's clear evidence that a horse is attracting support, there's no reason for not waiting as long as possible; especially when backing outsiders, which usually ease up much nearer to the off in any case. And while many of these may never appear to exceed their starting prices, it should often be possible to improve on that price when betting on-course, by looking around.

Taking Prices Conclusion

To secure the best prices therefore, it's necessary to have some idea of the likely pattern, if any, of the betting beforehand. Then as the betting gets under way, to note which prices are being taken and which aren't, and how this is likely to affect the price of your own selection. All of which is that much easier, when betting on-course.

Whereas anyone betting off-course and having to rely on SIS or Teletext betting shows, is clearly at a disadvantage in this respect; when the first indication they often have of any interest being shown, is when a price shortens up again. And so given this lack of information, there's possibly more excuse for their sometimes jumping in too early, and taking a price which maybe then drifts out by a point or two.

And two different remedies are sometimes suggested for this. The first is to only take a price once it's been taken, and so has already shortened up. But while this might help avoid further short-term disappointments, deliberately seeking out second-best prices, hardly seems to be a recipe for long-term success. While the other suggestion is to have an extra bet or bets at the bigger price(s). However this not only undermines the principle of level staking recommended in chapter 4, but it could also be seen simply as a vain attempt, to compensate for the earlier miscalculation.

Half-and-Half Staking

One possible approach which seems to avoid the very worst of these disadvantages, is to instead split the stake in two. And then only stake half at the first price taken, and then the other half, or possibly quarter if the price starts to drift, at the next available price. Or if there's no further change before the off, then to again take the original price.

3:Hedging

This chapter covers the topics of hedging, coupling prices, and also making a backer's book. And while all three of these subjects can often overlap to some extent, in this account as far as possible, they've each been treated separately.

Hedging means covering a risk, and so in that sense most bookmaking is already a form of hedging anyway. But other than that, it occurs most often when bookmakers lay off large liabilities on particular horses, by backing them themselves with other book-makers. And there's also another more spec-ulative kind of hedging, which is the preserve of the bookmakers and independent tic-tacs who work in the ring. Here, by virtue of their knowledge of the market and speed of reac-tion, they're often in a position to exploit any price changes the moment they occur: by maybe laying a horse at one price to one firm, while almost simultaneously backing it at a marginally better price elsewhere. And while maybe not as widespread as it once used to be, the possibility of such

hedging activity should never be overlooked when it comes to interpreting market moves.

Backers on the other hand have two main opportunities for hedging individual bets; either when they concern horses which are subsequently involved in photo-finishes, or objections, or horses that have already been backed ante-post.

Hedging on Photo-Finishes

On-course backers may have the chance of hedging, if their original selection is involved in a photo-finish, or more rarely in an objec-tion. This is possible because in really close finishes, whether the favourites are involved or not, the bookmakers will often be keen to lay one or both runners; both so as to drum up some extra business, and if possible to balance their books. Which is why for over twenty years, Alec Bird was able to back his judgement by coolly wagering tens of thousands of pounds on the outcome of photo-finishes, very often at extremely short prices. But whether hedging, as

3 : Hedging

opposed to just betting on photo-finishes is a good idea, is another matter entirely.

The problem here, is that if the original selection which is now in theory at least, an even-money chance, has previously been backed at odds-against, then this is already a favourable bet of a kind which must prove profitable in the long run. And even assuming that the bookmakers were prepared to lay even-money against the other runner, this would still only be a fair price. So that unless the original bet was struck at odds-on, hedging can only reduce the overall rate of return. Although admittedly, in the face of an impending cashflow crisis, or loss of confidence following ten consecutive losers, a short term guaranteed return of both cash and morale, may indeed be more to the point.

Hedging Ante-Post Bets

On the face of it, the same problem of a reduced rate of return would seem to apply equally well when hedging ante-post bets. There can though be an important difference; as some ante-post bets may only be struck in the first place, in the hope of hedging some or all of them at a later stage.

For instance anyone who's certain that a quoted horse is being targeted at a specific race and is therefore sure to run, may want to back it early on. Then, once this information became more widely known, and other more speculative entries dropped out of the reckoning, its price could be expected to shorten. So that regardless of whether it was actually expected to win, by the day of the race it should be possible to hedge some or all of the original bet at a profit: as shown in the following example.

Having originally been backed ante-post at 4/1 to take out £100, Vittorio the original selection has shortened to 7/4 on the day of the race. The prices and percentages of the three other remaining runners are shown below, together with the stake needed to again take out £100.

Backing Vittorio ante-post at 4/1, and then each of the three remaining runners on the day of the race to take out £100, would therefore require a total stake of £93.57: which gives an assured profit of £6.43 on the race, regardless of the result.

	price	percentage	stake	takeout
Vittorio	4 / 1		£20	£100
	(7 / 4)	36.36		
Marquita	5 / 2	28.57	£28.57	£100
Tamorn	3 / 1	25	£25	£100
Charlemagne	4 / 1	20	£20	£100
		109.93	**£93.57**	

One alternative to backing each of the three remaining horses individually, would be to take a price against the field instead. So that in this case, with their price percentages adding up to 73.57, this would give an equivalent price for the field of around 4/11, as shown in the table below. And taking the 4/11 against the field would be exactly the same as laying Vittorio back to the bookmaker at 11/4.

So that whether a hedging bet of some kind is still possible by the day of the race, will depend on how much would need to be staked on the remainder of the field either individually or collectively, to take out the required sum.

	price	percentage	stake	takeout
Vittorio	4 / 1	20	£20	£100
Field	4 / 11	73.57	£73.57	£100
			£93.57	

Takeout Tables

To save time in working out the necessary stakes there's a series of takeout tables beginning on page 143, giving the stake which would be needed to take out six different sums between £25 and £1000 at 92 different prices.

Coupling Prices

A coupled price is the price that results when backing two or more horses in the same race, and the price of 4/11 against the field in the previous race is a good example of this. Or again, if £10 was wagered at 2/1 on two different horses in the one race, then if either of them won the return would be £30; which when the £20 stake is deducted gives winnings of £10, and a coupled price for the pair of 1/2. Which can be confirmed by adding together the two price percentages of 33.3% and 33.3%, to give a total of 66.6%; which is equivalent to 1/2.

Unfortunately, as with the 4/11, not all coupled prices work out exactly. However starting on page 129, there's a series of tables which give the nearest recognised price when coupling any other two prices.

There's also a way of working out approximate coupled prices, by subtracting their combined percentage from 100. So that in the case of the 66.6% just mentioned, this could also be represented as 33/66, which is clearly equivalent to 1/2. And similarly in the example on the next page, prices of 7/4 and 4/1 represent a combined percentage of 56.36 - which when subtracted from 100 leaves 43.6, which rounded-off gives a price of 44/56; to which the nearest recognisable price is 4/5. And a reverse table giving the nearest equivalent price for the whole range of percentages can be found on page 122.

Coupled Price Strategies

Price coupling isn't just confined to ante-post hedging, but can be used when betting on any race. However despite claims to the contrary, and entire books seem to have been based on just this one idea, price coupling doesn't offer any guaranteed route to success, despite its being unfamiliar to many backers. To show some of the many possibilities, the table below describes four different ways of coupling horses in the one race. And as usual each horse is being backed to take out the same amount, which again is £100.

	s p.	%	A	B	C	D
Nomme De Guerre	7 / 4	36.36	36.36	36.36		36.36
Vittorio	4 / 1	20.00	20.00	20.00	20.00	
Senechal	11 / 2	15.38		15.38	15.38	
Marquita	6 / 1	14.29			14.29	
Tamorn	9 / 1	10.00			10.00	
Charlemagne	10 / 1	9.09			9.09	
Goldrush	16 / 1	5.88			5.88	5.88
New Liskeard	66 / 1	1.49			1.49	
		112.50	**56.36**	**71.74**	**76.13**	**42.24**

Coupling The First and Second Favourite - Column A
For backers who are convinced that the race is solely between Nomme De Guerre and Vittorio, their prices of 7/4 and 4/1 represent a total percentage of 56.36, and a coupled price of 44/56; which is approximately 4/5.　　(All percentage prices are rounded-off to the nearest whole number.)

Coupling The Top Three in the Betting - Column B
Narrowing the race down to the top three in the betting means coupling prices of 7/4, 4/1 and 11/2, to give a percentage price of 28/72; which is near enough 2/5.

Coupling The Field Against the Favourite - Column C
This is similar to the previous example where the field was backed against a favourite who'd been backed ante-post. Taken together, the other seven runners' prices add up to 24/76 or just over 1/3; so clearly any doubts about the favourite would need to be well founded.

Coupling the Favourite and An Outsider - Column D
This is quite a popular strategy anyway, and in this instance the coupled prices of 7/4 and 16/1 give a percentage price of 58/42; which works out at around 11/8.

Making A Backer's Book

The earlier hedging exercise was an example of making a backer's book. That is, backing one or more runners in some future race at comparatively generous ante-post odds; in the hope that by the start of the race every runner will have been backed so as to show an overall profit - and even after possibly allowing for one or two bets on non-runners.

The objective when making a backer's book therefore, is the exact opposite of what the bookmaker is trying to achieve; namely to end up with field money or a total stake which is smaller, rather than bigger, than the takeout or projected total return for each of the runners. But whether or not this proves possible in the end, to stand any real chance of success it's still essential to back every horse to take out the same amount; otherwise the overall position may soon become impossible to unravel, let alone retrieve.

However, as the day of the race begins to approach, damage limitation rather than profitability may well have become the name of the game. But it's still necessary to back every runner, no matter how negligible its chances may appear to be. And because the Tote can often pay better on outsiders, with books which look set to lose anyway, it may be worth waiting until the day of the race. And then, by backing any remaining outsiders for the nearest round figure to the required stake on the Tote, rather than taking a price, if any of them did manage to win, they might yet still save the day.

The Royal Hunt Cup 1922

As for me, I can't help admitting that I backed three horses for the Hunt Cup. I backed Crumbenmore because I thought he was going to win, Scamp because I had already lost money on him in the Derby, and Varzy for a reason which will appeal to anyone who realises in what a very uncertain world we live.

I think I should have decided that his chance of winning the Cup was small enough, if I hadn't looked up at the notice-board and seen beside his name the name of his jockey, Lynch. Because, on the previous day, I had had a letter through the post on the envelope of which my name was misspelled "Robert Lynch".

"These things" said an American lady to me about something else the other day, "are not accidents - they're meant."

R.L.

(Varzy won at 16/1)

The Grand National 1922

It was one of those rainy days on which Liverpool is of a gloomy, nondescript colour - the colour of wet flagstones that shine just enough to show the blurred reflections of the passers by. "It was a hundred times worse," declared one man "the day Troytown won. I shan't forget it. I had to lay in bed for six months afterwards."

This will give you some idea of the strength of character race-going develops in the young. It was a pneumonia day, a pleurisy day, at the very least a chill- on-the-liver day. Yet even those who had had the bitter experience of going to race-meetings on such a day in the past were exposing themselves to the elements as freely as if they had been paid money to do so.

I found an advertisement in one of the sporting papers that may help explain their hardihood. " WHY WORK ? " ran a tipster's appeal. "By availing yourself of our information you can live in ease and comfort without."

As an alternative to work, racing has undoubted advantages. It is more exhausting than work, but it is not so deadly monotonous. Even one's salary grows monotonous. The racing man's income is never the same for two day's running.

R.L.

4:Staking Systems

The majority of backers probably don't worry too much about staking plans and betting banks, as they're quite happy to finance their day-to-day betting out of income. And while they may be steadily losing small amounts week by week, because their betting is being kept within limits, they can carry on like this more or less indefinitely.

So that it's often only after deciding to take a more systematic approach to their betting, that many backers find their losses really starting to mount. Because while a succession of poor selections may lose manageable amounts in the short run, blindly following the dictates of an unsatisfactory staking plan or selection system might well result in continuing losses of much greater magnitude over the longer term; until it's finally and often reluctantly abandoned.

And so this chapter examines five of the most popular alternatives to level staking, and compares the claims which are sometimes made for them, with what's just as likely to happen in practice.

Retrieve Staking

The idea behind all retrieve staking, is for the stake to be increased sufficiently after each losing bet, to ensure that when there finally is a win, the proceeds will be enough both to recover all the past losses and also produce a profit as well.

An example of this is the martingale, used for betting on the even chances in roulette, where the stake is doubled after each losing bet. The real problem with all such systems though, isn't actually the astronomical size of the bank that would be needed in theory to cover the inevitable losing runs; but the fact that the table limits could be expected to come into effect well before reaching that point. Because casinos usually set their minimum and maximum limits so as to make it impossible to double up more than seven or eight times in a row.

Where horse-racing is concerned, one of the most popular systems is to back successive favourites at a meeting until there's a winner; increasing the stake each time so as to win a specific amount.

But the spectre which should really haunt all favourite backers, are the events of the Cheltenham National Hunt Festival of 1962; when over the three whole days of racing not a single favourite won.

Favourite backers will have gone on to Cheltenham in high spirits, after the favourite Herbalist won the last race at Worcester, the principal meeting on the previous afternoon. But what they weren't to know of course, was that not only would all 18 favourites fail at Cheltenham, but that the favourites would also go down in the first four races at both meetings on the following Friday, at the former Hurst Park and Manchester racecourses. Which made 22 successive losing favourites in all.

The following table shows what can happen in the space of just three days, to backers setting out with the relatively modest aim of winning just £10 - equivalent to around £60 in today's money - on every successful favourite. The columns give the starting price, the amount which needed to be won to clear any losses and win the £10, the stake required to win this amount, and the running deficit if the selection loses.

Cheltenham Tues March 13th..1962 2.15 Gloucestershire Hurdle Div I

1st. Tripacer 20/1   Fav. Trelawney 9/4 unplaced

s.p.	to win	stake	running deficit
9/4	£10.00	£4.44	£4.44

Cheltenham Tues March 13th..1962 2.50 2 Mile Champion Steeplechase

1st. Piperton 100/6   Fav. Scottish Memories 1/2 unplaced

s.p.	to win	stake	running deficit
1/2	£14.44	£28.89	£33.33

Cheltenham Tues March 13th. 1962 3.30 National Hunt Steeplechase

1st. Go Slow 10/1   Fav. Flying Wild 11/4 unplaced

s.p.	to win	stake	running deficit
11/4	£43.33	£15.76	£49.09

Cheltenham Tues March 13th. 1962 4.05 Nat. Hunt Handicap Steeplechase

1st. Longtail 100/7 Fav. Brown Diamond 9/2 unplaced

s.p.	to win	stake	running deficit
9/2	£59.09	£13.13	£62.22

Cheltenham Tues March 13th. 1962 4.40 Gloucestershire Hurdle Div II

1st. Clerical Grey 100/8   Fav. Python 9/4 Unplaced

s.p.	to win	stake	running deficit
9/4	£72.22	£32.10	£94.32

Cheltenham Tues March 13th. 1962 5.15 Broadway Steeplechase
1st. Caduval 11/2   Fav. Brittas 9/2 3rd

s.p.	to win	stake	running deficit
9/2	£104.32	£23.18	£117.50

Cheltenham Weds March 14th 1962 2.15 Cotswold Steeplechase
1st. Prudent Barney 20/1   Fav. Ruperini 6/4 Fell at 1st.

s.p.	to win	stake	running deficit
6/4	£127.50	£85.00	£202.51

Cheltenham Weds March 14th 1962 2.50 United Hunts' Challenge Cup
1st. Mr Teddy 7/2   Fav. Chaos 3/1 3rd

s.p.	to win	stake	running deficit
3/1	£212.51	£70.84	£273.34

Cheltenham Weds March 14th 1962 3.30 Champion Hurdle Challenge Cup
1st. Anzio 11/2   Fav. Another Flash 3rd 11/10

s.p.	to win	stake	running deficit
11/10	£283.34	£257.58	£530.92

Cheltenham Weds March 14th 1962 4.05 Kim Muir Memorial Challenge Cup
1st. Carrickbeg 7/1   Fav. Willow King 13/8

s.p.	to win	stake	running deficit
13/8	£540.92	£332.88	£863.80

Cheltenham Weds March 14th 1962 4.40 Cheltenham Grand Annual Steeplechase
1st. Moretons 100/8   Fav. Sandy Abbott 100/30 4th

s.p.	to win	stake	running deficit
100/30	£873.80	£262.14	£1,125.94

Cheltenham Weds March 14th 1962 5.15 Birdlip Handicap Hurdle
1st. St Stephen 100/6   Fav. High Tempo 2/1

s.p.	to win	stake	running deficit
2/1	£1,135.94	£567.97	£1,693.91

Cheltenham Thurs March 15th 1962 2.50 Cathcart Challenge Cup
1st. Hoodwinked 8/1   Fav. Mariner's Dance 1/1

s.p.	to win	stake	running deficit
1/1	£1,703.91	£1,703.91	£3,397.82

Cheltenham Thurs March 15th 1962 3.30 Cheltenham Gold Cup
1st. Mandarin 7/2   Fav. Pas Seul 9/4

s.p.	to win	stake	running deficit
9/4	£3,407.82	£1,514.59	£4,912.40

Cheltenham Thurs March 15th 1962 4.05 Spa Hurdle
1st. Merry Deal 7/1   Fav. Stenquill 5/2

s.p.	to win	stake	running deficit
5/2	£4,922.40	£1,968.96	£6,881.37

Cheltenham Thurs March 15th 1962 4.40 County Handicap Hurdle
1st. Sky Pink 100/8   Fav. Irish Imp 11/2

s.p.	to win	stake	running deficit
11/2	£6,891.37	£1,252.98	£8,134.34

Cheltenham Thurs March 15th 1962 5.15 Mildmay of Flete Challenge Cup
1st. Sprint Greeting 100/8   Fav. Richard of Bordeaux 9/4

s.p.	to win	stake	running deficit
9/4	£8,144.34	£3,619.71	£11,754.05

And so to the last race......

Cheltenham Thurs March 15th 1962 5.45 Foxhunters' Challenge Cup
1st College Master 9/2   Fav. Pegle 2/1

s.p.	to win	stake	total lost
2/1	£11,764.05	£5,882.02	**£17,636.07**

It's likely that in one way or another, most backers will have dropped out well before reaching this stage. But just as a matter of interest, the four further losers and the eventual winning favourite at Hurst Park on the Friday are as follows, with the deficit carried forward.

Hurst Park Friday March 16th 1962 2.00
1st. Solo Flight 8/1   Jt. Favs Incomparable, Jet Ace at 11/2
equivalent to single fav at 11/ 4

s.p.	to win	stake	running deficit
11/4	£17,646.07	£6,416.75	£24,052..83

Hurst Park Friday March 16th 1962 2.30
1st. Anner Loch 11/2   Fav. Clear Round 6/4

s.p.	to win	stake	running deficit
6/4	£24,062.83	£16,041.88	£40,094.71

Hurst Park Friday March 16th 1962 3.00

1st. Barbizon 11/2 | Fav. A and N 9/4 | | |
| s.p. | to win | stake | running deficit |
| 9/4 | £40,104.71 | £17,824.32 | £57,919.03 |

Hurst Park Friday March 16th 1962 3.30

1st. Desert Fort 9/1 | Fav. Superfine 13/8 | | |
| s.p. | to win | stake | running deficit |
| 13/8 | £57,929.03 | £35,648.63 | £93,567.66 |

Hurst Park Friday March 16th 1962 4.00

1st Autumn Poem 4/1 | **Fav. Winner !** | | |
| s.p. | to win | stake | total money at risk |
| 4/1 | £93,577.66 | £23,394.41 | **£116,962.07** |

So that finally, after paying off the odd £93,000 that was owing, there was still going to be that tenner left for some rounds of drinks on the Saturday night after all!

Clearly what happened in 1962 was something of an exception. But it does point up the real danger in all retrieve staking; in fostering the belief that continuing losses can simply be regarded as being on loan to the bookmaker, until the inevitable winner finally comes along

Progressive Staking

Aside from simply doubling-up, there are a number of alternatives again mainly associated with roulette, where the stake is increased and decreased more gradually according to various rules. And many such systems which go under a variety of exotic names and often date from the 19th century, were expressly designed in a vain attempt to correct flaws which gradually became apparent in existing systems. Because aside from the fact that with roulette, no system can overcome the game's unfavourable odds anyway, there's the further complication that with many such systems, the final outcome can often be crucially dependant on the order in which wins and losses occur. And this alone may account for their initial popularity, as it isn't too difficult to produce sets of results for almost any kind of system which show it to be clearly outperforming level stakes. While many of the system's less obvious drawbacks may take that much longer to emerge.

The two tables overleaf show the same series of seven wins and thirteen losses arranged in two different ways, with the outcome in each case both of using level stakes, and following a progressive system. The rules of the system are that the initial stake is £10, which is increased by £10 after each losing selection until there's a winner; after which it reverts to £10. The opening bank is set at £100 in each case.

Progressive Staking Series 1

No	price	result	level stake		staking system	
			stake	bank won/lost	stake	bank won/lost
1	2/1	Lost	£10.00	£100.00	£10.00	£100.00
				- £10.00		- £10.00
2	2/1	Won	£10.00	£90.00	£20.00	£90.00
				+ £20.00		+ £40.00
3	2/1	Lost	£10.00	£110.00	£10.00	£130.00
				- £10.00		- £10.00
4	1/1	Won	£10.00	£100.00	£20.00	£120.00
				+ £10.00		+ £20.00
5	2/1	Lost	£10.00	£110.00	£10.00	£140.00
				- £10.00		- £10.00
6	4/1	Lost	£10.00	£100.00	£20.00	£130.00
				- £10.00		- £20.00
7	9/4	Won	£10.00	£90.00	£30.00	£110.00
				+ £22.50		+ £67.50
8	5/1	Lost	£10.00	£112.50	£10.00	£177.50
				- £10.00		- £10.00
9	6/4	Won	£10.00	£102.50	£20.00	£167.50
				+ £15.00		+ £30.00
10	7/1	Lost	£10.00	£117.50	£10.00	£197.50
				- £10.00		- £10.00
11	3/1	Won	£10.00	£107.50	£20.00	£187.50
				+ £30.00		+ £60.00
12	2/1	Lost	£10.00	£137.50	£10.00	£247.50
				- £10.00		- £10.00
13	2/1	Lost	£10.00	£127.50	£20.00	£237.50
				- £10.00		- £20.00
14	2/1	Won	£10.00	£117.50	£30.00	£217.50
				+ £20.00		+ £60.00
15	2/1	Won	£10.00	£137.50	£10.00	£277.50
				+ £20.00		+ £20.00
16	2/1	Lost	£10.00	£157.50	£10.00	£297.50
				- £10.00		- £10.00
17	6/4	Lost	£10.00	£147.50	£20.00	£287.50
				- £10.00		- £20.00
18	1/1	Lost	£10.00	£137.50	£30.00	£267.50
				- £10.00		- £30.00
19	5/1	Lost	£10.00	£127.50	£40.00	£237.50
				- £10.00		- £40.00
20	2/1	Lost	£10.00	£117.50	£50.00	£197.50
				- £10.00		- £50.00
				£107.50		**£147.50**

No	price	result	level stake stake	level stake bank won/lost	staking system stake	staking system bank won/lost
1	2/1	Won	£10.00	£100.00 / + £20.00	£10.00	£100.00 / + £20.00
2	1/1	Won	£10.00	£120.00 / + £10.00	£10.00	£120.00 / + £10.00
3	9/4	Won	£10.00	£130.00 / + £22.50	£10.00	£130.00 / + £22.50
4	2/1	Lost	£10.00	£152.50 / - £10.00	£10.00	£152.50 / - £10.00
5	4/1	Lost	£10.00	£142.50 / - £10.00	£20.00	£142.50 / - £20.00
6	2/1	Lost	£10.00	£132.50 / - £10.00	£30.00	£122.50 / - £30.00
7	6/4	Lost	£10.00	£122.50 / - £10.00	£40.00	£92.50 / - £40.00
8	7/1	Lost	£10.00	£112.50 / - £10.00	£50.00	£52.50 / - £50.00
9	2/1	Lost	£10.00	£102.50 / - £10.00	£60.00	£2.50 / - £60.00
10	2/1	Lost	£10.00	£92.50 / - £10.00	£70.00	-£57.50 / - £70.00
11	5/1	Lost	£10.00	£82.50 / - £10.00	£80.00	-£127.50 / - £80.00
12	2/1	Lost	£10.00	£72.50 / - £10.00	£90.00	-£207.50 / - £90.00
13	3/1	Won	£10.00	£62.50 / + £30.00	£100.00	-£297.50 / + £300.00
14	5/1	Lost	£10.00	£92.50 / - £10.00	£10.00	£2.50 / - £10.00
15	6/4	Won	£10.00	£82.50 / + £15.00	£20.00	-£7.50 / + £30.00
16	2/1	Won	£10.00	£97.50 / + £20.00	£10.00	£22.50 / + £20.00
17	1/1	Won	£10.00	£117.50 / - £10.00	£10.00	£42.50 / - £10.00
18	2/1	Won	£10.00	£107.50 / + £20.00	£20.00	£32.50 / + £40.00
19	2/1	Lost	£10.00	£127.50 / - £10.00	£10.00	£72.50 / - £10.00
20	2/1	Lost	£10.00	£117.50 / - £10.00	£20.00	£62.50 / - £20.00
				£107.50		**£42.50**

Progressive Staking Conclusions

With wins and losses occurring as shown in the first sequence, progressive staking was the clear winner producing 40% more profit than level staking. However in the second sequence, while the same set of results in a different order again produced a level stake profit of £107.50, progressive staking now produced a loss of £57.50: a full £65 short of level staking.

What these two sequences indicate, is that for any system in which the stake is increased after each loser to produce a better return than level staking, it's necessary for winners to occur at fairly regular intervals; rather than being clustered together in groups, with long sequences of losing bets in between.

With wins in the first sequence at 2,4, 7, 9,11,14, and 15, the stake in six out of the seven winning bets was bigger than the initial £10; and the longest losing sequence was the five which occurred right at the end. Whereas the second sequence opened with a cluster of three wins at the minimum £10, followed by nine consecutive losers and an accumulated loss of £450; so even the £100 staked on a 3/1 winner couldn't quite recover. And with two further consecutive winners at 15 and 16, this meant that only three of the seven winners in the second sequence were staked for more than the initial £10.

And so given the impossibility of producing winners and losers to order, progressive staking may well prove disappointing, even when that same series of bets would have shown a good profit at level stakes.

And while it may not be as ruinous as retrieve staking, it's still possibly worth pointing out that by the 13th bet in the second sequence, the bank faced a cumulative loss of £497 - the original £100 bank, further losses of £297 and £100 for the next stake. Whereas at the same point the level stake bank still stood at £52, facing a loss of just £48.

Larger Trial

When this same set of results was subject to a further 10,000 trials where their order was decided at random, using the same set of rules and the same £100 opening bank each time, the outcome was as follows.

With busted banks being financed and allowed to stay in operation, the averaged final outcome was £165 per series. However this involved busting the bank at some stage in approximately 25% of all series, with the record in the 10,000 trials being a running deficit of £790 following a run of 12 consecutive losses. Whereas if credit was denied and the series was ended when the bank went bust, the average return was reduced to £97.40 per £100 starting bank; again compared with £107.50 for level staking.

Proportional Staking

Rather than increasing the stake after each losing bet, with proportional staking the size of each stake is set as a fixed fraction* of the current betting bank; so it decreases after a loss and increases after a win. This system is sometimes recommended as a way of playing up profits and stemming losses, and so seems to offer some advantages over level stakes.

However, as the two tables on pages 30

and 31 show, neither of these claims is necessarily true. These again use the same set of twenty results as were used for the previous example, but arranged in two different ways; so that the level stake profit in each case is £7.50, the same as before. The level stake is £10 throughout, while the proportional stake for each bet is set at 1/10th of the current capital.

The first point to note is that because of the different arrangement of wins and losses in each series, the size of the proportional stake from no.4 onwards, is different as well. However, the outcome for proportional staking is exactly the same in both cases, a closing bank of £88.48 and a loss of £11.52.

So that whereas before with progressive staking, the order of wins and losses was of crucial importance, when using proportional staking it makes no difference at all. And so despite the fact that the series once more shows a level stake profit of £7.50, with a proportional stake set at 1/10th of the current bank, there's a loss of £11.52, no matter in what order the wins and losses occur. Both of which findings may come as something of a surprise.

Using a Different Fraction

One effect of using a smaller fraction as the proportional stake, is to narrow the gap between level and proportional staking. So that using the same series of results, with stakes set at 1/20th of the bank, the final outcome was £98.67; a loss of only £1.33, although still £8.83 short of the outcome from level staking. The results from this, and another three fractions are as follows:

1/20 th	£98.67
1/30 th	£100.21
1/40 th	£100.58
1/50 th	£100.67

Proportional Staking Conclusion

The real drawback with all proportional staking, is that it only performs better if there's already a very high rate of return at level stakes. So that in this series, with stakes set at 1/10th. of the bank and easing prices gradually, proportional staking only produced a better return, when there was already a level stake profit of £82, an 82% return on the £100 opening bank.

---

* Fixed fraction systems are sometimes referred to as Kelly systems, after John L.Kelly Jr. a mathematician who made a study of their underlying principles. However it seems Kelly wasn't interested in betting on the horses but in data transmission down telephone lines, as his work first appeared in the "Bell System Technical Journal" for July 1947. Which is somewhat ironic, given that many of the best betting coups have often involved either monopolising phone-boxes or cutting all the telephone lines to remote racecourses. Until that is, some bright-sparks had to come along and develop the mobile phone. (See page 192)

Proportional Staking Series 1

No	price	result	level stake stake	level stake bank won/lost	proportional staking stake*	proportional staking bank won/lost
1	2/1	Lost	£10.00	£100.00 -£10.00	£10.00	£100.00 £10.00
2	2/1	Lost	£10.00	£90.00 -£10.00	£9.00	£90.00 £9.00
3	5/1	Lost	£10.00	£80.00 -£10.00	£8.10	£81.00 £8.10
4	9/4	Won	£10.00	£70.00 +£22.50	£7.29	£72.90 +£16.40
5	2/1	Lost	£10.00	£92.50 -£10.00	£8.93	£89.30 -£8.93
6	1/1	Won	£10.00	£82.50 +£10.00	£8.04	£80.37 +£8.04
7	6/4	Lost	£10.00	£92.50 -£10.00	£8.84	£88.41 -£8.84
8	2/1	Lost	£10.00	£82.50 -£10.00	£7.96	£79.57 -£7.96
9	2/1	Lost	£10.00	£72.50 -£10.00	£7.16	£71.61 -£7.16
10	7/1	Lost	£10.00	£62.50 -£10.00	£6.45	£64.45 £6.45
11	2/1	Lost	£10.00	£52.50 -£10.00	£5.80	£58.01 -£5.80
12	3/1	Won	£10.00	£42.50 +£30.00	£5.22	£52.20 +£15.66
13	5/1	Lost	£10.00	£72.50 -£10.00	£6.79	£67.87 -£6.79
14	4/1	Lost	£10.00	£62.50 -£10.00	£6.11	£61.08 -£6.11
15	2/1	Won	£10.00	£52.50 +£20.00	£5.50	£54.97 +£10.99
16	2/1	Won	£10.00	£72.50 +£20.00	£6.60	£65.97 +£13.19
17	6/4	Won	£10.00	£92.50 +£15.00	£7.92	£79.16 +£11.87
18	1/1	Lost	£10.00	£107.50 -£10.00	£9.10	£91.03 -£9.10
19	2/1	Lost	£10.00	£97.50 -£10.00	£8.19	£81.93 -£8.19
20	2/1	Won	£10.00	£87.50 +£20.00	£7.37	£73.74 +£14.75

(*Stakes were calculated to 6 decimal places but are shown rounded to 2.) **£107.50**   **£88.48**

No	price	result	level stake		proportional staking	
			stake	bank won/lost	stake	bank won/lost
1	2/1	Lost	£10.00	£100.00	£10.00	£100.00
				-£10.00		-£10.00
2	6/4	Lost	£10.00	£90.00	£9.00	£90.00
				-£10.00		-£9.00
3	2/1	Won	£10.00	£80.00	£8.10	£81.00
				+£20.00		+£16.20
4	9/4	Won	£10.00	£100.00	£9.72	£97.20
				+£22.50		+£21.87
5	5/1	Lost	£10.00	£122.50	£11.91	£119.07
				-£10.00		-£11.91
6	1/1	Won	£10.00	£112.50	£10.72	£107.16
				+£10.00		+£10.72
7	4/1	Lost	£10.00	£122.50	£11.79	£117.88
				-£10.00		-£11.79
8	1/1	Lost	£10.00	£112.50	£10.61	£106.09
				-£10.00		-£10.61
9	2/1	Won	£10.00	£102.50	£9.55	£95.48
				+£20.00		+£19.10
10	2/1	Lost	£10.00	£122.50	£11.46	£114.58
				-£10.00		-£11.46
11	7/1	Lost	£10.00	£112.50	£10.31	£103.12
				-£10.00		-£10.31
12	5/1	Lost	£10.00	£102.50	£9.28	£92.81
				-£10.00		-£9.28
13	2/1	Lost	£10.00	£92.50	£8.35	£83.53
				-£10.00		-£8.35
14	6/4	Won	£10.00	£82.50	£7.52	£75.18
				+£15.00		+£11.28
15	2/1	Lost	£10.00	£97.50	£8.65	£86.45
				-£10.00		-£8.65
16	2/1	Won	£10.00	£87.50	£7.78	£77.81
				+£20.00		+£15.56
17	2/1	Lost	£10.00	£107.50	£9.34	£93.37
				-£10.00		-£9.34
18	2/1	Lost	£10.00	£97.50	£8.40	£84.03
				-£10.00		-£8.40
19	2/1	Lost	£10.00	£87.50	£7.56	£75.63
				-£10.00		-£7.56
20	3/1	Won	£10.00	£77.50	£6.81	£68.06
				+£30.00		+£20.42
				£107.50		£88.48

Fixed-Takeout Staking

When using this system, all selections are staked to take out a specific amount, in the same way as was done earlier when coupling prices and making a backer's book. And on the face of it, this seems quite a good idea. Because reducing the stake on selections with the lowest strike rate, while increasing the stake on those with the highest, should in theory at least, even out the risk. Unfortunately though, there's one big drawback with fixed-takeout staking, as can be seen in the two tables opposite, where the level stake is set at £10, and the fixed-takeout stake is set to take out £20; the equivalent of a £10 level stake at even-money.

Fixed-Takeout Staking Conclusion

While as expected, the level stake return is the same in both cases, in the first sequence where the winners have bigger prices than the losers, fixed-takeout staking does considerably worse than level stakes. However in the second sequence where there are short priced winners and bigger priced losers it does much better.

Because the real problem with fixed-takeout staking is that it only seems to offer any sort of an advantage, when all the short priced selections can be expected to win, and when most of the losers are expected to be at bigger prices. But as nobody sets out to back losers at whatever price, this isn't of much real help. In fact all that fixed-takeout staking really seems to achieve, is to cancel out any benefit there might have been in backing big-priced winners in the first place, rather than simply favourites.

Value Staking

This method compares the prices on offer for the runners in any particular race, with a set of "true" or "fair" prices which have been estimated beforehand, by using some kind of system. And then, if the price which is available for any of the runners is better than its estimated price, then that becomes the selection; with the size of the stake being proportional to the difference between the two prices.

And indeed if any of this were possible, then it would seem to represent a truly scientific approach to the problem of selection and betting. Which may be why so many of the computer based systems which have been appearing on the market since the mid 1980s, have made extensive use of such ideas. Not that any of this does them any good however: for reasons which can be found in the discussions of prices generally on page 57, of Timeform prices on page 67, and strike rates and computer systems on pages 85-87. But in the meantime, possibly the continued prosperity of the bookmakers over the same period offers proof enough.

Graded Staking

Possibly the least systematic approach to variable staking is one where the size of the stake is mainly determined by the degree of confidence the backer has in any particular selection; and which for want of anything better, could be described as graded staking.

At its simplest, this is based on the idea of standard and maximum bets, the latter being restricted to selections in which the backer has the utmost confidence.

Series 1				Level Stake		Fixed Takeout	
				stake	bank	stake	bank
	1	1/1	Lost	£10	£100	£10	£100
					-£10		-£10
	2	1/1	Lost	£10	£90	£10	£90
					-£10		-£10
	3	1/1	Lost	£10	£80	£10	£80
					-£10		-£10
	4	1/1	Lost	£10	£70	£10	£70
					-£10		-£10
	5	1/1	Lost	£10	£60	£10	£60
					-£10		-£10
	6	1/1	Lost	£10	£50	£10	£50
					-£10		-£10
	7	1/1	Lost	£10	£40	£10	£40
					-£10		-£10
	8	3/1	Won	£10	£30	£5	£30
					+£30		+£15
	9	3/1	Won	£10	£60	£5	£45
					+£30		+£15
	10	3/1	Won	£10	£90	£5	£60
					+£30		+£15
					£120		**£75**
Series 2				stake	bank	stake	bank
	1	1/1	Won	£10	£100	£10	£100
					+£10		+£10
	2	1/1	Won	£10	£110	£10	£110
					+£10		+£10
	3	1/1	Won	£10	£120	£10	£120
					+£10		+£10
	4	1/1	Won	£10	£130	£10	£130
					+£10		+£10
	5	1/1	Won	£10	£140	£10	£140
					+£10		+£10
	6	1/1	Won	£10	£150	£10	£150
					+£10		+£10
	7	1/1	Lost	£10	£160	£10	£160
					-£10		-£10
	8	3/1	Lost	£10	£150	£5	£150
					-£10		-£5
	9	3/1	Lost	£10	£140	£5	£145
					-£10		-£5
	10	3/1	Lost	£10	£130	£5	£140
					-£10		-£5
					£120		**£135**

However, this does raise the question of why, if the standard bets are already showing a profit, the maximum isn't being staked on these as well. In fact, the idea that anyone without access to specialised or inside information, has the luxury of being able to choose between highly profitable, and marginally profitable bets is scarcely credible anyway: when all too often, the likely success of any selection seems to be inversely proportional to the size of the stake and the degree of confidence shown beforehand. So that singling out certain bets for special treatment, may simply be giving yet another hostage to fortune. Which is one more good reason for choosing level stakes.

Staking Systems Conclusion

What all these examples have shown, is that almost any reasonable sounding staking system can sometimes outperform level stakes, but usually only under fairly specific conditions. However, because none of these conditions can be anticipated, let alone produced to order, it's clear that no type of staking system could be relied on to consistently outperform level staking in the long run.

The series used for the examples in this chapter were chosen from a much larger sample, and the results of using these systems on a further 30 series can be found on page 117.

The Names of Horses

There was a curious item of news in the paper the other day concerning a race which was run at Lewes. One of the horses that took part was named League of Nations. It came in last of a field of eleven horses. The winner of the race was a horse called Thoughtless. Thus does life compose her ironic fables, and the very Turf is ablaze with warnings to the heedless tribe of men.

The victory of Thoughtless is not I am afraid an isolated incident in the year's racing. I have taken the trouble to look up a sporting calendar, and I find that on the whole the results of the season's races have been painfully discouraging to the angels. One of the most victorious animals of the year has been the filly Stupidity. Another winner has been Nonentity. Aimless has won, while Be Serious (whose dam was Don't Wink) has never managed better than second. Progress seems only to have run once, and to have been all but last in a race won by Musket Ball. While in this same race, Demagogue was another of the horses that defeated Progress.

R.L.

5:The Betting Bank

Once having decided on a level stake, the only other question which still needs to be resolved, is the size of that stake in relation to the betting bank. And so it's this which is the subject of this chapter.

Before going any further it's necessary to distinguish between **betting capital**, which is the total amount which could be made available for betting purposes at any one time, and the current **betting bank**, which should only ever represent a part of this capital. The reason for this, is that if staking levels are set so low as to protect the bank at all costs, then this is also likely to remove much of the interest too. Whereas if stakes are set at more competitive levels, there's not only more chance of winning worthwhile amounts, but also of losing the bank altogether. But so long as the entire betting capital hasn't been put at risk, this needn't be the end of the world.

So that basically the betting bank is a unit of account. It can remain in existence until it goes bust, to be followed possibly by a rethink; or until it grows so unwieldy that it's necessary to either take out a profit or increase the size of the stake. Or if neither of these things happens, then it could simply be carried on indefinitely. And because betting capital can always be added to, or taken out and used for other purposes, it's the current state of the betting bank which alone represents the true position.

The Staking Ratio

When deciding on the ratio between the stake and the betting bank, it can be a mistake to pay too much attention to the evidence of losing runs. For instance, because there's only a 1 in 1024 probability of ten successive losses on an even-chance such as spinning a coin, it might seem that an opening bank set at ten times the stake would offer some degree of security. But unfortunately this isn't so, as can be seen in the table on the next page. Losing run statistics do have their uses however, which is why some are included on page 92.

5 : The Betting Bank

Because the fact is, that the majority of backers aren't wiped out by catastrophic losing runs at all, but simply by a lack of profitability. So that the betting bank is gradually being eroded, not just by losing bets but also by winning bets which never quite recover losses. Until a point comes when there's simply nothing left.

The way this can so easily come about, is shown in the following table, which covers the first 64 spins of a coin from a simulated series which has been generated at random.

The opening bank has been set at £10, with £1 being bet on heads each time, and all winning bets are being settled at the fair odds of even-money.

no.	result	bank	no.	result	bank	no.	result	bank
1	Head	£11.00	23	Head	£9.00	45	Head	£9.00
2	Tail	£10.00	24	Head	£10.00	46	Head	£10.00
3	Tail	£9.00	25	Head	£11.00	47	Tail	£9.00
4	Tail	£8.00	26	Head	£12.00	48	Tail	£8.00
5	Tail	£7.00	27	Head	£13.00	49	Tail	£7.00
6	Tail	£6.00	28	Tail	£12.00	50	Tail	£6.00
7	Head	£7.00	29	Tail	£11.00	51	Tail	£5.00
8	Head	£8.00	30	Tail	£10.00	52	Head	£6.00
9	Tail	£7.00	31	Head	£11.00	53	Head	£7.00
10	Tail	£6.00	32	Tail	£10.00	54	Tail	£6.00
11	Tail	£5.00	33	Head	£11.00	55	Head	£7.00
12	Head	£6.00	34	Tail	£10.00	56	Tail	£6.00
13	Head	£7.00	35	Head	£11.00	57	Tail	£5.00
14	Head	£8.00	36	Tail	£10.00	58	Tail	£4.00
15	Head	£9.00	37	Head	£11.00	59	Tail	£3.00
16	Tail	£8.00	38	Head	£12.00	60	Head	£4.00
17	Head	£9.00	39	Tail	£11.00	61	Tail	£3.00
18	Tail	£8.00	40	Head	£12.00	62	Tail	£2.00
19	Head	£9.00	41	Tail	£11.00	63	Tail	£1.00
20	Head	£10.00	42	Tail	£10.00	**64**	**Tail**	**£0.00**
21	Tail	£9.00	43	Tail	£9.00			
22	Tail	£8.00	44	Tail	£8.00			

Despite the fact that the longest losing run in this series is five, and all bets are being settled at fair odds, the bank is still lost after only 64 spins. The reason for this, is that by this stage, with 27 heads and 37 tails overall, there are already ten more losers than winners. And with all winning bets being settled at even-money, and therefore all previous pairs of winners and losers cancelling each other out, as soon as the surplus of losers over winners exceeds the size of the opening bank, the bank is lost.

And indeed, experiments with spinning coins should soon convince anyone that it's a much easier proposition to spin ten more tails than heads overall, than it is to spin ten successive tails. So much so in fact, that after the first 20 spins there's already a 1 in 32 chance of having busted a 10 point opening bank.

This does however overlook the fact that when spinning a coin at fair odds, there's no built-in profit for either side. Successful backers on the other hand, would normally expect to be betting at favourable prices and therefore making a profit in the long run. And so maybe if these profits were being continually ploughed back into the bank, this might affect how long it could be expected to survive.

Betting Bank Tables

To test out this idea, results were generated for a very large number of races in which the overall proportion of winners to losers for each chance was correct, but where the order in which they occurred was determined at random. In all, 10,000 sequences

of 100 and 200 races were generated for 3 different chances; evens, 2/1 and 4/1.

Using a £10 level stake throughout, for each chance there are two different sizes of opening bank, set at £100 and £200 for even chances, £150 and £300 for 2/1 chances, and £200 and £400 for 4/1 chances.

Then in each of these categories, results were produced for 5 different rates of return between -5% and +20%. These rates are all based on turnover, so that for example in the case of even-money chances showing a 5% profit, each of the £10 winning singles returned £20.10 in total.

The measurement used was the percentage of opening banks which were busted, doubled, and won or lost overall in each category; a bank being busted when it fell below the £10 needed for the next stake.

And because the final outcome for each series could still be subject to very large random fluctuations which might undermine the validity of any comparisons being made, a level £1 stake was also placed on every selection at the appropriate fair price. Then successive series were generated for each category, 12 in one instance, until a final level stake bank was produced which was within plus-or-minus £1000 for that series; which over 1,000,000 races is less than 0.1 % on turnover. And these are the series which were then used as the basis for the tables.

5 : The Betting Bank

Even Chances

10,000 sequences of 100 races
£100 opening bank £10 stake

percentage return	percentage of busted banks	percentage of doubled banks	percentage of banks won/lost
-5%	49.41	14.3	-35.11
fair	31.53	31.78	0.25
+5%	22.16	48.49	26.33
+10%	15.05	65.77	50.72
+20%	6.38	86.94	80.56

final level stake balance + £810 : + 0.081%

Even Chances

10,000 sequences of 100 races
£200 opening bank, £10 stake

percentage return	percentage of busted banks	percentage of doubled banks	percentage of banks won/lost
-5%	10.84	0.98	-9.86
fair	4.51	5.03	0.52
+5%	2.50	12.04	9.54
+10%	1.16	25.89	24.73
+20%	0.30	60.39	60.09

final level stake balance + £716 : + 0.071%

Even Chances

10,000 sequences of 200 races
£100 opening bank, £10 stake

percentage return	percentage of busted banks	percentage of doubled banks	percentage of banks won/lost
-5%	68.63	19.68	-48.95
fair	44.44	45.01	0.57
+5%	28.20	64.20	36.00
+10%	16.31	79.87	63.56
+20%	5.94	93.73	87.79

final level stake balance + £708 : + 0.035%

Even Chances

10,000 sequences of 200 races
£200 opening bank, £10 stake

percentage return	percentage of busted banks	percentage of doubled banks	percentage of banks won/lost
-5%	35.89	3.13	-32.76
fair	15.77	15.83	0.06
+5%	6.57	36.64	30.07
+10%	2.40	61.99	59.59
+20%	0.29	92.40	92.11

final level stake balance - £658 : - 0.032%

2/1 Chances

10,000 sequences of 100 races
£150 opening bank, £10 stake

percentage return	percentage of busted banks	percentage of doubled banks	percentage of banks won/lost
-5%	60.10	24.05	-36.05
fair	42.59	41.60	-0.99
+5%	30.97	56.97	26.00
+10%	21.10	70.14	49.04
+20%	9.78	87.90	78.12

final level stake balance - £623 : - 0.031%

2/1 Chances

10,000 sequences of 100 races
£300 opening bank, £10 stake

percentage return	percentage of busted banks	percentage of doubled banks	percentage of banks won/lost
-5%	24.17	4.15	-20.02
fair	12.76	12.65	-0.11
+5%	6.81	26.90	20.09
+10%	3.61	43.72	40.11
+20%	0.99	74.52	74.53

final level stake balance - £164 : - 0.016%

5 : The Betting Bank

2/1 Chances

10,000 sequencesof 200 races
£150 opening bank, £10 stake

percentage return	percentage of busted banks	percentage of doubled banks	percentage of banks won/lost
-5%	59.73	24.16	-35.57
fair	42.36	41.62	-0.74
+5%	30.53	56.98	26.45
+10%	20.48	71.08	50.60
+20%	9.67	88.02	78.35

final level stake balance + £910 : + 0.045%

2/1 Chances

10,000 sequences of 200 races
£300 opening bank, £10 stake

percentage return	percentage of busted banks	percentage of doubled banks	percentage of banks won/lost
-5%	23.60	4.02	-19.58
fair	11.92	12.71	0.79
+5%	6.73	26.31	19.58
+10%	3.33	43.58	40.25
+20%	1.08	75.91	74.84

final level stake balance - £272 : - 0.013%

4/1 Chances

10,000 sequences of 100 races
£200 opening bank, £10 stake

percentage return	percentage of busted banks	percentage of doubled banks	percentage of banks won/lost
-5%	56.61	29.42	-27.19
fair	44.55	42.72	-1.83
+5%	35.99	53.66	17.67
+10%	27.85	63.69	35.84
+20%	17.54	78.62	61.08

final level stake balance - £820 : - 0.082%

4/1 Chances

10,000 sequences of 100 races
£400 opening bank, £10 stake

percentage return	percentage of busted banks	percentage of doubled banks	percentage of banks won/lost
-5%	21.82	7.70	-14.12
fair	14.50	15.83	1.33
+5%	9.67	25.39	15.72
+10%	6.14	37.71	31.57
+20%	2.62	62.68	60.06

final level stake balance + £35 : + 0.0035%

4/1 Chances

10,000 sequences of 200 races
£200 opening bank, £10 stake

percentage return	percentage of busted banks	percentage of doubled banks	percentage of banks won/lost
-5%	56.83	29.09	-27.74
fair	44.73	42.48	-2.25
+5%	35.34	53.36	18.02
+10%	27.24	64.47	37.23
+20%	16.93	79.64	62.71

final level stake balance + £175 : + 0.0085%

4/1 Chances

10,000 sequences of 200 races
£400 opening bank, £10 stake

percentage return	percentage of busted banks	percentage of doubled banks	percentage of banks won/lost
-5%	22.51	7.62	-14.89
fair	15.31	15.96	0.65
+5%	10.13	25.66	15.53
+10%	6.43	38.15	31.72
+20%	2.79	62.60	59.81

final level stake balance + £210 : + 0.01%

Betting Bank Conclusion

These tables confirm that profitability can indeed play a major part in the survival of a betting bank. However what's also worth noting is that even at the most favourable rates of return, there's still a theoretical possibility of losing the bank in the short term; which is why it's unwise to put the entire betting capital at risk. While at the other extreme, even with a negative rate of return, it's still possible in theory to occasionally double the bank.

The tables also confirm that betting banks set at 10 and 20 times the stake at even-money, are roughly equivalent to banks set at 15 and 30 times the stake at 2/1, and 20 and 40 times the stake at 4/1.

These figures should at least provide some idea of what can be expected from any particular staking ratio; better than could be obtained from either losing runs or guesswork, anyway.

Money Management

But whichever ratio is chosen, it will still then be necessary to decide between three basic approaches to managing the bank.

A first possibility would be **retaining profits,** in which all winnings are added directly to the betting bank. Maintaining the original stake as the bank increases, will gradually lessen the possibility of it ever being completely wiped out; thus making this the safest option of all.

A second would be **taking profits**, so that winnings are taken out immediately they're produced, leaving just the original bank and the same level of staking.

While the final option would be **doubling stakes**; where after sufficient winnings have been added to the bank to double it in size, the stakes are then doubled also; but which differs from proportional staking as staking levels aren't subject to individual results. This is clearly the way to accumulate the largest sum of money in the shortest possible time, but it's also the most hazardous; as the possibility of losing the entire bank, including all previous winnings, increases as the series progresses. And so in view of this, one possible strategy might be to aim for a specific target, and then cash in the bank immediately it's reached, and revert to the original stake.

Psychological Aspects of Staking

As well as application, attention to detail, and a certain amount of luck, successful betting also requires the right temperament. And ideally this would encompass among other things, unshakeable confidence, a steady nerve, plus a degree of indifference to the real value of money.

Otherwise as stakes are being gradually increased, a point can be reached, possibly when the average stake is beginning to approach a week's or a month's salary, where inhibitions about losing so much on the one bet can begin to undermine judgement and confidence; no matter how large the sums which may have already been won. And unfortunately, this is something which it's much easier to be born with, than to deliberately acquire. So it's maybe as well to recognise this limitation from the outset, and the fact that stakes will still need to be kept within comfortable limits, regardless of the dictates of any chosen staking plan.

Betting on Account

While there's no doubting the convenience of being able to bet by telephone or over the internet, it's important not to overlook the potential pitfalls.

A first point to bear in mind about all account betting whether credit or debit, is that like the use of chips in casinos, it puts the backer at one remove from actual cash. And so by reducing the pain of losing, it may allow him to stake much more than he might otherwise have been prepared to do.

A second consideration with all credit, betting whether settlement is to be weekly, fortnightly, or monthly, is that the imposition of artificial deadlines can also undermine staking discipline. Because anyone who's losing, may be tempted to increase their stakes in an attempt to break even before settlement day. Whereas anyone who's already ahead, may be inclined to try and play up their winnings even further; by making free with what they may wrongly come to regard as the bookmaker's money.

A third difficulty faced by anyone betting by telephone, is that once having partially committed themselves by ringing up and enquiring about a price for a horse, they may be more inclined to accept that price than they would be if it was simply available on the racecourse or in the betting shop.

While even on the racecourse, account customers of rails bookmakers who in any case may have nowhere else to go, may find themselves faced with a similar dilemma.

But in any case, at the end of the day, what better feeling could there possibly be, than leaving the racecourse or the betting shop clutching a carrier bag stuffed-full of readies? Or at least so they say.

Another Practical Aspect Of Staking

Backing horses to take out specific amounts as described in chapter three and elsewhere, can often involve staking the bet for quite awkward sums of money which may even include the pennies. However what's always worth bearing in mind, is that the stakes are only the size they are, because they're specifically intended to take out a round figure, whereas a stake which was either rounded up or down, might in its turn take out an equally awkward amount anyway. Most on-course bookmakers are likely to recognise the significance of any such stake, but in the betting shop, there's no harm in adding "To take out £100" or whatever, in brackets beneath the stake.

Going to the Derby 1921

There were so many people there that there was no room for anybody...There was simply a crush - an enormous, sweltering, and appallingly silent crush. Even the bookmakers seemed to be awed by it. They stood on their stands beside blackboards full of horses names and mystical figures, but they did not yell at you hoarsely, bullyingly, as bookmakers ought to do. If having looked at the elephantine portrait advertisement of one of them, you wished to bet with him, he would consent in a listless way, and say wearily to his clerk: "Nine-nine-one, seventy shillings to a dollar Polumetis," as he handed you a blue, red and green card. I do not blame him for not being enthusiastic. I am myself no longer enthusiastic about Polumetis....

And indeed, all the jockeys as they paraded down the field before the race seemed to have robbed a rainbow. They brought meaning and beauty into an otherwise bald and unconvincing mob. I assure you that I love horse racing - if I could see it. But of all the people who congregated on the little crooked hills of Epsom, I doubt if ten people in a hundred saw it. You knew that the horses had started only because, as you lay dreaming, the million people in the stands suddenly made you jump with a loud, sharp, and terrifying bark, which said: "They're off!" in one syllable.

Then there was deep silence, and somebody near me said: "The favourite can't be leading or they would be shouting." Then from the stands came a murmur like bees, a muttering as of a man talking in his sleep, a growling as of wind in a cave. This only served to intensify the silence of a defeated people. One knew that something awful must be happening. Perhaps even Polumetis was winning...

But I did not really know who had won till the numbers were put up on the board. Then a badly shaven man in a bowler cried : "Spion Kop has won ! Bravo !" and clapped his friend on the back. The rest of us looked at him with contempt.

R.L.

6:Multiple Betting

This chapter describes three of the biggest problems with all types of multiple bet*, and why in general they should be avoided. And it also gives an account of related contingencies, which are one of the few areas where multiple bets can in fact confer some sort of an advantage.

Depending on how they're defined, any bet in which winnings are carried forward from one selection to the next, such as a double or a treble, is either an accumulator or a multiple bet. And in the same way, bets such as Yankees, Heinz's, or Union Jacks which cover a number of selections in

different arrangements of doubles, trebles, and bigger accumulators, can again be either multiple or combination bets.

But regardless of their actual definition, all multiple and combination bets suffer from at least three basic flaws. These are often overlooked though, because on the surface at least, all such bets may appear to offer an improved rate of return, when compared with winning singles.

This can be seen in the example on the next page, where two selections Senechal and Goldrush have been backed in two £10 singles and one £10 double. Both horses are

---

* The first bookmaker to recognise the profit potential of multiple bets is said to have been William Crockford (1775 - 1844), an unprepossessing former fishmonger and later styled the "Napoleon of the Turf". As well as regularly attending the races, in 1827 Crockford also established the Gaming Rooms in St.James's Street Piccadilly which bore his name; and where he catered for among others, the more

sporting elements among the landed gentry and aristocracy. As a result of his activities both on the racecourse and in his Gaming Rooms, Crockford is sometimes credited as being responsible for the greatest redistribution of wealth by a private individual, to have taken place in England between the Dissolution of the Monasteries in the 16th century, and the introduction of Death Duties in the 20th.

priced at 6/4 against, although it's been assumed that they're really even-money chances. This gives the four possible outcomes as set out in the table.

	Senechal 6/4	Goldrush 6/4	single stakes	winning singles	single returns	double stakes	winning doubles	double returns
1	Win	Win	£20	2	£50	£10	1	£62.50
2	Win	Lose	£20	1	£25	£10	-	-
3	Lose	Win	£20	1	£25	£10	-	-
4	Lose	Lose	£20	-	-	£10	-	
			£80	**4**	**£100**	**£40**	**1**	**£62.50**

Staking this bet therefore, requires eight £10 singles totalling £80, and four £10 doubles totalling £40.

The four winning singles each yield £25 for a total of £100, giving a return of 25% on the £80 staked.

The one winning double however yields £62.50, which appears to represent a return of 64% on the £40 stake; which is more than twice as much as the singles. And so on this basis alone, it seems that backers would be much better off if they simply concentrated all their resources on doubles.

However, it's only when each of the four doubles is broken down into two separate bets, that a more accurate picture emerges. So that as with the singles, four £10 bets are placed on the first leg of each of the doubles. Two of these bets then win, and yield a total of £50, which represents a 25% return on the original £40 staked.

This £50 is then reinvested with £25 going straight onto each of the second legs of the two surviving doubles. And then,

when one of these wins it yields £62.50, which again represents a return of 25% on the £50 staked on the second leg.

And so the only reason why the rate of return first appeared to be 64%, was because this £50 which was staked on the second leg was being totally overlooked. And this neatly illustrates the first point about all multiple bets. Which is that any stakes which are being carried forward, still remain just as much a part of the betting bank, as they would be if they were actually money in hand. And so the fact that they're being retained by the bookmaker in the meantime shouldn't be allowed to obscure this fact.

The first two objections to multiple bets, therefore, are that they undermine the principle of level staking, and the relationship between the stake and the betting bank.

In this particular double for instance, while both Senechal and Goldrush are presumably thought worth backing, by the nature of the bet, the stake on Goldrush is always going to be that much bigger than the stake on Senechal. Because apart from ante-post bets, the size of the stakes on the subsequent legs of all multiple bets are totally arbitrary; being solely determined by the prices of previous winners.

Stress was also placed earlier, on the need to establish a satisfactory ratio between the stake and the betting bank. However with multiple betting, where the stakes are of all different sizes, this is clearly an impossibility. And what's more, multiple betting also magnifies the risk-reward ratio when compared to single bets. So that either the initial stakes are going to have to be set that much smaller in relation to the size of the bank to start with, or if not, then there's a far greater possibility of breaking the bank than there would be with singles.

A third and equally irrational feature of all multiple bets, is the way in which all subsequent bets depend on the success of previous selections. So that in this example for instance, whether Senechal is backed at all in the second race, depends solely on whether Goldrush has already won the first. And yet given that these are totally unconnected events, what possible reason can there be for imposing this extra condition?

In effect, all multiple betting can be seen as some kind of crazy system, in which all the most important questions are being determined on a more-or-less random basis. And while this may be an ideal arrangement when the main objectives are entertainment, and the excitement which can be generated by such uncertainty, in any other circumstances such deficiencies are rather more difficult to overlook.

Related Contingencies

While the last two races featuring Senechal and Goldrush were totally unconnected events, this needn't always be the case. For instance, a stable which seems to be returning to form, might well send out a number of different runners on the same day. And if one of them wins, then this in itself may make it that much more likely that the others will also win, and vice versa. So that backing those horses in doubles or trebles, could well generate a much better return than would singles alone. Making this one of the few occasions when multiple bets can be positively recommended.

Events that are connected in this way are known as related contingencies; and for the reason just given, they can often be of interest to backers. And two other instructive examples concern tricast dividends, and the Classic Double.

On Saturday May 20th 1989 the 1.15 at Thirsk, the 6 furlong Dick Peacock Sprint Handicap was won by Miss Daisy at 20/1, with Halvoya second at 25/1, and Roysia Boy third at 33/1; while Crofters Cline the 4/1 favourite was unplaced. But none of this would be of interest if it weren't for three facts. First, that out of a field of 23 runners the first three home were drawn 21, 22, and 23. Second, that the tricast dividend for correctly forecasting the first three in correct order paid £13,637 to a £1 stake. And third, that Paul Cooper, a professional backer is reputed to have won around £250,000 on the race.

This wasn't simply down to luck however, as the perceptive Mr. Cooper had already noticed the effect which artificial watering was having on the draw at Thirsk; and so he had the foresight to cover all the highest drawn runners in tricast combinations. But the reason why the dividend was so big in the first place, was because under such circumstances, the tricast dividend offered full multiplied odds against what in fact were related events.

So that in the Thirsk race, given what was known about the effect of watering on the draw, if a highly drawn outsider with little apparent chance on form made the frame, then there was a strong possibility that the other two places would be filled by highly drawn runners as well. And in this case they also happened to be outsiders.

In other words, the first three placings weren't independent events, but were all the result of the bias in the draw. However the tricast formula is based on starting prices which are intended to reflect the winning chances of individual horses, rather than the chances of groups of similarly drawn horses filling the first three places.

So that while, from a bookmaker's point of view, it may have been perfectly acceptable to lay odds of 20/1 against a highly drawn outsider winning the race, if it were in fact to win, then the chances of two other highly drawn horses being placed would be an awful lot shorter than the tricast odds of 13,636/1 against. Hence the need for the constant tinkering with the tricast formula.

Where the Classic Double is concerned, the related events are the result of the first race, and the effect this is likely to have on the prices quoted for the second. So that for

example, a horse may be quoted in the Spring at evens for the Guineas and 3/1 for the Derby. However, if it then goes on to win the Guineas, then regardless of whether this actually improves its chances, its price for the Derby may well shorten, from say 3/1 to 6/4. Which would also mean that anyone who'd obtained the full multiplied odds of 7/1 for the double beforehand, would now benefit twice over from the horse's having won just the one race.

Because not only would they double their original stake on the first half of the bet, as would anyone who backed it in a single; but with its Derby price halving to 6/4 as a result of its winning the Guineas, this also enhances the value of the second leg of the bet. As they now also stand to win twice as much as anyone who backed it afterwards at its post-Guineas price. Hence the reluctance of bookmakers to lay the full multiplied odds beforehand.

Obtaining full multiplied odds against related events can often present backers with a real advantage, which is why such situations are always worth looking out for. And aside from just racing, in sports betting generally there can often be opportunities. For instance by backing the same individual or team to win two or more events; all the more so if one of them just happens to be a qualifying event for one of the others.

7:Each-Way Betting

One of the problems with each-way betting, is that while there are various strategies, such as backing the second favourite each-way, in fields of eight runners with odds-on favourites, and betting each-way in handicaps with sixteen runners, the reasoning behind such ideas is often sketchy, if not absent altogether. And so this chapter tries to correct that deficiency, not just by identifying the most promising areas for each-way betting, but also by examining some of the underlying principles; and whether some of them mightn't be more widely applicable.

Opportunities in each-way betting are believed to arise, because the place price offered against a horse is a fixed fraction of its win price, and so may bear little or no relation to its actual chance of being placed. The difficulty of course, lies in not knowing exactly what any horse's chances of winning or being placed actually are; exactly the same problem as also arises when weighing up prices. And so as a way around this, two different approaches are being proposed .

The first of these involves using place overrounds to identify which types of race are most likely to produce the best each-way returns overall, and why. The second approach, is to then use starting price data to produce estimates of the win and place chances of the runners in broad categories of races, on the basis of their prices alone. And these estimates can then used to identify which patterns of prices and which positions in the betting are likely to yield the best each-way returns, in races which are already known to be overbroke on places. And to illustrate some of the main points, 57 such estimates in the form of race profiles have also been included.

Place Overrounds
Up until now overrounds have only been calculated for the prices offered against horses winning races, but exactly the same principle can be applied to place prices. And in fact calculating place overrounds should prove even more worthwhile,

because while it's rare to find overbroke win prices, overbroke place prices aren't that uncommon in certain types of race.

Place Prices and Percentages

One of the main features of place betting is that while the terms of 1/4 and 1/5th the odds apply to the actual fractional prices, they don't always have the same impact on the underlying percentages; as in the case of the 1/7 favourite in the first example.

As far as the actual prices are concerned where the terms specify 1/4 the odds a place,

the equivalent place price is the win price with the right hand side multiplied by four. So that 5/1 becomes 5/4; 16/1 becomes 16/4 or 4/1; 7/4 becomes 7/16, and so forth. And the same applies with 1/5th the odds a place. The place price percentages can then be worked out from these in the same way as are win price percentages, as is further explained on page 120.

Otherwise, to save time in calculating place overrounds, a full list of place prices and percentages at both 1/4 and 1/5th the odds can be found on page 124.

Race 19 *	8 Runners 3 Places at 1/5 the odds		
win		**place**	
1/7	87.50	1/35	97.22
12/1	7.69	12/5	29.41
20/1	4.76	4/1	20.00
20/1	4.76	4/1	20.00
25/1	3.85	5/1	16.67
25/1	3.85	5/1	16.67
25/1	3.85	5/1	16.67
25/1	3.85	5/1	16.67
	120.11		**233.31**

*All race numbers refer to the corresponding profiles from which the figures are derived.

The Impact of Odds-On Favourites

In a race paying three places, such as in the above example, the total chances of the eight runners being placed add up to 300%. So that while the win prices for this race are 20 percent overround, the place prices are seriously overbroke to the tune of 22.2 percent ; that is, the total overbroke margin of 66.69 out of 300 percent, divided by three.

This can be explained by the fact, that

while the place percentages for all the other prices increase by a factor of three or four at one fifth of the odds, because the favourite's win percentage is already so large to start with, the change from 1/7 to 1/35 can only ever have a marginal effect. And this in turn limits the amount of possible increase in the total place percentage. Which is why races with odds-on favourites are among the most likely to be overbroke on places.

And this doesn't just apply to races with eight runners either. Because they pay only two places, races with seven runners are usually considered among the least promising prospects for each-way betting. But if the favourite is short enough, even these can be overbroke on prices. As can be seen in the following race, where a deficit of 13.26 out of 200%, means that the two places can still end up 6.63 % overbroke.

Race 13   7 Runners 2 Places at 1/4 odds

win		place	
2 / 9	81.82	1 /18	94.74
5 / 1	16.67	5 /4	44.44
14 / 1	6.67	7 /2	22.22
25 / 1	3.85	25/4	13.79
100 / 1	0.99	25/1	3.85
100 / 1	0.99	25/1	3.85
100 / 1	0.99	25/1	3.85
	111.98		**186.74**

And likewise with ten runners and a win overround of 16, the place prices can still work out at 9.93 percent overbroke.

Race 33   10 Runners 3 Places at 1/5 odds

win		place	
4 /9	69.23	4 / 45	91.84
6 /1	14.29	6 / 5	45.45
11 / 1	8.33	11 / 5	31.25
12 / 1	7.69	12 / 5	29.41
16 / 1	5.88	16 / 5	23.81
25 / 1	3.85	5 / 1	16.67
33 / 1	2.94	33 / 5	13.16
50 / 1	1.96	10 / 1	9.09
100 / 1	0.99	20 / 1	4.76
100 / 1	0.99	20 / 1	4.76
	116.15		**270.20**

7 : Each-Way Betting

Besides races with odds-on favourites, the other main category which is most likely to be overbroke on prices features handicaps with sixteen or more runners, in this case simply because of the terms and conditions.

12 16 runners 4 places at 1/4 the odds

	win		place	
4 / 1	20.00		1 / 1	50.00
9 / 2	18.18		9 / 8	47.06
8 / 1	11.11		2 / 1	33.33
9 / 1	10.00		9 / 4	30.77
10 / 1	9.09		5 / 2	28.57
12 / 1	7.69		3 / 1	25.00
14 / 1	6.67		7 / 2	22.22
25 / 1	3.85		25 / 4	13.79
25 / 1	3.85		25 / 4	13.79
50 / 1	1.96		25 / 2	7.41
50 / 1	1.96		25 / 2	7.41
50 / 1	1.96		25 / 2	7.41
66 / 1	1.49		33 / 2	5.71
66 / 1	1.49		33 / 2	5.71
100 / 1	0.99		25 / 1	3.85
	120.29			**352.03**

Because four places are being paid at 1/4 the odds, this race is 11.99 percent overbroke on places; despite having a win overround of 20.29. And overbroke place prices can even be found in a race with 24 runners, as in race 55 on page 187.

Individual Chances

Without taking into account any bias in prices it's clear that overall, betting each-way in races with overbroke place prices should produce a better return than would betting win-only. The only real problem with this approach though, is that it treats all the runners in each race alike, in assuming that their chances of being placed will be in proportion to their prices, when the evidence all clearly suggests otherwise.

However, as was mentioned in the intro-duction, a way was found of using starting price data, to estimate the win and place chances of the runners in broad categories of race on the evidence of those prices alone, the idea being that these estimates could then form the basis of race profiles.

And then by examining a large number of such profiles, it should be possible to identify which positions in the betting and which patterns of prices, are most likely to yield the best each-way returns.

However because all this proved to be quite a long drawn out process, the details of all the various calculations have been given a separate chapter of their own, "Estimating Win and Place Chances" which begins on page 98.

Below is the profile of the seven runner race which was introduced earlier, one of 57 such profiles which begin on page 153.

race 13   7 runners   2 places at 1/4 the odds

s.p.	s.p. win %	s.p. place %	nearest fair price	fair win%	fair place%	win	returns e/w	place
2 / 9	81.82	94.74	2 / 9	82.30	98.33	0.59	2.19	3.79
5 / 1	16.67	44.44	15 / 2	11.92	68.05	-28.50	12.31	53.12
14 / 1	6.67	22.22	28 / 1	3.64	21.13	-45.43	-25.17	-4.91
25 / 1	3.85	13.79	66 / 1	1.55	9.02	-59.78	-47.19	-34.61
100 / 1	0.99	3.85	500 / 1	0.20	1.16	-80.03	-74.99	-69.96
100 / 1	0.99	3.85	500 / 1	0.20	1.16	-80.03	-74.99	-69.96
100 / 1	0.99	3.85	500 / 1	0.20	1.16	-80.03	-74.99	-69.96
	111.97	186.74		100.00	200.00			

The columns are as follows -

s.p.	The returned starting price.
s.p. win %	The starting price as a percentage.
s.p. place %	The equivalent place price as a percentage.
nearest fair odds	The nearest equivalent fair recognised price.
fair win %	The horse's fair win chance.
fair place %	The horse's fair place chance.
win return	Percentage return on win bets.
e/w return	Percentage return on each-way bets.
place return	Shows the place contribution to each-way returns.

Favourable Patterns of Prices

Probably the most significant feature to emerge from the profiles, was the effect which different arrangements of prices could clearly have on individual returns.

This was most marked where there was a significant jump in the prices; such as in race 1 below, where this occurs between the second and third favourites; or in race 27 between the third and fourth favourites; or again in race no 2 between the fourth and fifth favourites. Because, as can be seen in all these examples, the each-way returns on the intermediate runners - those between the favourite and the jump in prices - are significantly better than where there's simply a smooth progression, such as occurs in race 10.

Race no. 1 5 runners		Race no. 27 9 runners		Race no. 2 17 runners		Race no. 10 16 runners	
s.p.	e.w. return	s.p.	e.w. return	s.p.	e.w. return	s.p.	e.w. return
2 / 17	+ 1.01	1 / 3	+ 4.22	8 / 11	- 0.25	9 / 4	+ 2.80
13 / 2	**+ 47.31**	6 / 1	**+ 18.68**	9 / 2	**+ 16.24**	7 / 2	+ 4.66
40 / 1	- 58.66	10 / 1	**+ 19.52**	7 / 1	**+ 19.79**	7 / 2	+ 4.66
40 / 1	- 58.66	20 / 1	- 22.27	7 / 1	**+ 19.79**	13 / 2	+ 5.06
50 / 1	- 59.04	25 / 1	- 30.50	14 / 1	- 5.58	7 / 1	+ 4.83

Each-way Betting Conclusions

To judge by the earlier examples, it would certainly seem to be worth calculating place overrounds for selected races. However as far as the profiles are concerned, besides the fact that these aren't intended to apply to individual races anyway, and would take much longer to produce, the existing data should already provide more than enough evidence, as to what to look out for.

One of the most common objections to each-way betting is that it can foster an over-cautious attitude, with stake money being wasted on unnecessary insurance in the form of each-way bets, when it would be far better employed win-only.

But even disregarding everything that's been said up to now, this still overlooks one significant fact; which is that the bookmakers themselves are unwilling to accept place-only bets. And why? Because they've known all along that under the right circumstances, place-only bets would give backers a better return than would betting to win. Which means that betting each-way on such races would provide an improved rate of return as well; especially once it's possible to identify for certain exactly which races they are.

Part Two:
Selection

The Intellectual Side of Horse Racing I

Our teachers used to apologise for teaching us Latin Grammar and mathematics by telling us that they were good mental gymnastics. If education is only a matter of mental gymnastics, however, I should recommend horse racing as an ideal study for young boys and girls. The sole objection is that it is so engrossing; it might absorb the whole energies of the child. The safety of Latin Grammar lies in its dullness.

No child is tempted by Latin Grammar into forgetting that there are other duties in life besides mental gymnastics. Horse racing, on the other hand comes into our lives with the effect of a religious conversion. It is the greatest monopolist among the pleasures. It affects men's conversation. It effects their entire outlook. The betting man's is indeed a dedicated life.

R.L.

8:An Alternative View

Profitable betting doesn't just depend on finding winners, but on those winners being backed at favourable prices. So that in order to be consistently successful, it's necessary to be better informed, either in terms of doing more homework or having access to better sources of information, than are the majority of the other participants in the betting market. Because it's only by acting on such information whenever they're in a position to do so, that backers can be certain of securing a favourable price. So that obtaining value should really be seen as an inevitable consequence of effective selection methods, rather than as an end in itself.

However as already noted on page 32, there's a totally different approach to selection, in which value and price are seen as the main criteria. And to this end, a number of different systems have been put forward which, so it's claimed, are capable of estimating fair prices for horses, which can then be compared with the prices which are actually on offer. So that in effect, the actual selection process can be left to take care of itself. Which indeed at first glance may seem like an eminently logical approach. But unfortunately it isn't. And to show up the fallacy behind this entire line of reasoning, its only necessary to consider this whole question of price as it's applied to horses.

Our Idea of a Fair Price

At one time or another when weighing up form, almost everyone believes they've got a good idea of what a fair price for a particular horse should be. A 5/2 favourite might look more like a 6/4 chance for instance; or the 20/1 on offer against another runner may seem particularly appealing. And this isn't really surprising, because this habit of weighing up the likelihood of all sorts of events is a basic feature of human intelligence; and whether we're conscious of it or not, it's probably something we're doing instinctively all the time. Although whether it's really up to the fairly complex task of pricing up racehorses, is another matter.

8 : An Alternative View

Take for instance, someone who's firmly convinced that the favourite just mentioned, really is a 6/4 chance. In reality of course, this can't simply apply in isolation, but will depend on the chances of all the other runners in the race as well. So that in theory at least, he should be equally convinced that a fair price for the field against the favourite should be 4/6: and not just because the favourite's a 6/4 chance, but because he's worked out all the other runners' chances independently. However it's doubtful whether many such backers, in taking such a view of the chances of an individual horse, will have genuinely weighed up the chances of even half of the other runners in the race. And certainly not in enough detail so as to produce a full set of prices about which they could be equally confident, and which came anywhere near to totalling 100 percent.

And for similar reasons, the chances of horses whose form is studied first, or in the greatest detail, can often be overestimated in comparison with the rest of the field; especially where outsiders are concerned. Because even in a big field, 20/1 may well seem like an attractive price for a horse with respectable form when viewed in isolation; and before the chances of all the other runners have been fully taken into account. Whereas to backers who've straightaway latched onto a selection at a seemingly attractive price, there may seem little point in looking any further.

Yet despite all this, maybe it's still possible that our knowledge of prices may just come with experience, almost subconsciously; in the same way we seem to learn

about a lot of other things. However, before getting too carried away with this idea, it's maybe as well to reflect on the backer's disadvantages in this respect, when compared with the odds-compiler. For example, the latter may forecast that the second favourite in a particular race should start at around 5/1 - and he's only trying to predict public opinion don't forget, not the actual result. So that as soon as the sp's are announced, he'll know straight away whether he was right or not, or how close he came. Which means that he's always in a position to learn from his mistakes. Whereas a backer who's also concluded that a fair price for the horse should be around 5/1, has no way of ever discovering whether he was right or not; as a single result can prove nothing either way. Especially when as in this case, a genuine 5/1 chance could only ever be expected to win one race in six anyway.

In fact when judging by results, the only way a backer can ever be certain he's obtaining favourable prices, is if he's making a profit in the long run. But even then, all this really indicates is that at least some of his winning selections must have been at favourable prices, but not necessarily which ones. As it's always possible that at least some of the winning bets may have been at unfavourable prices; to say nothing of some favourably priced losers as well. The point being that there's just no real way of knowing. So that in the short term at least, it's difficult to see how backers could possibly be learning anything useful about prices on the basis of results; whether this was all being done subconsciously or not.

Possibly the only real alternative to this, would be to try and adopt a more methodical approach by calculating the runners' chances directly from their form. And this presumably would have to involve strike rates at some stage. However, as explained in detail on page 85, there are numerous problems with strike rates and similar quantitative approaches to the study of form, which render them totally unsuitable for selection and betting purposes. So there doesn't really seem to be too much scope in that direction either.

What all these arguments are intended to show, is that a number of assumptions about prices, and the way they're determined, can't really stand up to any close examination. Although what can't be denied of course, is that there does in fact seem to be quite a close correlation between starting prices and actual results. And presumably the factors just mentioned must play some part in this, although to what precise extent isn't clear. However because all the various processes which actually determine prices are proving so difficult to pin down, there doesn't seem to be much prospect of finding an alternative method of estimating prices, which could be expected to outperform the market, either in the long or the short term. Not that any of this is necessary anyway.

Taking An Alternative View

As already mentioned, if backers are to be consistently successful, then they'll need to be better informed than are the majority of the other participants in the betting market. So that they always need to be on the lookout

for an angle which might sometimes provide them with an alternative view. And so the following two chapters are mainly concerned with those aspects of form and conditions, which most easily lend themselves to such an approach. But first, there are two specific examples of an alternative view. The first kind is based on the type of specialised knowledge which in theory at least it should be possible for anyone to acquire. While the other is based on the sort of inside information, which by its very nature is only ever known to a select few.

Specialised Information

Before he went on to establish Timeform, Phil Bull had already developed his own scientific approach to the problem of timing racehorses. So that by taking into account such variables as wind speed and direction, going, and weight, and using his own hand-timings and calculations he was able to pinpoint horses, especially two-year-olds, which had put up particularly good performances. And he began supplying lists of these horses to subscribers in 1938, under the name of the Temple Racetime Analysis. And these selections showed a good level stake profit in six out of their seven years of operation.

But what's really of interest here, is that all Bull's clients were specifically instructed to back all these selections at Tote odds. So that when they came to place their bets they'd have had no idea whether they'd be obtaining a favourable price or not; something that runs totally contrary to all the conventional wisdom regarding value. Which is somewhat ironic, given that much of this seems to have subsequently originated from Phil Bull himself. However, and this is the real point, because his Racetime clients knew something about the real ability of those horses that the rest of the market didn't, they were more or less certain to obtain favourable prices anyway. Prices that is, which could not only compensate for the 16% deducted from the Tote win pool and still show a profit, but which could also compensate for the overround as well; as perhaps not surprisingly, the selections also showed a good profit when backed at starting price.*

The reason for this, is that after allowance is made for bias and the overround, on average market prices can be said to offer a fair reflection of the horses' chances based on all the generally available information. So what was formerly a fair price for a horse based on all that generally available information, should now represent a

---

* And it was through the continuing success of his Temple Racetime clients that Bull first met William Hill, with whom he struck up the immediate rapport which was to develop into a lifelong friendship. In fact so impressed was he with Bull's patient and detailed explanation of his scientific methods, that Hill, perhaps not surprisingly given the potential threat this posed to his business, immediately closed down or placed restrictions on the accounts of all Bull's clients.

As well as thinking he could get an even break from William Hill, apparently many years later Phil Bull was also under the impression he could ask Alex Higgins around to his house, for a nice relaxed game of snooker.

---

favourable price for anyone in possession of additional information, which suggests that a horse's chances are even better than is generally recognised.

Any attempt to promote value as a main selection criterion therefore, seems to be rather undermined by the fact that it isn't just difficult but well nigh impossible for backers to ever be certain whether any particular price is really favourable or not. Whereas it shouldn't be too difficult for them to recognise when they're acting on relevant information, which is apparently being ignored by almost everybody else; and when by so doing they're almost guaranteed a favourable price anyway. So that to repeat the point made earlier, if the proper selection criteria are in place, then the prices can be more or less left to take care of themselves. Whereas if they're not, then there's very little prospect of success anyway.

Inside Information

Because market prices are determined largely by generally available information, it follows that the best kind of alternative view would be one based on information which was known only to a select few. And it was in order to secure a steady supply of such information, that a group of wealthy establishment figures at the turn of the century formed the Druids' Lodge Confederacy; the name being that of the isolated stables, which they'd had built on Salisbury Plain. And as a reward for their efforts they landed among others, what's still regarded as probably the biggest single coup in the history of the British Turf, when backing their filly

Hackler's Pride to win the Cambridgeshire in 1903, at prices from 25/1 down; and she started as the 6/1 2nd favourite on the day.

And yet despite all the expense and years of careful preparation, the fact remains that the success of the whole enterprise was still dependent on Hackler's Pride being entered in unsuitable races beforehand, so as to finish well down the field and achieve a low handicap mark. Tactics which on the face of it, wouldn't stretch the resources of even the humblest one-man operation; whether with or without the assistance of his proverbial dog. Although the fact that Hackler's Pride also won the following year's race when carrying an additional 23lbs, even allowing for an extra 7lbs in weight-for-age, does suggest she had plenty in hand on the day.

Which may indeed have been just as well, because all such coups can still depend for their success, on the fact that nobody else has been working along similar lines. And the number which may have failed for that very reason can only be guessed at. So that given all the trouble and expense which can be involved, it's maybe not surprising that genuine inside information of this kind simply isn't for sale at any price. And even if it were, there's still be no real guarantee that things would always work out as planned.

In fact, what very often passes for inside information, concerns news of horses' work on the gallops, and whether or not this has pleased connections. And while this in itself may provide useful confirmation of a horse's fitness in the lead up to a race, much of it could probably be gleaned from a careful reading of the racing press anyway.

A Matter of Degree

An alternative view needn't necessarily be diametrically opposed to the prevailing view, but may simply be a matter of degree. The Temple Racetime selections for instance, were hardly unexposed, having already put up useful racecourse performances. And so the only real question was just how good those performances were; one which Phil Bull, with his stopwatch and calculations was in the best position to answer.

And a similar point can apply to prices. A knowledge of the betting market, and of the bias in favour of shorter prices, can often support an alternative view; even in races where there's already general agreement as to the likely winner. Which isn't to say that short-priced runners can be supported indiscriminately, but that contrary to all the received wisdom, a short price in itself needn't act as a deterrent: but rather it could even be seen as an incentive, when there are already enough other positive factors in favour of a selection. Providing of course, that it's taken at the right time.

An Alternative View on Form

In the absence of either inside or specialised information, the only other source for an alternative view will have to be from among the mass of potentially confusing information, which is readily available in various forms concerning almost every runner in every race. And while much of this material is going to be totally irrelevant most of the time, on other occasions even the smallest detail can assume real significance; and it's on being able to recognise such details that success or failure can depend. However, in the vast majority of races it usually turns out that there's simply no scope for an alternative view, no matter how much additional information is brought to bear on the problem. Either that, or there are just too many imponderables to form a judgement of any kind. So that most of the time spent studying form is inevitably going to be devoted to races which are subsequently rejected for betting purposes. Hence the need for patience, and the sort of disciplined approach, which isn't, admittedly, to everyone's taste.

Form and Conditions

At its most basic, form is the record of a horse's past performances on the racecourse, in terms of the distances it finished in front of, or behind other horses, and the weights they all carried. Of far more interest for betting purposes however, are all the various factors or conditions which may well have affected those performances either way. Because if horses could reproduce the same level of performance under all sorts of different conditions, in terms of say going, or distance, then the results of many races would either be a foregone conclusion, or in the case of handicaps, decided solely by chance, with very little scope for serious betting.

But while very few horses can meet such an ideal of consistency, this doesn't mean that the majority of them mightn't reproduce their best form under the right conditions. And so one of the main objectives is to try and discover as far as possible just what those conditions are, and then to judge their ability mainly on that basis.

This isn't helped though, by the fact that horses' racecourse appearances are strictly limited, as may be the range of conditions they're likely to meet on those infrequent visits. Or by the possibility that changes in conditions, may well affect different horses to a greater or lesser extent.

The real point though, is that while such changes in conditions can sometimes have a profound effect on the relative abilities of different horses, it seems that the market can sometimes fail to fully recognise this. And so it's always worth trying to discover the conditions under which each horse performs best, and then to only support those who seem to be especially well suited by the prevailing conditions, more especially when they're opposed by others who clearly aren't.

And because it's horses with the more obvious form qualifications, such as having won last time out, or having already won over the distance, which are less likely to be favourably priced to start with, it will be necessary to concentrate mainly on horses whose form may require more careful interpretation. Which means studying all these various factors and conditions in possibly greater detail, than might be needed to support a more conventional view.

9:Conditions 1

Handicaps and Weight

In racing, weight is used both as a great leveller and as a measure of ability. And to this end, there are standard scales for converting distances into weight, and to compensate for the differences in ability between horses of different ages. So that at it's simplest, if one horse beats another of the same age at level weights by two lengths over six furlongs, then the winner would be allotted a handicap weight or rating six lbs higher than the second. This being considered the equivalent to two lengths, in races of up to a mile. And if the two were to next meet in a handicap, with the former winner now carrying that extra six lbs, then while the result mightn't be the dead heat which it should be in theory, it should at least be much closer than before.

So that on the face of it, handicapping would seem to be a fairly straightforward mathematical exercise which if carried out correctly shouldn't leave any of the runners with a better than average chance. Which is usually the main reason given, when backers are advised to avoid handicaps altogether. However, if things really were that simple, then there'd be no such things as handicap favourites, and very little serious betting interest either, as their results would be largely determined by chance. But while this might seem to apply to some sprint handicaps, more often the whole point of betting in such races is the realisation that for various reasons, the handicapper is often faced with an almost impossible task. So that rather than actually equalising all their chances, the best he can often hope for, is to try and prevent the same one or two horses from carrying off all the best prizes; which from the point of view of the owners of the other runners, may be one of the main purposes of handicaps anyway.

Many of the handicapper's difficulties stem from the fact that in allotting a weight or rating to a horse, he doesn't just need to be objective, but to be seen to be objective as well; certainly where owners and trainers are concerned. Therefore he'll want to base his judgements as far as possible on the concrete evidence of the form book. Rather than on speculation and supposition, no matter how well informed, as to how far that form may or may not truly represent the abilities of those horses. In other words, in order to keep things as simple as possible at this stage, the handicapper will want to assume that every horse is being run on its merits in truly run races. And under conditions which, as far as they can be expected to know, its owner and trainer believe will allow it to do itself justice. And it's only later on, when the ratings are being updated, and anomalies begin to appear, all of which will somehow have to be reconciled, that the handicapper will really need to draw on all his interpretative skill and judgement.

Nobody else though apart from the handicapper, is under any similar obligations; either to refrain from speculation about horses' real or potential abilities, or to be totally consistent in their opinions of those horses from day to day. And there are probably three main areas where this advantage can be exploited fairly readily; these being optimum weight, improvement, and the possible effect of the conditions.

Relative and Specific Weight

All handicap ratings are relative, and so the fact that a horse has a particular rating doesn't refer to a specific amount of weight, but only to how much weight the horse would have to carry in relation to other rated horses. And so the only specific weights which actually apply in any handicap, are the maximum and minimum limits laid down in the Race Conditions in accordance with the Rules of Racing. And the imposition of such limits may well give rise to one or two unintended consequences.

Maximum and Minimum Weights

One observation which often crops up in relation to handicapping, is that while at the top end of the scale giving more weight to a fast horse should eventually succeed in slowing it down, at the other end taking weight off a slow horse won't necessarily make it run any faster. And it's here that the effect of having a maximum weight can be most clearly seen; if it makes it impossible to give the fastest horses enough of a burden, to slow them down sufficiently for them to be caught by the slower runners, no matter how little weight the latter are set to carry. Which may go some way to explaining the disproportionate success of top weights, and horses in the top half of the handicap generally.

While at the other end of the scale, because all handicaps have a stipulated minimum weight, any horse which is allotted less than this amount in the handicap, will still have to carry sufficient extra weight to bring him up to that minimum figure. However, if taking weight off a horse - by for instance reducing its weight from 7st 7lbs to 7st won't necessarily make it run any faster, then by the same token, giving it an additional 7 lbs to bring it up to the minimum 7st 7lbs flat race limit, mightn't succeed in slowing it down either. And this seems to be supported by the fact, that horses running a stone or more out of the handicap - and so carrying 14lbs more than the handicapper originally intended - have shown themselves quite capable of winning races.

Optimum Weight

Clearly specific amounts of weight will affect different types of horse to a greater or lesser extent. So that for example, a well furnished and muscular horse should have less trouble carrying a big weight than would a similarly rated but more lightly framed individual. So that regardless of his rating, every horse will presumably have an optimum weight; above which any additional burden will really begin to have a discernible effect; but below which there will be something of a plateau, where any equivalent reduction in weight won't necessarily be accompanied by any parallel improvement.

So that at the top end of the scale, any horse which can carry a top-weight of 10 st to victory in a competitive handicap, must have an optimum weight in excess of that 10st. While at the other end, horses who win from out of the handicap, must have an optimum weight in excess of the 7st 7lbs minimum limit. But other than that, when reviewing a horse's past races it may or may not be possible to identify the point at which increasing amounts of weight clearly began to have a serious effect on its performance.

The way horses perform in handicaps therefore, mightn't simply be determined by the weight they've been allotted by the handicapper when compared with the other runners, but also by how close that weight comes to their optimum weight, when compared with how close the other runners' allotted weights come to theirs. And so while at times, the whole question of weight and ratings may already seem quite complicated enough, nevertheless if the idea of optimum weight can help to explain some of the more puzzling aspects of handicaps, then maybe it's worth bearing in mind.

And finally, in terms of absolute weight, regardless of how much weight a horse is set to carry in comparison with the other runners or with a private handicap rating, it's always worth checking that the horse has already carried that amount of weight successfully; ideally in a comparable race run under similar conditions.

Weight and Improvement

The handicapper can only ever base his judgement on a horse's past performances on the racecourse, not on how well he may think it's likely to perform in its next race. So that in the case of an improving horse, its handicap rating can only reflect any improvement it may have shown in the period up to and including its last race. But obviously it can't take account of any further improvement that may have occurred in the meantime. And so to this extent, the handicapper will always find himself one step behind an improving horse.

It's two-year-olds though which can often show the most marked improvement, both in terms of physique and ability, especially in the latter half of the season. And it's at this stage that the top-weights in nursery handicaps can really start attracting some serious attention.

Weight and Conditions

It has already been noted, that while the prevailing conditions may have a big effect on a horse's performance, in order to remain objective, the handicapper will want to ignore these as far as possible. So that if a horse puts up a string of poor performances, whether or not this is as a result of encountering unsuitable conditions, his official handicap rating can be expected to reflect the fact. All of which opens up any number of possibilities which haven't entirely gone unnoticed down the years.

The real point though, is that horses whose poor recent form can definitely be attributed to their having raced under unsuitable conditions, are already good candidates for an alternative view whenever more satisfactory conditions prevail. And by easing their burden even further in response to those poor performances, the handicapper is tipping the balance even further in their favour; which can only really be to the advantage of their supporters too.

Universal Handicaps Ratings

In addition to making for more competitive racing, weight in the form of ratings can also function as an objective measurement of the abilities of horses both in the same, and arguably across different generations. And yet given the Victorians' enthusiasm for statistics of all kinds, what's maybe surprising is that this idea of a universal handicap covering every horse in training was only conceived as late as 1942; by Dick Whitford, who at the time was serving as a Naval Officer on North Atlantic convoys*.

Today, as well as Timeform and their commercial rivals, the chief of which is the Raceform Private Handicap, there are numerous other sources of ratings including the racing press. And the Jockey Club itself has been producing official ratings derived from a centralised handicap since the 1970s. However no matter how many resources are devoted to them, none of these enterprises is ever going to be completely immune to the kinds of problems already mentioned. So there are still likely to be marked discrepancies in the ratings which they sometimes assign to particular horses.

And yet despite all these difficulties, the fact remains that a rating figure is probably the closest it's possible to get, to a single

---

* Although Whitford was already supplying ratings to both Raceform and the "Daily Express", wartime difficulties hindered further progress. So that it was only after the war in collaboration with Phil Bull, that his idea became a commercial reality in the guise of the Timeform Ratings. However, having failed to gain the recognition or partnership he felt was his due, Whitford decided to part company with Bull and Timeform in 1949; and he later went on to produce ratings for the "Sporting Life" in the 1970's.

Another racing enthusiast who was serving on convoys at the time, was Able Seaman Alec Bird. According to his autobiography, Bird regularly turned up for duty in his SS Jaguar Saloon, which he would park ostentatiously on the dockside, so as to deliberately upstage the officers. And hopefully it hasn't gone unnoticed, that there are no inexcusable references to "naval ratings", anywhere in this account.

---

objective measurement of a horse's ability both within and across generations; if that is what's actually required. But as far as favourable prices are concerned, it seems probable that the likes of racing journalists and odds-compilers will have been among the first regular subscribers to both Time-form and the Raceform Private Handicap; and presumably they remain so to this day.

Do-It-Yourself Handicapping

In the light of all this, it's now necessary to consider the misguided but popular notion, that it's possible for the real enthusiasts to usefully wile away the hours by compiling their own sets of handicap ratings.

Because in reality, there's very little chance that any one person, no matter how knowledgeable and resourceful they might be, and no matter how specialised their field, could ever really hope to match the output of the Jockey Club, or that of any of the leading commercial ratings services; especially given all the resources these en-terprises have at their disposal, both on and off the racecourse. And for handicapping to ever make sound financial sense, the output would need to be sold in some way. Which in turn means having to employ other people, so as to maintain the necessary standards from day to day.

And there are two other points maybe worth remembering in this context. Firstly that Dick Whitford began work on his hand-icap in wartime; when there were severe restrictions on racing, and far fewer horses in training than there would be under more normal conditions. And secondly, given his

relative isolation in the middle of the North Atlantic, such a project would have been an ideal way of maintaining an active interest in racing, in the absence of any realistic alternative.

Converting Ratings into Prices

The Holy Grail for most value enthusiasts, would probably be some sort of formula, which could convert ratings such as those supplied by Timeform or Raceform directly into prices. However as anyone who's ever tried this with a pencil and paper knows, it's often difficult to avoid simply ending up with 5/1 favourites, and 8/1 outsiders.

As it turns out, to convert ratings into anything resembling normal prices involves calculations using 16-plus digit numbers. And unfortunately these were beyond the scope of pencil and paper, electronic calcu-lators, and even the software supplied with the earliest personal computers. However, once the right software became available, it wasn't too difficult to devise a fairly simple formula, which could convert ratings into prices which bore some real similarity to those that were actually on offer. Although whether in the end it was all worth the wait is another matter.

The first problem was that the number of noticeably overpriced market leaders was relatively small. And what's more, many of these could be explained by reference to such factors as unsuitable conditions, or an unfavourable draw. While in bigger fields with more open betting, sometimes upwards of six or seven of the runners might appear to be marginally overpriced. But usually by not nearly enough, for the occasional winners to offset the steady losses being incurred on the other, far more numerous losers.

The second main difficulty lay in how to deal with unrated horses; which depending on the time of year could amount to three or more per race. The point here was that giving such horses an average rating, a minimum rating, or even a zero rating, might well make a significant difference to the prices allotted to the rest of the field. And unfortunately, it proved impossible to devise any truly satisfactory and consistent method for deciding between the three.

The Going

Although the going is usually regarded as second only to weight in its potential effect on performance, the fact is that many horses are relatively indifferent to the state of the ground and so can perform well under a variety of conditions; while at the height of the summer it may hardly enter into the picture at all.

However if the ground is going to be a factor, especially when more extreme conditions prevail, then horses who are especially suited by such conditions can often turn out to be favourably priced. It may be because any late changes in the going could immediately wrong-foot all their forecasts, that the press usually choose to ignore its effects as far as possible. And if this is then reflected in how the betting-public comes to view a race, then it can only really suit the odds compilers too. But whatever the actual reason, it's clear that the advantage which some types of going can confer on particular horses, isn't always being fully reflected in their prices.

Because of their undulating nature and problems with watering and drainage, many racecourses can exhibit two or more distinct states of going at any one time, even across the width the track; and this is something which the introduction of more precise measuring equipment such as the French penetrometre, would do very little to solve.

So that it would probably be a mistake to ever base selection decisions on over-precise going requirements, or to worry too much about the imperfect nature of going reports as they're produced at present. And in any event, where the ground is going to be a factor, it's horses who require extremes of going who can provide the best betting opportunities, as they're more likely to spend most of their time running up unimpressive form under unsuitable conditions. And of these, it's those who require soft or heavy ground who tend to have longer careers; and any who've shown themselves capable of carrying big weights under such testing conditions probably have the biggest advantage of all.

There can be any number of possible explanations, as to why different types of horses seem to be best suited by certain types of ground. So that horses with bigger feet, or a higher action, and lighter individuals generally, are seen as best able to cope with soft or heavy ground; while those with a daisy cutter action which skims across the surface are best equipped to handle firm or hard conditions. But whatever the truth of any of these theories, all that really counts in the end is what appears in the form book. Because unlike in the case of distance, the question of going offers very little scope for informed guesswork of any kind.

Over the jumps, ground that is either too firm or too soft mightn't just affect a horse's action between the obstacles, but may also undermine its confidence when jumping them as well. Therefore in National Hunt Racing, a change in the going may well lead to much bigger turnarounds in the form than might be the case on the flat.

Distance

On the face of it, the question of whether a horse is suited by a particular distance might seem to be quite straightforward, but there are at least two reasons why it isn't.

First, there are the different demands which can be made on a horse's stamina, when covering the same nominal distance under the varying conditions which can apply on different racecourses, in terms of gradients, pace, and going

In order to appreciate the potential effect of gradients on stamina, it's only necessary to compare races with stiff uphill finishes on courses such as Cheltenham, Newcastle or Salisbury, with equivalent distances over essentially flat courses such as Kempton, Haydock or Redcar. And while undulating courses may allow for breathers on the down-hill gradients, the constant renewal of effort needed to tackle the uphill sections can make them far more of a test than flatter courses; because while the pace may be more unrelenting there's less call for any

stamina sapping changes of gear. Although rather paradoxically, on flat courses, races over straight distances are often considered to be more testing than races over the equivalent distance at courses that incorporate one or two bends, as these may allow for a momentary drop in pace.

Clearly pace and distance are intimately connected, and a horse's ideal distance is the one that makes the best use of both its speed and its stamina. For instance, if a horse struggles to keep up with the pace in a six furlong race, only to drop right away at the furlong pole, then it's likely it would be much better suited by the easier pace of a longer trip. Whereas if the horse was fighting for its head and contesting the lead for most of the race, only to again drop away, then clearly it would be better suited to racing over five furlongs.

However it's still always worth bearing in mind that jockeys will usually try and time their effort so as to get the best out of their mounts, rather than show up their limitations. And also that in borderline cases, the suitability of the tempo and pace in the first half of a race can clearly affect any horse's ability to fully last out the trip,

Testing ground can make additional demands on stamina whatever the distance; and horses with proven ability over longer distances on soft or heavy ground, are almost always worth supporting whenever similar conditions prevail.

The second main obstacle to determining any horse's ideal trip concerns the fact that sprinters apart, its distance requirements can generally be expected to increase as it develops to full maturity whether this on the flat or over the jumps. While at any age and for whatever reason, a horse's attitude to racing can sometimes seem to change; as may its style of running and its ideal distance, as compared with before.

And so because of the interplay between these various factors, a horse's ideal distance mightn't be immediately obvious at any stage of his career. But this also offers plenty of scope for informed guesswork, especially to those not overburdened with expectations concerning the horse's projected career path or its ideal distance, based perhaps mainly on its pedigree, or on its original cost in the sales-ring.

But whatever the actual reason may be, there always seem to be plenty of examples around, of horses of all ages being repeatedly raced over what appear to be the wrong distances. So that it often seems as if every other possibility is explored first; in terms of trying the horse over different going, using different tactics, and even putting up different riders, before the horse is finally entered in a race over a more suitable distance. And none of this is going to make its recent form look too impressive either. So that when it's finally entered in a more appropriate race, such a horse is far more likely to be favourably priced than are the majority of so-called proven distance winners.

The Intellectual Side of Horse Racing II

It is when we come to the question of form that we realise most fully the amazing intellectualism of the betting life. In the study of form we are faced by problems that can be solved only by the higher algebra. Thus if Jehosaphat, carrying 7st. ran third to Jezebel, carrying 8st. 4lb. in a mile race, and Jezebel carrying 8st.4lb., was beaten by a neck by Woman and Wine, carrying 7st.9lb., over a mile and a quarter, and Woman and Wine carrying 8st.1lb., was beaten by Tom Thumb carrying 9st. in a mile 120 yds., and Tom Thumb carrying 9st.7lbs was beaten by Jehosaphat over seven furlongs, we have to calculate what chance Tom Thumb has of beating Jezebel in a race of a mile and a half on a wet day... And the sincere betting man has to make such calculations daily.

R.L.

10:Conditions 2

The Draw and Field Sizes

Although the draw can sometimes have a big influence on the outcome of races, its likely effect may depend on three totally separate factors. Firstly, over shorter distances around curving tracks such as Chester and Brighton an outside draw is a clear disadvantage, simply because so much more ground has to be covered by horses racing around the outside; either that, or lengths have to be sacrificed at the start in dropping in behind. Secondly, the positioning of likely front runners in the field can confer an advantage on horses drawn alongside them; and so may affect the whole pattern of the race. And thirdly, as has already been noted, for various reasons the going can vary significantly across the width of the track, to the extent that one side may ride many lengths faster than the other.

Now the first of these factors is fairly straightforward, in the sense that over shorter distances no amount of early pace or faster ground can ever really overcome the handicap of an outside draw around a curving track; thus allowing the chances of any such horses to be safely written off.

However the influence of the other two factors isn't as clear-cut, if only because of a lack of statistics concerning front-runners. But it's likely that both going and early pace may have an effect in big fields, although to an extent which will vary from race to race.

As to the effect of early pace on the shape of the race, it can often prove useful to make a list of the participants in draw order, and then highlight all the likely front-runners.

Any overall advantage in the draw may be apparent in the statistics which are featured in the racing press, and in specialist publications. But because these can often overlook such factors as the possible re-positioning of the stalls and any artificial watering prior to the race, they don't always give the complete picture. In fact, as in the case of the Thirsk race described on page 47, under the right conditions at certain courses, races can be decided solely by the draw irrespective of the form book. So here's one area offering plenty of scope for the use of specialised knowledge.

And big fields can also provide a positive advantage, at least to backers of well drawn selections who are capable of making all the running. Because not only will the more fancied of the other runners be attracting support, but the more numerous they are, the greater the possibility of their impeding each other as well. However where there's no clear advantage in the draw and known front runners are posted on either side, there's always the possibility of the field splitting into two or more groups. Which may then turn the outcome into even more of a lottery than it might otherwise be.

Bends and Gradients

At the last count there were 59 Flat and National Hunt racecourses in Great Britain, 35 left-handed, 22 right-handed, and two, Windsor and Fontwell in the form of figures of eight, with turns in both directions. And while some of these courses such as Kempton Park are more or less flat, having being specifically laid out as racecourses, others such as Epsom, Brighton, and Goodwood, simply follow the natural contours of the existing downland landscape. And not only does this variety contribute to the unique character of racing in the British Isles but it can also provide a useful selection criterion as well.

Generally speaking, it's courses such as Brighton and Epsom with their pronounced undulations and tight bends, which are seen as best suited to the short-striding, handy type of horse. Whereas flattish tracks with easy bends such as Newmarket and York, favour the long-striding galloping type. However because the average horse is less likely to be inconvenienced by a galloping track than by a sharp one, it's at the latter, that previous course, and course and distance winners, can be expected to have the most marked advantage. A fact which isn't always necessarily reflected in their prices.

To maintain his balance while negotiating bends at speed, a horse needs to lead with the correct leg. And this could prove difficult for horses who may have got into the habit of favouring a particular leg, maybe as a result of a long forgotten injury or schooling problems. While even on straight courses, horses that hang towards the rail will tend to cover less ground. So that the marked preference shown by some horses for courses running in one particular direction isn't simply an aberration, but has a solid basis in fact; and so it shouldn't be ignored.

Galloping uphill can provide a good test and good exercise for any horse and so it shouldn't present any problems. Whereas being asked to gallop downhill can unsettle and unbalance some horses, even if this is only into the seemingly innocuous Dip, on the Rowley Mile. And downhill gradients can have even more significance over the jumps, as horses will naturally try to shorten their stride in their approach to downhill fences. It's this which can make them such a good test, and why form shown at flat tracks such as Kempton or Aintree, mightn't necessarily be reproduced over the demanding gradients to be found at the likes of Cheltenham or Sedgefield.

In order to help discover whether a horse is suited by one particular type of track, starting on page 110 there are some outline lists of all British and Irish racecourses, in which they've been broadly classified according to the three factors just mentioned here. And there are also some other suggestions, as to how this idea might be taken further.

Tempo and Pace

A comparison of record, standard, and actual race times suggests that it's often the race tempo, rather than out-and-out pace, which decides the outcome. One reason is that the riders of the best horses, especially in better class races, are often unwilling to set a fast early pace themselves, if this simply sets up the race for the opposition. And secondly, while the uniform nature of the tracks in the USA makes it possible to train horses there against the clock, so as to naturally develop an optimum tempo, the variable nature of the racecourses in the British Isles clearly rules out any such approach.

In fact, except over shorter distances, the more usual pattern is for a fairly leisurely start as the runners sort themselves out, to be followed by a gradually quickening tempo as the race progresses, culminating in an all-out effort in the final one or two furlongs. Which is a pattern best suited to horses who are capable of producing one or more changes of pace, and sustained bursts of acceleration, especially towards the end of a race.

So that given that the tempo in so many races can be such a hit-and-miss affair, unless a horse is capable of setting its own pace, the fact that it may have put up an exceptional time in the past, offers no guarantee that it will necessarily get the chance to make use of that speed in the future.

However with two-year-olds, the main priority is usually to familiarise them with racing without blunting their natural enthusiasm; and so more straightforward tactics can often be applied. So that two-year-olds' race times are more likely to reflect their real ability than might be the case with older horses. And for the same reason, any two-year-olds which have already put up a good time, will also be that much better placed to capitalise on that speed, at least until the end of the season.

Only a minority of horses are capable of taking the lead, and even fewer can stay in front for any length of time before eventually losing concentration. Which means that in any field, there are only ever likely to be a handful of runners capable of setting the tempo; and all the rest are going to be dependant on them, whether this suits them or not. So that in longer races where tempo is likely to be a factor, the horses with the biggest advantage are going to be those capable of setting their own tempo, by maybe leading from start to finish; and those with enough pace and acceleration to pull away and win races, whether from three furlongs out, or inside the last hundred yards.

Race Tactics

The ideal tactics for a jockey, would be to ride his horse in such a way as to make the best use of whatever speed and stamina it had, throughout the entire course of a race, which would be close to its best distance.

However with any number of horses having to run at the wrong tempo and over unsuitable distances, this can often prove to be an impossibility. And so the influence of tactics on the outcome of most races is probably best ignored as far possible.

Jockeys Trainers and Double Counting

When weighing up a horse's chances, it may seem only reasonable to give some consideration to the jockey and trainer; but this can often be both unnecessary and misleading. Because even if a horse is from a leading stable and is being ridden by a top jockey, these facts in themselves don't necessarily improve its chances if the same team have already been responsible for its progress up until that point. As their contribution will already be reflected in the horse's form.

Jockeys

With only a limited number of really good horses to go around, most of which will be concentrated among a small number of leading owners and trainers, it's inevitable that the jockeys retained by those stables are going to ride a disproportionate number of winners. And that when they're available they're also likely to pick up the cream of the outside rides as well. So that with many more perfectly competent riders around than there are good horses, the fact that a particular jockey isn't in the top half of the table or has a low winning percentage, could just as easily be the result of a shortage of winning opportunities, as of any real lack of ability. And so the most important question concerning the jockey, isn't his

position in the table, but whether he's familiar with the horse, and has already ridden it with any degree of success. While horses to be especially wary of are those which appear to need special handling, but whose regular partner is unavailable through either injury, suspension, or whatever.

Before reading too much into a leading jockey's choices of outside rides, it's also worth noting that many may accept an unpromising mount simply to stay in the good books of a particular owner or trainer; as paying attention to such details, may have got them where they are in the first place. While on other occasions, a top jockey may be engaged, simply in order to give a second, or even third opinion, concerning a horse's ability and potential; or what may be more to the point, its apparent lack of either.

If there's one area of racing where almost everyone appears to be a real expert, it's in their ability to spot jockeys' mistakes, whether real or imagined, the moment they occur. So that even if they couldn't pick a winner to save their lives, the confirmed losers at least have the consolation of having somebody else to point the finger at; while at the same time salvaging another ready-made excuse, for possible future use. (See also page 107)

Jockeys Trainers and Prices

Given the number of backers who blindly follow top jockeys and stables, in theory there should be a price advantage when backing form horses from smaller stables, being ridden by lesser-known jockeys. And while the overall statistics don't seem to bear this out, this is probably only because they're not comparing like with like; as on average, horses from bigger stables could already be expected to have a better chance on form anyway.

Trainers and Statistics

More than any other aspect of racing, the performance of trainers most easily lends itself to the kind of statistical analysis pioneered by Peter Jones with his "Trainers' Record" and much imitated since. And where this approach comes into its own is in the insights it can provide, into trainers and their methods; their most successful times of year, their record with first-time-out-runners, their favoured courses and so on. These are factors which might not otherwise jump out of the form book by themselves, but once they've been identified they can provide useful pointers as to what to look out for in future, in the form of horses from particular yards. So that training statistics, like statistics in general, are likely to yield the best results when used in conjunction with other sources of information, rather than when simply looked at in isolation.

Dangers in Following Stables

While following particular stables may provide extra interest, it's unlikely to prove profitable in the long run. This is because it can lay backers open to the twin perils of selective attention and misguided loyalty; so that the valid claims of opposing horses may be subconsciously down-played if not ignored altogether, while the abilities of horses from the chosen stables are being consistently overestimated by comparison.

A Change of Scenery

While horses are creatures of habit and so can easily adapt to routine, perhaps paradoxically they can also welcome a change of scenery. For a trainer there are probably few more galling experiences, than to have horses removed following a disagreement of some kind, only to have them run out of their skins on their first racecourse appearance following their change of address. Because while this might appear to vindicate the owner and reflect badly on their former trainer, the fact is that moving them to different boxes in an adjacent yard might well have had precisely the same effect. But regardless of this, horses actually changing stables are certainly worth watching out for, as this can often signal a temporary improvement in form.

The Virus

Equine virus or "flu" is a catch-all term which can cover a number of different conditions, which may last for an entire season or for just a few days. And in the same way, while at one extreme victims may show obvious symptoms of a high temperature, low blood-count, coughing, and general lethargy, at the other end of the spectrum infected animals may show no clinical symptoms at all: so that the only indication that something is wrong is a succession of disappointing performances from fancied stable runners.

Whenever bigger stables are suspected of having the virus this usually invites plenty of media comment and speculation anyway. But whatever the size of the stable, it's still always advisable to check the trainers' table for any conspicuous lack of success with fancied runners in recent weeks; as clearly any such stables will need to be avoided until there's an evident return to form. And it's then that an interesting possibility may arise. As some horses, having finally mustered the strength to shake off the effects of the virus, may also show some temporary improvement over their pre-virus form.

Two Kinds of Fitness

As with humans, unfit horses will usually run out of breath well before their muscles tire, because in effect there are two main stages of fitness. First, there's basic physical or muscular fitness, which is built up at the start of each season, and then maintained by a daily program of walking, trotting, cantering, and finally galloping. Then secondly, there's full racing fitness, where the horse's breathing and circulation are such as to allow it to fully extend itself when matched against other fit individuals. And this can only be achieved and maintained by regular and sustained effort on the gallops, and then subsequently on the racecourse. And so the difficulty is, that while a horse may look in the peak of physical condition as it walks around the paddock, it might yet still lack that extra edge in its breathing, that one or two further gallops would have given.

However, given a suitable temperament and barring injuries, there's no reason in principle why any horse which races regularly in handicap company, can't be kept fully fit and ready to race throughout an entire season. Whereas horses of Group or Championship class on the other hand, may be aimed at only six or seven races in a season, with gaps of six or eight weeks in between. And so their feeding and exercise will need to be carefully regulated so as to keep them quietly ticking over between races.

Further Questions About Fitness

Planned absences such as these though, present much less of a problem than do prolonged absences due to illness or injury. Because not only will the horse lose racing fitness fairly quickly, but with insufficient exercise it will start to lose physical condition as well; something which it may take weeks or even months of painstaking effort to restore. So that any horse returning from injury or illness presents backers with three separate questions - Is it fully recovered? Is it racing fit? And has its overall level of performance been badly affected by the illness or injury? All of which questions can only really be fully answered after the race.

But even in the absence of serious problems, no horse, no matter how fit and how well cared for, can always be guaranteed to be entirely free of the sort of minor injuries and infections, which while fairly insignificant in themselves, could sometimes make all the difference in a really close finish.

And likewise, while it's not generally the practice to deliberately race unfit horses, as this may do more harm than good, common sense suggests that a horse probably won't be as fit going into what's clearly intended as a preparatory race, as it will be going into its target race to be held in maybe two or three weeks time.

While finally, there are always horses who no matter what may be asked of them at home, will only ever fully extend themselves on the racecourse. And so they can't always be guaranteed to be at the peak of fitness, when returning from an absence.

The most convincing evidence of a horse's fitness would clearly be a good racecourse performance, or an impressive piece of work on the gallops, in the period immediately leading up to a race. But in the absence of either of these, and while bearing in mind the exceptions just noted, it still seems reasonable to assume that any horse that has been sent to the races, will most likely have been judged fit enough by his connections, to do himself justice on the day.

Class

Class as it applies to races can be difficult to pin down as it's determined by at least three different factors: the actual category of the race, the status of the racecourse where it's taking place, and the amount of prize money involved. It can be of real significance though, as previous wins no matter how impressive, may count for little once a horse steps up in class. But on the other hand, because the market is usually sceptical of any such horse's chances of succeeding they're often priced accordingly. And of all the big-priced winners whose success can be explained with the benefit of hindsight, it's probably horses who've succeeded in stepping up in class which form the largest group. This can also be confirmed by comparing the performance of various selection systems, as it's often only those which deliberately ignore class altogether, which succeed in throwing up any really big-priced winners.

So that while it's important not to underestimate the relevance of class in weighing up form, from a price point of view it can be worth looking out for horses which seem capable of defying the sceptics by successfully stepping-up in class. Which is really only an extension of the previous idea, of supporting improving horses.

While moving in the other direction, with the possible exception of horses being sent out by selling-race specialists, in general horses are often dropped in class because of a problem of some kind, including a lack of fitness. And so they're usually best avoided.

Over The Jumps

National Hunt Racing is held over two types of obstacles, hurdles and fences. Hurdles, which have a minimum height of 3ft 6ins are relatively flimsy affairs and much more forgiving than are fences. And while it can help for horses to meet the hurdles in the right stride, it's speed rather than jumping ability that's usually at a premium in hurdle races. Which is why they can attract horses from the flat, in addition to dedicated hurdlers, and intended steeplechasers not yet old or mature enough to tackle the bigger obstacles.

Apart from the Grand National and the water jump, all steeplechase fences have a minimum height of 4ft 6ins and are quite substantial affairs. Constructed of tightly packed birch, they may be 6 feet or more deep at the base, tapering off to around 18 inches at the top. And it's the stiffness of the birch at the top of the fence and the resistance it offers, rather than the height in itself, which accounts for the varying difficulty of the fences at different courses.

The ideal when jumping is for a horse to meet the fence in its natural stride, taking off from approximately 9 ft away. This should then allow it to both clear the fence with a minimum of effort, and maintain its forward momentum on landing. But if this isn't possible, then there are two other options. The horse could be checked so as to get in an extra stride; but in taking off so much closer to the fence it will need to jump higher, and so may well lose momentum on landing. The other alternative would be for it quicken and lengthen its stride in the run up, taking off from maybe 12ft away; but with a fall the almost inevitable outcome if its hind legs fail to properly clear the fence.

The best position from which to watch jumping in order to compare the style and fluency of different horses and riders, is at the take-off side of the fence. It's just unfortunate, that because of the need to stay up with the action, it isn't normally possible to cover jumping from this angle on TV. So that in order to get a better idea of what's actually involved, it's really necessary to go to the races and stand at the take-off side of a fence as the horses approach.

Three factors which can impact on a horse's jumping, are the going, gradients and tiredness towards the end of a race. And in addition, there are some courses which can present horses with particular problems. Haydock and Aintree for instance with their drop fences which fall away at the landing side, and Sandown Park with its series of seven closely-spaced "railway fences" down the back straight.

As much as anything else, successful jumping requires concentration. Especially when this is being done at speed, possibly in company with other horses, and when all involved are coming under pressure. And in order to win races it's necessary for a horse to maintain this throughout, despite tiredness and distractions. Because no matter how well it may have jumped up until that point, it may only take one mistake for it to forfeit any chance of winning.

It sometimes seems as if backers can be rather too forgiving of horses who get into the habit of making the occasional mistake; certainly when their prices are compared with those of other horses of similar ability who manage to always keep themselves out of trouble. So that purely from a price point of view, the ability to jump consistently and avoid mistakes would probably be among the first requirements for any selection.

Pedigree

For owners, breeders, and trainers, or indeed anyone else who may be concerned with the buying and selling of horses, especially unraced ones, the question of pedigree can be all-important. Because whatever it's bearing on results in the short term, a good pedigree is sure to command an extra premium when it comes to sales-prices and stud-fees. However from a backer's point of view the exact opposite can often apply, as horses with impressive pedigrees are seldom favourably priced for that very reason.

Breeding can also come to the fore in the run-up to the Classics, and the perennial question concerning the stamina limitations of particular horses. But even here, as was mentioned earlier, a horse's style of running can often give as good an indication of its stamina potential as can its pedigree.

So that in general, time spent studying pedigrees is probably much more likely to reward buyers and sellers of horses than it is backers; who should already have access to plenty of other information anyway.

Why Horses Run, Or Maybe Don't

Any account of form and conditions can't totally ignore the question of how horses can be persuaded to race at all. The most common explanation for this is flight, the suggestion being that because horses are essentially prey animals, their first instinct will always be to flee in the face of danger, whether real or imagined; which is a throw-back to their origins on the plains of Central Asia, and the ever-present danger posed by wolves and bears and suchlike.

However the behaviour of racehorses is clearly more complex than that, showing plenty of evidence of play and displacement activity, mimicry, mating, and herd behaviour, and the exuberance which is deliberately fostered by a carefully controlled regime of both diet and exercise.

So the fact that horses can be persuaded to race at all, let alone run in straight lines and actually win, is really owing to a fortu-nate combination of circumstances of which we still only have very limited understand-ing, and even less control. So that when

horses begin to lose interest, or simply no longer perform at their best, there's often no one simple explanation or guaranteed cure.

Form and Conditions Conclusion

As already noted, racecourses are too varied to ever function satisfactorily as the sites of scientific experiments; and its hard to think of a subject less suited to such experiments than the thoroughbred racehorse anyway.

So that as far as questions of form and conditions are concerned the best that can usually be hoped for is informed guesswork, although with the emphasis always being on the informed. But whereas before with questions of staking, it was possible to make categorical statements based on concrete evidence, any worthwhile observations con-cerning form will still need to be hedged around with plenty of qualifications. And so any suggestion that the whole business can be reduced to a purely logical exercise, based solely on incontestable evidence, proof, and deduction, is simply wishful thinking.

What is fairly clear however, is that to judge by the results of backing certain types of horses over the longer term, horses that is, which seemed to have been especially well suited by the prevailing conditions in maybe one of the ways described here, it's possible to conclude that a fair proportion of them must have been favourably priced at the time that the bets were struck. And so it's on this basis that any observations about favourable prices have been made. Although whether some of the suggested explanations for these discrepancies are all equally sound, is altogether another question.

System Advert (1947)

It's too late now of course, but if only Dad or Granddad had had the foresight to send off that £2 postal order for the Pro Handicap Method back in 1947. Starting off with £10 and a 1,200% annual rate of return on the Flat - after all, there's no point in being too greedy - in just 15 years they could have amassed over £1,848,842,588,950,364,300 and in 1962 money as well! The mind boggles to think just how much Mr. Collision's descendants must be worth by now - but its clearly a case of eat your hearts out Bill Gates, and the Sultan of Brunei!

11:Selection Systems

On October 14th 1997, the $1m Nobel Prize for Economics was awarded to Robert Merton of Harvard, and Myron Scholes of Stanford University, for their mathematical work in devising a formula for pricing stock options and futures which, so it was claimed, would eliminate much of the risk in stock-market trading.

In order to exploit their discovery, Merton and Scholes had already helped establish a firm called Long Term Capital Management, whose main business was to be hedging stock and option trades. And in its first three years of operation everything went according to plan, with the firm posting an average 40% return on invested funds. However things began to change rapidly for the worse with the collapse of successive Far-Eastern Stock-Markets, and the Rouble.

So that by October 1998, exactly one year after the award of the Nobel Prize, Long Term Capital Management held options on $1 trillion worth of trades - equivalent to the annual turnover of the entire U.S government -

which they were no longer able to finance, owing to their plummeting value. All of which left the firm and its clients facing a cumulative loss of $4.4 billion. And it took a $3.3 billion bailout by a consortium of banks and institutions to prevent a total meltdown of the New York Financial Markets. And while this might seem to have very little to do with racing, in fact Long Term Capital Management seemed to fall prey to exactly the same kind of delusions as can beset the users of amost any type of system.

Pattern recognition is a basic feature of human intelligence. So it's maybe not surprising if there's often a real feeling of euphoria following the discovery of a hidden pattern or equation, which can apparently make sense of what was formerly a mass of seemingly unconnected data. All the more so, if it also seems to offer a way of making easy money. And it's this infectious sense of euphoria which can sometimes have such a devastating effect on the judgement of even the most highly intelligent people.

So that in the case of Long Term Capital Management it seems it was impossible for any of the participants to admit at any stage, either to themselves or to anyone else, that despite mounting losses and spiralling costs, the system wouldn't be able to cope with any further falls in the Far Eastern Stock Markets. Something that a slightly more sceptical outsider, might well have recognised straight away. To say nothing of any possible similarity between the call for the $3.3 billion bailout, and the legendary begging telegram - SYSTEM WORKING FINE PLEASE SEND MORE MONEY

One final irony is that even prior to its official publication and right up until the present, the Merton and Scholes formula has been used successfully by the more street-wise dealers on the New York Futures Markets. But only as a way of evaluating short-term trades rather than as the basis for a global market strategy. An acknowledgement perhaps of the truism, that while almost any reasonable-sounding system can be expected to work at least some of the time, no system can ever be guaranteed to work all of the time.

Simple and Compound Systems

There are any number of simple systems around, based on following a single rule; and included among these might be backing the outsider in fields of three, favourites, or most tipped selections. But of maybe more interest in this context are what might be called compound systems, which are based on combinations of different rules. Because it's this type of system which often provides the most regular betting opportunities, while at the same time appearing to be the most logical and scientific in its approach.

And with so many different questions of form reducible to a straight yes-or-no answer, there's certainly no shortage of possibilities. The table shown on the opposite page which is probably far from complete, lists 61 such questions or rules, formed into 20 separate groups covering different aspects of form; so that no system would need to include more than one rule from any single group.

It might come as a surprise to learn that anyone thinking of assembling a system made up of just five of these rules from different groups, would have a total of 3,899,139 different combinations to choose from. While adding a sixth rule would take the total to 29,801,389. And having such a vast range of choice can create problems all of its own.

61 Possible Rules for Inclusion in Systems

1	1	Last 3 form-figures 111.
	2	Last 3 form-figures 112.
	3	Last 3 form-figures 122.
	4	Last 3 form-figures below specified total.
2	5	Won last time out.
	6	Won at least once this season.
3	7	Timeform top rated.
	8	Timeform top two rated.
	9	Other top rated.
	10	Other top two rated.
4	11	Best Timeform speed-figure.
	12	Best other speed-figure.
5	13	50% plus place ratio.
	14	25% plus place ratio.
6	15	50% plus win ratio.
	16	25% plus win ratio.
7	17	Specified price or better.
	18	Favourite.
	19	In top three in betting.
	20	Not in top three in betting.
8	21	Has won over the distance.
	22	Has won over a similar distance.
	23	Has performed well over this distance.
9	24	Has won on this going.
	25	Has won on similar going.
	26	Has performed well on this going.
10	27	Has won over this course.
	28	Has won over a similar course.
	29	Has performed well on this course.
	30	Has won over this course and distance.

11	31	Has won within the last 7 days.
	32	Has won within the last 14 days.
	33	Has won within the last 28 days.
12	34	Has run within the last 7 days.
	35	Has run within the last 14 days.
	36	Has run within the last 28 days.
13	37	Has won a more valuable race.
	38	Has won a race of equivalent value.
14	39	Won an equivalent race with more weight.
	40	Won an equivalent race with same weight.
15	41	Has won most prize-money.
	42	Has averaged most prize-money per victory.
16	43	Top trainer at this course.
	44	Trainer in top three at this course.
	45	Trainer in top three this season.
	46	Trainer in top three this month.
17	47	Top jockey at this course.
	48	Jockey in top three at this course.
	49	Jockey in top three this year.
	50	Jockey in top three this month.
18	51	Selected by most tipsters in this race.
	52	Selected by at least 3 tipsters.
	53	Is today's most tipped horse.
	54	Selected by current leader of naps table.
	55	Selected by longest losing tipster.
19	56	Is well drawn.
	57	Less than a specified percentage of falls.
	58	Has never fallen.
20	59	Less than 8 runners.
	60	Between 8 and 16 runners.
	61	Number of runners within specified range.

11 : Selection Systems

The betting bank calculations on page 38 have already shown how it's possible, even with an overall negative rate of return, for the odd series of 100 races to still show enough profit in the short term to occasionally double the bank. And so working along similar lines, the following table shows the results from 10,000 series of 100 races, in this case using six built-in rates of return.

But unlike before, where the measurement used was that of busted or doubled banks, this time it's simply the overall percentage of series, which were either winning or losing after the first 100 races.

Even Chances
10,000 sequences of 100 races at 6 different rates of return
£100 opening bank £10 stake.
Percentage of trials showing a profit or loss after 100 races

rate of return	winners	losers
-20%	0.66%	99.34%
-15%	4.61%	95.39%
-10%	14.18%	85.82%
-8%	19.27%	80.73%
-5%	31.55%	68.45%
fair	48.39%	51.61%

Assuming that most system selections start at prices between 5/6 and 3/1, then on the evidence of the price-band data on page 152 they're likely to be losing between 7.8% and 10.1% overall. So that according to these figures, most systems already have between a 1 in 5, and 1 in 7 chance of showing some sort of a profit after the first 100 races.

And even if they don't, it should only be necessary on average to make between 4 and 6 rule changes to turn things around, which with so many possible alternatives to choose from, shouldn't present too much of a problem. In systems terminology, this juggling of different rules until a satisfactory outcome is achieved is often referred to as "fine tuning" the system. However this isn't really tuning at all, when improved results can't necessarily be linked to any particular rule changes but are almost inevitable anyway, provided enough changes are made.

And unfortunately, it's systems which appear to follow the most logical rules, that are by their very nature the most misleading. Firstly, by generating mainly short priced selections, they're more likely to produce favourable runs of results in the short term anyway. And secondly, because the system rules appear to be so logical, it's then that much easier to believe that they alone might be responsible for any favourable runs of results that do occur.

Two Further Problems With Systems

Because most systems tend to follow fairly logical-sounding rules, they're unlikely to be producing too many favourably priced selections in the first place; despite the occasional favourable runs.

This is because market prices will almost certainly be taking account of the very sort of form criteria which can be most easily incorporated in such rules. And so, because all such systems can be largely expected to point towards unfavourably priced selections anyway, they could hardly be expected to generate an overall profit in the long term.

And on those occasions when a system does succeed in throwing up a big-priced winner, when seeking an explanation it can often be worth looking at those factors which weren't covered by the system, rather than just at those which were. Class being a good case in point.

The other main problem concerns the fact that systems are expressly designed to simplify the study of form by applying the same set of rules to every runner; and regardless of whether those rules are at all relevant in determining that horse's actual chances. While at the same time they may be deliberately overlooking other factors, which may have real significance in individual cases. Whereas what's often required, is almost a different set of rules for every horse. So that for any system to be capable of producing a profit in the long run, it would probably need to be so complicated and incorporate so many different rules, that it would no longer be really recognisable as a system as such, any more.

Winners Last-Time-Out

price band		runners	winners	percent	capital	pc return
		1152	225	19.53		
1 / 28 -	7 / 2	539	165	30.61	-21.74	-4.03
4 / 1 -	100 / 1	613	60	9.79	-111.46	-18.18

The Real Problem With Strike-Rates

It was mentioned earlier in relation to value and prices, that strike-rates could prove useful in any systematic approach to form study. Because in measuring how particular factors may be affecting a horse's overall chances of success, they should make it possible to determine exactly what a fair price for that horse should be. Wrong!

For instance, as shown in the above table, a sample of 5000 races produced 1152 runners who'd won last-time-out. And of these, 225 went on to win their next race; which gives winners last-time-out a success rate of 19.5%, and therefore presumably a "fair" price of just over 4/1.

However anyone who backed all the 613 runners at "fair" or "value" prices of 4/1 or better, would have lost 18% of their total stake; whereas those who'd backed the 539 which started at prices of 7/2 or less, would have lost only 4% of theirs,

So that of the 225 winners last-time-out which then went on to win their next race, 73% of them started at prices shorter than their supposed fair price of 4/1; while those starting at "favourable" prices bigger than 4/1 accounted for only 26.6%.

And exactly the same applies to favourites. In the sample of 12,800 races shown below, there were 14,099 favourites including joint-favourites of which 4726 - 33.52% won; thus giving a "fair" price for favourites of around 2/1. However as the table also shows, anyone backing favourites at prices in excess of 2/1 would have lost 11.24% of their total stake, while backers of favourites at 2/1 or less, would have lost only 6.73%. of theirs.

All favourites (including joint favourites)

price band			favourites	winners	percent	capital	pc return
			14099	4726	33.52		
1 / 28	-	2 / 1	7781	3399	43.68	-523.71	-6.73
85 / 40	-	16 / 1	6318	1327	21.00	-709.83	-11.24

What's evident from both of these examples, is that there are clearly additional factors over and above having won last-time-out, or favouritism, which make some of these runners two or three times more successful than others. And these other factors are also being reflected in their shorter prices.

And unfortunately there's no reason why this shouldn't always be the case, no matter how many additional rules or combinations of rules are applied. So that it's the shortest priced qualifiers, those who on the face of it appear to offer the least "value", who'll still generate the best rate of return because of additional factors which still aren't being covered by those further rules.

The main reason why strike-rates are so popular, is that while they're relatively easy to calculate, they can still lend a spurious air of scientific credibility and precision, to what are often totally bogus arguments.

And they're certainly much easier to compile than are profit-or-loss figures, which in the context of betting are the only statistics that are of any real value. Whereas strike rates, no matter how impressive they might appear on the surface, are really about as much use as the proverbial chocolate teapot.

DIY Computer Systems

It's an unfortunate fact that the unquestioning faith that many people place in selection systems, can all too easily be matched by a similar susceptibility towards the supposed mystique and power of computers.

So that computer systems can often come to represent the worst of all possible worlds. Because not only do they appear to satisfy the instinctive need to find hidden patterns in all sorts of things, and to assign probabilities to all kinds of events, but in order to do so, they're apparently able to draw on the resources of an infinitely adaptable calculating machine, boasting capabilities that would have been undreamed of even 20 years ago - and while also making money in the process. So it's maybe no wonder that the poor old bookmakers are all quaking in their boots!

Garbage In Garbage Out

Computers to be fair, are invaluable when it comes to handling large amounts of data; and without the help of a computer to do all the calculations, and lay out the tables and text, this book simply wouldn't have been possible at all. However by the same token, they're equally capable of transforming the worst kind of nonsense into neat columns of figures, all calculated to two or three decimal places. And while this should always be a concern wherever computers are being used to process and present information, with racing systems it can be almost guaranteed. That no matter how impressive the output may appear on the surface, underneath it's still not going to make any more real sense, than it did before it first went in.

Off-The-Shelf Computer Systems

There always seem to be plenty of these on the market, and the sort of names they go under - "Bookie Buster Mark IV" , or "New Improved Moneymaker Gold", suggest they may have undergone plenty of "fine tuning" along the way. But anyone tempted to spend their money on such things need only ask themselves one question. Why would anyone who discovered a genuine winning system, ever want to sell it to anyone else?

Private handicappers and work-watchers may often have to put in many hours of effort, before discovering anything remotely useful, either to themselves or to anyone else. And so they may well need to sell some of this information just to cover their expenses.

Whereas anyone who's discovered a real winning system has no further expenses to worry about at all. And any they'd incurred up until that point they could recoup easily enough, by simply operating the system for themselves. So why would they ever need to sell it, when by so doing they'd be effectively cutting their own throats?

The Betting Man

Not that racing men have much time to spare for thoughts about social problems. Theirs is a busy life. They enjoy little of the leisure that falls the lot of statesmen and shopkeepers. Their anxieties are a serial story continued from one edition of the day's paper to another. Nor does the last edition of the evening paper make an end to their anxieties. It is not an epilogue to one day so much as a prologue to the next. The programme of races for the following day suggests more problems than a Summit Conference itself could settle in a month....

R.L.

12:When Things Go Wrong

The Uncertainty of Racing

Mention has already been made of races where there are so many imponderables, that it's impossible to make any sensible predictions about the outcome of the race at all. But at least it should be possible to identify such races beforehand. And so this shouldn't be confused with the uncertainty of racing, which results from all the unpredictable factors which can affect the outcome of any race at any time; and which from a psychological point of view anyway, can be seen as almost always working in the bookmakers' favour.

This is because it's backers rather than bookmakers whose fortunes are generally dependant on individual results, which is something the latter specifically set out to try and avoid. So that while this uncertainty needn't necessarily be damaging in a financial sense, and certainly not at level stakes, it can still have the effect of constantly undermining the confidence and morale of backers, as they see one race after another not working out quite as expected. And this is never more evident, than when a long-odds-on shot gets beaten.

The late Sir Gordon Richards was not only the most successful British jockey of all time, winning the Jockeys' Championship a record 26 times and achieving an unsurpassed 269 victories in a single season; but he was also a paragon of integrity. Quite possibly unique among jockeys, Richards was raised as a Primitive Methodist in a mining community; and so he was made well aware from a very early age, of the virtues of modest living and hard work, and of the pernicious effects of gambling in any form. And these were ideals that he demonstrably lived up to for the rest of his life.

Chepstow was undoubtedly a lucky course for Gordon Richards, as it was at a meeting here in 1933 that he not only went through the card on the first day, but rode the first five winners on the second day as well. None of which presumably, will have been lost on those of his loyal band of

12 : When Things Go Wrong

followers who regularly backed all his mounts. Such as for instance Glendower, which started at odds of 1/20 in the 4.00 at Chepstow on June 28th 1947 - which incidentally, was to be his record breaking year. But unfortunately, on this occasion their confidence was to be short-lived.

Chepstow June 28th. 1947
4.00 Chepstow Stakes 1m.4f.

| 1 Markwell | K.Mullins | 20/1 |
| 2 Glendower | G.Richards | 1/20 |

Only 2 ran

After coming under Starter's Orders, Glendower was unnerved by something at the start, reared up and unseated Richards, and was therefore unable to take any further part in the proceedings.*

And then in the September of the following year, there was to be similar confidence in another of Richards' mounts, the Coventry Stakes winner Royal Forest which started at odds of 1/25 in the Clarence House Stakes.

Ascot September 23rd. 1948
4.00 Clarence House Stakes 6f.

1 Burpham	T.Burn	33/1
2 Royal Forest	G.Richards	1/25
3 Vineyard	W.Evans	33/1

4 ran   dist. 1/2 length, 6 lengths

One explanation given for Royal Forest's defeat was that it may have been stung by a wasp, and it convincingly reversed the placings with Burpham when afterwards winning the Dewhurst Stakes at 5/4.

The real point here though, is that this explanation for Royal Forest's defeat only came to light, because the horse was an odds-on favourite which was confidently expected to win. And so it's quite possible that other less well-fancied horses may be suffering similar mishaps all the time, but with the resulting poor performances being simply put down to a straightforward lack of ability, or bad form on the day. And even with beaten favourites, the speed at which races are run means that the riders themselves, as in the case of Gordon Richards and Royal Forest, may be totally unaware of what actually happened at the time.

But while the form-book alone may give no real idea of the extent to which such incidents may be influencing results, the fairly close correlation between prices and results overall does still suggest that form appears to be working out most of the time.

So that while it should never be forgotten that there's simply no such thing as a racing certainty at any price, such uncertainty as there is, is unlikely on its own to be responsible for continuing losses or any great calamities. At least certainly not when betting at level stakes.

---

* And it isn't just highly-strung thoroughbreds that are so easily startled. Apparently the Irish playwright George Bernard Shaw was once knocked off his bicycle by a cart-horse, after it had bolted when a passer-by suddenly opened an umbrella.

And while still on the subject of umbrellas, St Simon (1881 - 1908), who is regarded as one of the most influential stallions in the history of British bloodstock, became increasingly temperamental with age; but it seems he would immediately calm down on being shown, among other things, a furled umbrella.

Losing Run Probabilities

It's already been established that losing run probabilities are of very little help in deciding staking ratios. However what has also emerged, is that even when betting at favourable prices it's still quite possible, as the betting bank calculations show, to suffer really bad runs of results in the short term. And while the financial impact of such runs can be minimised by the use of level staking, this doesn't mean that a long succession of losing bets mightn't still have a bad affect on morale. And so it's in this context, that the losing run probabilities on the next page may come in useful, by providing some idea of what can be expected, in terms of successive losing bets under various circumstances.

Because the emphasis up to now has been based on outperforming the betting market, the whole question of probabilities has never really arisen. However if the tables are to be of any real use, then it will clearly be necessary to decide into which category most typical selections are likely to fall.

In order to avoid possible misunderstandings, in the tables there are two figures given for each value, the actual probability and the expected frequency. So that for example, in the case of even-chances, because there's a 1 in 8 probability of 3 successive losses, it shouldn't be thought that this is only likely to occur once in every 24 races. In fact, because each successive race marks the start of a new sequence, as shown in the example below, on average three successive losses can be expected to occur once in every 10 races - and so this is what's meant by the expected frequency.

1	2	3						
	2	3	4					
		3	4	5				
			4	5	6			
				5	6	7		
					6	7	8	
						7	8	9	
							8	9	10

12 : Losing Run Probabilities

1/2 losing run	probability	expected frequency
1	3.00	3.00
2	9.00	10.00
3	27.00	29.00
4	81.00	84.00
5	243.00	247.00
6	729.00	734.00
7	2187.00	2193.00
8	6561.00	6568.00
9	19683.01	19691.01
10	59048.98	59057.98

1/1 losing run	probability	expected frequency
1	2.00	2.00
2	4.00	5.00
3	8.00	10.00
4	16.00	19.00
5	32.00	36.00
6	64.00	69.00
7	128.00	134.00
8	256.00	263.00
9	512.00	520.00
10	1024.00	1033.00

6/4 losing run	probability	expected frequency
1	1.67	1.67
2	2.78	3.78
3	4.63	6.63
4	7.72	10.72
5	12.86	16.86
6	21.43	28.43
7	35.72	41.72
8	59.54	66.54
9	99.23	107.23
10	165.38	174.38

2/1 losing run	probability	expected frequency
1	1.50	1.50
2	2.25	3.25
3	3.38	5.38
4	5.06	8.06
5	7.59	11.59
6	11.39	16.39
7	17.09	23.09
8	25.63	32.63
9	38.44	46.44
10	57.67	66.67

5/1 losing run	probability	expected frequency
1	1.25	1.25
2	1.56	2.56
3	1.95	3.95
4	2.44	5.44
5	3.05	7.05
6	3.81	8.81
7	4.77	10.77
8	5.96	12.96
9	7.45	15.45
10	9.31	18.31

10/1 losing run	probability	expected frequency
1	1.10	1.10
2	1.21	2.21
3	1.33	3.33
4	1.46	4.46
5	1.61	5.61
6	1.77	6.77
7	1.95	7.95
8	2.14	9.14
9	2.36	10.36
10	2.59	11.59

13:A Day At The Races

Cost and Convenience

Entry to most Premier League Football Grounds nowadays can cost a minimum of £15 to £25 whereas admission to Tattersalls' or the Grandstand enclosure at a Grade One Course may still only cost £10, with even cheaper admission for family groups.

So that except for those living in favoured areas such as the South-East, who enjoy fairly easy access to a number of different courses, it's probably the travelling costs as much as anything else, rail fares especially, which prevent more people from going racing on a regular basis.

Food And Drink

Because racecourses can only hold a limited number of fixtures each year, the prices they charge for food and refreshments will sometimes tend to reflect this; but at least they've got more excuse in this regard than have motorway services and airports which can open all year round. But in any case, anyone wanting to make the most of their visit to the racecourse would do better by stopping-off and eating on the way.

When going anywhere for the first time by road, apparently the best way of deciding where to stop-off, is to first leave the motorway, and then make a good mental note of the first possible eating place you pass. You should then stop-off, at the next place you see which is a decided improvement on that first establishment. And it seems it's even possible to prove this with mathematics too.

The Parade Ring

Ideally, occasional visitors to the races should already have a fair idea of which horses they're going to back, well before they arrive at the course. So that nothing they see there should normally affect any decisions they'll have already made.

More experienced racegoers on the other hand, may already know what to look out for in terms of physical appearance and behaviour when it comes to particular horses. As the true significance of any of these factors can vary between different individuals, and so may only be apparent to those who've already seen them on their previous appearances.

So that if it's to be of any real use when it comes to selection, paddock watching probably needs to be done on a fairly regular basis. And for anyone who's able to do so, it could well then provide them with a very valuable source of specialised information.

But even so, by actually going to the races it's still possible to make the kind of direct comparisons between the different horses, which simply aren't practicable when watching on TV. And it shouldn't take any real expertise to spot a number of obvious differences, which while they mightn't be of much help in spotting likely winners, may at least provide a better idea of what the TV paddock commentators are sometimes referring to.

In The Betting Ring

All the main points concerning the best strategy to adopt when betting on-course have already been covered on pages 13, 14.

In deference to the good old days of gas lighting and rickets, most on-course bookmakers are still prepared to lay the marginally better fractional prices as described on page 11, some of which were abandoned in the run-up to decimalisation in 1970. So that if they're asked, they'll still lay 100/6 in place of 16/1, 100/7 instead of 14/1, 100/8 in place of 12/1 etc. While any overseas visitors might also like to try asking for 100/30 instead of 3/1. Of course nothing could ever be quite that simple, because to take

advantage of this concession while maintaining a level stake still means having to top-up the bet at the normal price as well.

Not all on-course bookmakers regularly bet each-way, and those who do will normally display a notice to that effect. So if you intend betting each-way at what's expected to be a busy meeting, it may be worth making a mental note of their whereabouts in the ring before the start of racing.

Televised Meetings

Attending a televised meeting can make a big difference, as it can be illuminating to record the racing, and then to afterwards compare your own impressions at the time with the same events as seen from the different perspective of the coverage on TV.

Over The Jumps

It's already been suggested that the best place from which to watch jumping is on the racecourse, by standing at the take-off side of a fence. If it's possible to walk around the outside of the course, then this shouldn't present too many problems, and anyway there should usually be a recognised crossing point situated somewhere in front of the stands. Failing that, the best plan is probably to keep an eye out for any other groups of people who seem to be setting off in the same direction and then to simply follow them.

A Day Out For All the Family

There's no doubt that a day at the races, out in the open air and with plenty of new things to see and do, can make an ideal family outing; and also that it's quite possible to back horses regularly without ever having to pawn the kiddies' toys. But nevertheless...

"Mummy Mummy, why does Daddy keep going off all the time?"

"But Mummy Mummy, I've already had a go on the bouncy castle."

"Mummy Mummy, why has Daddy gone all red?"

"But Mummy Mummy, that's twice I've been on the bouncy castle now."

"Mummy Mummy, why is Daddy shaking his fist and shouting at that man on the horse?"

"But Mummy Mummy, that's three times now."

"Mummy Mummy, why is Daddy groaning and punching the ground?"

"Oh please Mummy Mummy, why can't I go and help Daddy find his wallet?"

"But Mummy Mummy please, that's four times now, and I'm feeling sick."

"Oh Mummy Mummy look, why are those men over there driving away in our car?"

"Oh look Mummy Mummy, Daddy's started crying again."

"Oh Mummy Mummy please, I want something to eat."

"Oh please Mummy Mummy, why is everyone else going home?"

"Oh look Mummy Mummy, Daddy's started searching through all the bins."

"Oh dear Mummy Mummy, it's getting very dark. Is Granny going to be long?"

"But Mummy Mummy, why is my sandwich all squashed with bits missing?"

"Oh Mummy Mummy please, why won't Granny let Daddy into the car?"

"Oh look Mummy Mummy, poor Daddy's trying to run after us."

"Mummy Mummy I'm scared, why is Granny driving so fast?"

A Day At The Races II

The parade of the horses, the hoisting of the names of the starters and jockeys, the laying of the bets, and the climbing of the grand stand are all gone through over and over again. The betting man has no time even for a drink. To the casual onlooker a day's horse racing has the appearance of a day's holiday. But the racing man knows better. He is collecting information, coming to decisions, wandering among the bookies in the hope of getting a good price, climbing into the grand stand and descending from it, studying the points of the horse all the time, with as little chance of leisure as though he were a stockbroker during a financial crisis or a sailor on a sinking ship.

R.L.

Part Three:
Reference

14:Estimating Win and Place Chances

This chapter describes the methods which were used to produce the estimated win and place chances which form the basis of the race profiles.

When comparing starting-prices with actual results over large numbers of races it soon becomes clear, as was already noted in relation to the betting-market, that there is in fact quite a marked bias in favour of shorter prices from a backer's point of view. And in order to confirm this, the results and prices of 12,800 races covering two complete seasons of Flat and National Hunt Racing were assembled and analysed.

This bias can most easily be seen in the following table, which breaks down the 126,000 odd runners from those races into eight separate price-bands

A	B	C	D	E	F	G
Price band	runs	wins	percent	ratio	capital	pcreturn
1 / 28 - 2 / 5	386	304	78.76	1.01	5.46	1.41
40 / 95 - 4 / 5	1490	839	56.31	0.93	-108.45	-7.28
5 / 6 - 6 / 4	3524	1479	41.97	0.92	-277.17	-7.87
13 / 8 - 3 / 1	10971	2975	27.12	0.90	-1111.00	-10.13
100 / 30 - 15 / 2	28865	4204	14.56	0.88	-3553.17	-12.31
8 / 1 - 16 / 1	39534	2442	6.18	0.75	-10066.50	-25.46
18 / 1 - 60 / 1	35557	540	1.52	0.43	-20434.00	-57.47
66 / 1 - 500 / 1	5883	17	0.29	0.24	-4456.00	-75.74
	126210	12800	10.14		-40000.83	-31.69

The columns are as follows :-

A The price band.
B The number of runners.
C The number of winners.
D The percentage of winners.
E The ratio of winners to the average price pc.
F The outcome to one point staked.
G This outcome as a percentage of the total stake.

The ratio of the percentage of winners to the average price percentage for each price band in column E offers a simple measure of profitability; with a ratio of 1 representing fair prices, a figure greater than 1 favourable prices, and a ratio less than 1 unfavourable prices.

And while this bias in prices is useful in helping to explain a number of features of the betting market, the fact that it's so clearly defined, also suggests a fairly close relationship between starting-prices and results overall.

Full tables covering all 95 reported starting prices, can be found on page 149, and data for 4 of these is shown below. And apart from the prices, the columns are the same as those previously used for the price bands table.

In effect, the percentage success rate for each price as shown in the fifth column, represents the average chance of all the horses which started at that price.

However, as can be seen in the figures shown here, even over 12,800 races there are still large variations in the success rates for adjacent prices which clearly run contrary to the overall trend, and which therefore will all need to be averaged out, before proceeding on to the next stage.

price	percent	runs	wins	percent	ratio	capital	pcreturn
11 / 8	42.10	606	248	40.92	0.97	-17.00	-2.81
6 / 4	40.00	744	259	34.81	0.87	-96.50	-12.97
13 / 8	38.09	637	254	39.87	1.05	29.75	4.67
7 / 4	36.36	1106	359	32.46	0.89	-118.75	-10.74

And so to this end, successive adjustments were made to the individual percentages, which were then tested by applying their equivalent prices to all the runners in the original races, with the results being sorted into the same 8 price-bands as were used before. This process was then repeated, until results were produced which couldn't be improved on, as shown in the table below.

Applying prices derived from this final set of percentages, which can be found on the next page, produced a tax-free gain of 17 points, which is equivalent to 0.13% overall, with each price band showing a profitability ratio of 1, and no really pronounced bias now discernible, at either end of the price range.

Final set of Results Using Prices Derived From the Adjusted Percentages.

Price band			runs	wins	percent	ratio	capital	pcreturn
1 / 28	-	2 / 5	363	286	78.79	1.00	-1.77	-0.49
40 / 95	-	4 / 5	861	522	60.63	1.00	3.06	0.36
5 / 6	-	6 / 4	3049	1403	46.02	1.00	-8.26	-0.27
13 / 8	-	3 / 1	8714	2627	30.15	1.00	-15.25	-0.18
100 / 30	-	15 / 2	26638	4367	16.39	1.00	-46.33	-0.17
8 / 1	-	16 / 1	27617	2296	8.31	1.00	19.00	0.07
18 / 1	-	60 / 1	33400	1100	3.29	1.00	-26.00	-0.08
66 / 1	-5000 / 1		25568	199	0.78	1.00	93.00	0.36
			126210	12800	10.14		17.45	0.01

Revised Win Chance Percentages

price	percent	price	percent	price	percent
1 / 28	82.08	8 / 11	51.09	8 / 1	9.11
1 / 25	81.75	4 / 5	48.99	17 / 2	8.55
1 / 20	80.97	5 / 6	48.05	9 / 1	8.06
1 / 16	80.03	10 / 11	46.11	10 / 1	7.16
1 / 14	79.38	20 / 21	45.04	11 / 1	6.51
1 / 12	78.51	1 / 1	43.79	12 / 1	5.38
1 / 11	77.98	21 / 20	42.86	13 / 1	4.73
1 / 10	77.41	11 / 10	41.76	14 / 1	4.24
1 / 9	76.58	6 / 5	39.11	15 / 1	3.79
2 / 17	76.14	5 / 4	38.23	16 / 1	3.40
1 / 8	75.65	11 / 8	35.92	18 / 1	2.87
2 / 15	75.11	6 / 4	34.06	20 / 1	2.47
1 / 7	74.48	13 / 8	32.23	22 / 1	2.25
2 / 13	73.78	7 / 4	30.71	25 / 1	1.80
1 / 6	72.98	15 / 8	29.33	28 / 1	1.28
2 / 11	72.05	2 / 1	28.06	33 / 1	1.07
1 / 5	70.97	85 / 40	26.87	35 / 1	0.94
2 / 9	69.69	9 / 4	25.81	40 / 1	0.69
1 / 4	68.15	95 / 40	24.84	50 / 1	0.55
2 / 7	66.25	5 / 2	23.93	60 / 1	0.44
3 / 10	65.53	11 / 4	22.33	66 / 1	0.38
1 / 3	63.89	3 / 1	20.92	80 / 1	0.29
4 / 11	62.47	100 / 30	19.29	100 / 1	0.23
2 / 5	64.28	7 / 2	18.56	125 / 1	0.18
40 / 95	63.28	4 / 1	16.70	150 / 1	0.14
4 / 9	62.20	9 / 2	15.18	200 / 1	0.10
40 / 85	61.04	5 / 1	13.90	250 / 1	0.08
1 / 2	59.78	11 / 2	12.83	300 / 1	0.06
8 / 15	58.43	6 / 1	11.91	400 / 1	0.05
4 / 7	56.97	13 / 2	11.12	500 / 1	0.03
8 / 13	54.73	7 / 1	10.42	1000 / 1	0.02
4 / 6	53.00	15 / 2	9.72		

Further Adjustments

The way the percentages were applied, both in the tests and then in assembling the profiles, is shown in the following example.

A	B	C
5 / 4	38.23	40.39
6 / 4	34.06	35.98
5 / 1	13.90	14.69
10 / 1	7.16	7.57
33 / 1	1.07	1.13
100 / 1	0.23	0.24
	94.65	**100.00**

Column A shows the starting-prices for an actual race, while Column B lists the revised chance percentages for those prices taken from the table. And it can be seen straight away, that the percentages in Column B only add up to 94.65; which is maybe only to be expected, given that the overrounds in the original races ranged between 3 and 75. And so to convert these into figures which would more accurately reflect the runners' actual winning chances, it's necessary to multiply each of them by 1.056, the equivalent of 100 divided by 94.65. This then gives the figures in column C, which as expected, now total 100%.

So that as a result of these last calculations, the favourite has finally been given a 40.39% chance of winning. This isn't meant to imply however, that the horse really has a 40.39% chance of winning this particular race, nor even that any horse starting at 5/4 in a race with identical prices would

necessarily have a 40.39% chance of winning; but only that when judging solely on prices, this figure represents the best estimate of the winning chances of a 5/4 favourite in a race with identical, or at least broadly similar prices.

But in any case, the object of the exercise isn't to calculate the chances of individual horses, but to obtain some sort of estimate of the overall distribution of win and place chances, among the runners in races with similar arrangements of prices. And so now having arrived at a point where it's possible to produce estimates of the runners' winning chances, these figures can then be used as the basis for the place-chance calculations which begin on the next page.

Calculating Place Chances

Calculating place chances is complicated by the fact that a horse's place chance doesn't just depend on its own chance of winning, but on the winning chances of all the other runners in the race as well. So that to determine the place chances of all eight runners in a race paying three places, would require 336 separate calculations, a task that would normally require the use of equations.

However by instead choosing a race with only six runners paying two places, it's possible to work out the place chances using a calculator; and this should still give a fair idea of what's involved. The race in question is the one for which fair winning chances have just been calculated, and those prices and percentages are again as shown below.

A	C
5 / 4	40.39
6 / 4	35.98
5 / 1	14.69
10 / 1	7.57
33 / 1	1.13
100 / 1	0.24
	100.00

In any such race there are six possible winners, and whichever one it is, there is then going to be another separate race going on for second place among the remaining five runners.

So that by subtracting from the original total the win chance percentage of the horse that came first and recalculating the chance percentages of the other five so that they again total 100%, these will then represent their chances of winning any such race for second place. Then, when each of these figures is multiplied by the winner's chance of actually winning, this gives the probability of each runner coming second in a race won by that particular horse.

So that as shown in the first table on the opposite page, when the race is won by the 5/4 favourite, the percentage chances of the other five runners now total 59.61% - as shown in column B.

Then, when these percentages are recalculated to 100% - as shown in column C - the chance of the 6/4 winning any race for second place, coming second in other words, is now 60.36%.

However, because the favourite has only a 40.39% chance of winning anyway, the chance of the 6/4 coming second in a race won by that favourite is 60.36 ×.404, which works out at 24.39 %.

Then as shown, the chances of the other four runners coming second to the 5/4 favourite are calculated in a similar way.

This whole process is then repeated to cover each of the other five runners coming first, and the results of these calculations can then be added together to give their overall chances of being placed, as shown in the composite table on page 106.

The race is won by the 5 / 4 chance

A	B	C
6 / 4	35.98	60.36
5 / 1	14.69	24.64
10 / 1	7.57	12.70
33 / 1	1.13	1.90
100 / 1	0.24	0.40
	59.61	100.00

Chances of 5/4 winning 40.39%

Chances of 6/4 coming second to 5/4	60.36	× 0.404	=	24.39
Chances of 5/1 coming second to 5/4	24.64	× 0.404	=	9.95
Chances of 10/1 coming second to 5/4	12.70	× 0.404	=	5.13
Chances of 33/1 coming second to 5/4	1.90	× 0.404	=	0.77
Chances of 100/1 coming second to 5/4	0.40	× 0.404	=	0.16

The race is won by the 6 / 4 chance

A	B	C
5 / 4	40.39	63.15
5 / 1	14.69	22.91
10 / 1	7.57	11.81
33 / 1	1.13	1.76
100 / 1	0.24	0.37
	64.12	100.00

Chances of 6/4 winning 35.98

Chances of 5/4 coming second to 6/4	63.15	× 0.3598	=	22.72
Chances of 5/1 coming second to 6/4	22.91	× 0.3598	=	8.24
Chances of 10/1 coming second to 6/4	11.81	× 0.3598	=	4.25
Chances of 33/1 coming second to 6/4	1.76	× 0.3598	=	0.63
Chances of 100/1 coming second to 6/4	0.37	× 0.3598	=	0.13

14 : Estimating Win and Place Chances

The race is won by the 5 / 1 chance

A	B	C
5 / 4	40.39	47.34
6 / 4	35.98	42.18
—	—	—
10 / 1	7.57	8.87
33 / 1	1.13	1.32
100 / 1	0.24	0.28
	85.31	99.99

Chances of 5/1 winning 14.69

Chances of 5/4 coming second to 5/1	47.34	×	0.1469	=	6.95
Chances of 6/4 coming second to 5/1	42.18	×	0.1469	=	6.20
Chances of 10/1 coming second to 5/1	8.87	×	0.1469	=	1.30
Chances of 33/1 coming second to 5/1	1.32	×	0.1469	=	0.19
Chances of 100/1 coming second to 5/1	0.28	×	0.1469	=	0.04

The race is won by the 10 / 1 chance

A	B	C
5 / 4	40.39	43.70
6 / 4	35.98	38.93
5 / 1	14.69	15.89
—	—	—
33 / 1	1.13	1.22
100 / 1	0.24	0.26
	92.43	100.00

Chances of 10/1 winning 7.57

Chances of 5/4 coming second to 10/1	43.70	×	0.075	=	3.308
Chances of 6/4 coming second to 10/1	38.93	×	0.075	=	2.947
Chances of 5/1 coming second to 10/1	15.89	×	0.075	=	1.203
Chances of 33/1 coming second to 10/1	1.22	×	0.075	=	.092
Chances of 100/1 coming second to 10/1	0.26	×	0.075	=	.020

The race is won by the 33 / 1 chance

	A	B	C
5 / 4		40.39	40.95
6 / 4		35.98	36.39
5 / 1		14.69	14.86
10 / 1		7.57	7.66
		—	—
100 / 1		0.24	0.24
		98.87	100.00

Chances of 33/1 winning 1.13%

Chances of 5/4 coming second to 33/1	40.95	× 0.011	=	0.463
Chances of 6/4 coming second to 33/1	36.39	× 0.011	=	0.411
Chances of 5/1 coming second to 33/1	14.86	× 0.011	=	0.168
Chances of 10/1 coming second to 33/1	7.66	× 0.011	=	0.087
Chances of 100/1 coming second to 33/1	0.24	× 0.011	=	0.003

The race is won by the 100 / 1 chance

	A	B	C
5 / 4		40.39	40.49
6 / 4		35.98	36.07
5 / 1		14.69	14.73
10 / 1		7.57	7.59
33 / 1		1.13	1.13
		—	—
		99.76	100.01

Chances of 100/1 winning 0.24%

Chances of 5/4 coming second to 100/1	40.49	× 0.002	=	0.08
Chances of 6/4 coming second to 100/1	36.07	× 0.002	=	0.07
Chances of 5/1 coming second to 100/1	14.73	× 0.002	=	0.04
Chances of 10/1 coming second to 100/1	7.59	× 0.002	=	0.03
Chances of 33/1 coming second to 100/1	1.13	× 0.002	=	0.01

14 : Estimating Win and Place Chances

These figures can then be arranged in the form a table, giving each horse's chances of coming second to each of the other five runners, its total chance of coming second, its chance of winning, and finally its overall chance of being placed.

	5/4	6/4	5/1	10/1	33/1	100/1	2nd	win	place
5 / 4	.	22.72	6.95	3.30	0.46	0.08	33.51	40.39	**73.90**
6 / 4	24.39	.	6.20	2.94	0.41	0.07	34.01	35.98	**69.99**
5 / 1	9.95	8.24	.	1.20	0.16	0.04	19.59	14.69	**34.28**
10 / 1	5.13	4.25	1.30	.	0.08	0.03	10.79	7.57	**18.36**
33 / 1	0.77	0.63	0.19	0.09	.	0.01	1.69	1.13	**2.82**
100 / 1	0.16	0.13	0.04	0.02	0.003	.	0.35	0.24	**0.59**

Any slight discrepancies in the place percentages are due solely to the different way they were produced. **99.94** **100.00** **199.94**

Having estimated the win and place chances for a full set of prices, it then becomes possible to calculate the returns these would produce, and assemble this information into race profiles. Such as the following, one of 57 such profiles which begin on page 151.

9   6 Runners 2 Places at 1/4 odds

s.p.	s.p. win %	s.p. place %	nearest fair odds	fair win%	fair place%	returns win	e/w	place
5 / 4	44.44	76.19	6 / 4	40.39	**73.91**	-9.12	-6.05	-2.99
6 / 4	40.00	72.73	7 / 4	35.98	**70.00**	-10.05	-6.90	-3.75
5 / 1	16.67	44.44	6 / 1	14.69	**34.31**	-11.86	-17.34	-22.81
10 / 1	9.09	28.57	12 / 1	7.57	**18.34**	-16.85	-26.33	-35.82
33 / 1	2.94	10.81	80 / 1	1.13	**2.83**	-61.46	-67.64	-73.83
100 / 1	0.99	3.85	400 / 1	0.24	**0.61**	-75.38	-79.75	-84.13
	114.13	**236.59**		**100.00**	**200.00**			

The columns are as follows -

s.p.	The returned starting price.	**fair win %**	The horse's fair win chance.
s.p. win %	The starting price as a percentage.	**fair place %**	The horse's fair place chance.
s.p. place %	The equivalent place price as a percentage.	**win return**	The percentage return on win bets.
nearest fair odds	The nearest equivalent fair price.	**e/w return**	The percentage return on each way bets.
		place return	The place contribution to each way returns.

The Riders in the Stand

There's some that ride the Robbo style, and bump at every stride;
While others sit a long way back, to get a longer ride.
There's some that ride as sailors do, with legs and arms, and teeth;
And some that ride the horse's neck, and some ride underneath.

But all the finest horsemen out - the men to Beat the Band -
You'll find amongst the crowd that ride their races in the Stand.
They'll say "He had the race in hand, and lost it in the straight."
They'll show how Godby came too soon, and Barden came too late.

They'll say Chevally lost his nerve, and Regan lost his head;
They'll tell how one was "livened up" and something else was "dead" -
In fact, the race was never run on sea, or sky, or land
But what you'd get it better done by riders in the Stand.

The rule holds good in everything in life's uncertain fight;
You'll find the winner can't go wrong, the loser can't go right.
You ride a slashing race and lose - by one and all you're banned!
Ride like a bag of flour, and win - they'll cheer you in the Stand

A.B."Banjo"Paterson

System Advert (1938)
Yet another missed opportunity, it seems.

15:Courses For Horses

While it can often provide a useful selection criterion, the varied nature of the racecourses in the British Isles can present backers with two different problems.

Firstly, unless bets are to be restricted to existing course winners, it will be necessary to classify all these different racecourses in some way; so that compromises may have to be made which mightn't always do justice to their individual characteristics.

The following lists are based on information taken from a variety of sources, some of which disagree, particularly as to whether certain courses can accurately be described as undulating or not. In this context an undulating course is one which features at least one downhill gradient which could unsettle a horse, and on this basis it was possible to conclude that the Rowley Mile Course should qualify. But there are probably plenty of other entries in the lists which are equally open to question. And because any courses which feature both Flat and National Hunt racing have been treated as one, it follows that because these different tracks will either run inside or outside of one another, their bends will inevitably differ to some extent in their sharpness.

The second problem concerns the sheer quantity of this information. Because while it might be possible in theory to learn it all off by heart, the fact that not all of it will be needed on a daily basis, means that this isn't something many people would necessarily want to do.

One possible alternative to having to constantly thumb through racecourse directories or newspapers in search of the necessary information might be to assemble all the course details which are considered relevant and write them up on a wall chart, or possibly to keep all the details on cards. Otherwise, because such information isn't always immediately to hand there's often the temptation to overlook it altogether, and maybe miss something significant.

The lists, which are more or less self-explanatory, classify racecourses in terms of three different criteria, as a way of making it easier to see whether a horse seems suited to a particular type of track. While courses with an uphill finish have also been singled out, as horses that win well on such tracks can be worth noting as possible candidates for a step up in distance at an easier course. Among the other factors which could also be used to classify racecourses might be the stiffness or otherwise of the fences, the likelihood of extreme going of any kind, or simply their category and status .

And because there would be no obvious benefit from doing otherwise, the various racecourses of Britain and Ireland have all been listed separately.

British Racecourses Classified in Terms of Four Categories

a left hand or right hand   **b flat or undulating surface**
c sharp or easy bends   **d uphill finish**

	a	b	c	d		a	b	c	d
Aintree	L	F	E		Market Rasen	R	F	S	
Ascot	R	U	E	UF	Edinburgh	R	F	S	
Ayr	L	F	E		Newbury	L	F	E	
Bangor	L	F	E		Newcastle	L	U	E	UF
Bath	L	F	E		Newton Abbot	L	F	S	
Beverley	R	U	E		Newmarket July	R	F	E	UF
Brighton	L	U	S		Newmarket Rowley	R	U	E	UF
Carlisle	R	U	E		Nottingham	L	F	E	
Cartmel	L	U	S		Perth	R	F	S	
Catterick	L	U	S		Plumpton	L	U	S	UF
Cheltenham	L	U	E		Pontefract	L	U	E	UF
Chepstow	L	U	E		Redcar	L	F	S	
Chester	L	F	S		Ripon	R	U	S	UF
Doncaster	L	F	E		Salisbury	R	U	S	UF
Epsom	L	U	S		Sandown	R	U	E	UF
Exeter	R	U	E		Sedgefield	L	U	S	UF
Fakenham	L	U	S		Southwell	L	F	S	
Folkestone	R	U	E		Stratford	L	F	S	
Fontwell Chase	L,R	F	E		Taunton	R	F	E	
Fontwell Hurdle	L	F	E		Towcester	R	U	F	
Goodwood	R	U	S		Thirsk	L	F	S	

a left hand or right hand   **b flat or undulating surface**

c sharp or easy bends   **d uphill finish**

	a	b	c	d		a	b	c	d
Hamilton Park	R	U	E	UF	Uttoxeter	L	U	S	
Haydock Park	L	F	E		Warwick	L	F	S	
Hereford	R	U	S		Wetherby	L	F	E	
Hexham	L	U	E		Wincanton	R	U	E	
Huntingdon	R	F	E		Windsor	L,R	F	S	
Kelso	L	F	S	UF	Wolverhampton	L	F	E	
Kempton Park	R	F	E		Worcester	L	F	E	
Leicester	R	U	E		Yarmouth	L	F	E	
Lingfield	L	U	S		York	L	F	E	
Ludlow	R	F	E						

Left Handed Courses

Aintree	Doncaster	Newcastle	Uttoxeter
Ayr	Epsom	Newton Abbot	Warwick
Bangor	Fakenham	Nottingham	Wetherby
Bath	Fontwell Chase	Plumpton	Windsor
Brighton	Fontwell Hurdle	Pontefract	Wolverhampton
Cartmel	Haydock Park	Redcar	Worcester
Catterick	Hexham	Sedgefield	Yarmouth
Cheltenham	Kelso	Southwell	York
Chepstow	Lingfield	Stratford	
Chester	Newbury	Thirsk	

15 : Courses For Horses

Left Handed Undulating Courses   * with sharp bends

Brighton *	Chepstow *	Lingfield *	Sedgefield *
Cartmel *	Epsom *	Newcastle	Uttoxeter *
Catterick *	Fakenham *	Plumpton *	
Cheltenham	Hexham	Pontefract	

Left Handed Flat or Flattish Courses   * with sharp bends

Aintree	Fontwell Chase	Nottingham	Wetherby
Ayr	Fontwell Hurdle	Redcar *	Windsor *
Bangor	Haydock Park	Southwell *	Wolverhampton
Bath	Kelso *	Stratford *	Worcester
Chester	Newbury	Thirsk *	Yarmouth
Doncaster	Newton Abbot *	Warwick *	York

Right Handed Courses

Ascot	Hamilton Park	Edinburgh	Taunton
Beverley	Hereford	Newmarket July	Towcester
Carlisle	Huntingdon	Newmarket Rowley	Wincanton
Exeter	Kempton Park	Perth	Windsor
Folkestone	Leicester	Ripon	
Fontwell Chase	Ludlow	Salisbury	
Goodwood	Market Rasen	Sandown	

Right Handed Undulating Courses

		* with sharp bends	
Ascot	Folkestone	Leicester	Sandown
Beverley	Goodwood *	Newmarket Rowley	Towcester
Carlisle	Hamilton Park	Ripon *	Wincanton
Exeter	Hereford *	Salisbury *	

Right Handed Flat or Flattish Courses

		* with sharp bends	
Fontwell Chase	Ludlow	Newmarket July	Windsor
Huntingdon	Market Rasen *	Perth *	
Kempton Park	Edinburgh *	Taunton	

Courses in both Directions with an Uphill Finish

Ascot	Kelso	Plumpton	Sandown
Carlisle	Newcastle	Pontefract	Sedgefield
Cheltenham	Newmarket July	Ripon	
Hamilton Park	Newmarket Rowley	Salisbury	

Irish Racecourses Classified in Terms of Four Categories

a left hand or right hand   **b flat or undulating surface**

c sharp or easy bends   **d uphill finish**

	a	b	c	d		a	b	c	d
Ballinrobe	R	F	S		Limerick	R	U	E	UF
Bellestown	L	F	S		Listowal	L	F	S	
Clonmel	R	U	S		Mallow	R	F	E	
The Curragh	R	F	E		Naas	L	U	S	UF
Downpatrick	R	U	S	UF	Navan	L	U	E	UF
Down Royal	R	U	S		Punchestown	R	U	S	
Dundalk	L	U	S		Roscommon	R	U	S	UF
Galway	R	U	S	UF	Sligo	R	F	E	
Gowran Park	R	U	E		Thurles	R	U	S	UF
Kilbeggan	R	U	S		Tipperary	L	F	E	
Killarney	L	F	E		Tralee	L	U	E	UF
Laytown beach	straight flat				Waterford	R	U	S	
Leopardstown	L	F	E		Wexford	R	U	E	

Irish Left Handed Courses

Bellestown	Leopardstown	Navan
Dundalk	Listowal	Tipperary
Killarney	Naas	Tralee

Irish Left Handed Undulating Courses   * with sharp bends

Listowal*	Navan	Tralee

Irish Left Handed Flat or Flattish Courses

		* with sharp bends
Bellestown*	Killarney	Naas*
Dundalk*	Leopardstown	Tipperary

Irish Right Handed Courses

Ballinrobe	Gowran Park	Roscommon
Clonmel	Kilbeggan	Sligo
The Curragh	Limerick	Thurles
Downpatrick	Mallow	Waterford
Down Royal	Punchestown	Wexford
Galway		

Irish Right Handed Undulating Courses

		* with sharp bends
Clonmel *	Gowran Park	Roscommon *
Downpatrick *	Kilbeggan *	Thurles *
Down Royal *	Limerick	Waterford *
Galway *	Punchestown *	

Irish Right Handed Flat or Flattish Courses

		* with sharp bends
Ballinrobe*	Mallow	Sligo
The Curragh		

Irish Courses in both Directions with an Uphill Finish

Downpatrick	Naas	Thurles
Galway	Navan	Tralee
Limerick	Roscommon	

16:Staking Systems Series 1-30

Probably the biggest obstacle, when trying to compare the performance of various staking systems is the sheer volume of evidence.

For instance the series of races used in chapter 4, were based on only eight different prices. However as each of these prices could apply to either winners or losers, and because the prices of the losers are equally significant in fixed takeout staking, this gives 16 possible outcomes for every race. Which over a series of 20 races works out at 16^{20} - in other words - 1,208,925,819,614,629,000,000,000 different possibilities. And even with 10 series to the page these would still take up quite a fair amount of space - approximately 4,770 billion miles of shelving in fact! Not to mention the further complication that because with progressive staking, the order in which the results occur is of crucial significance, each of these series will in turn need to be multiplied by $20 \times 19 \times 18 \ldots \times 2 \times 1$. So it's down to the shop again, for even more brackets!

Nevertheless, by concentrating on just a small sample from among this incalculable number, it should still be possible to identify some general features of staking systems, as was already done in chapter 4. The following 30 series of 20 races were chosen from a very much larger sample, all generated at random using the same eight prices as were used before. The relative performance of the four systems as applied to each series can be seen as depending mainly on four different but clearly related factors; these being the return at level stakes, the frequency and distribution of winning bets, and finally their respective prices. However none of this contradicts the earlier conclusion that level stakes are to be preferred, if only because of the impossibility of producing results to order, in terms of price, frequency, or whatever.

As before, each final outcome includes the 100 pt opening bank. The prices and results for each series are shown in the two rows going across the page as picked out in bold type for series 1 opposite. The first column then gives the **level stake** outcome with 10 pts staked on each selection. The second column shows the outcome for **progressive** staking using the same rules as before, with an opening 10 pt stake which increases by 10pts after each losing bet. **The figure shown is the average after 10,000 trials** with the results generated in random order, and where busted banks were immediately terminated. The **proportional** stakes in columns 3 and 4 are set at **1/10** and **1/20** of the bank, while as before, the **fixed-takeout** stake in column 5 is set to take out 20 points, the equivalent of a 10 pt level stake bet at even-money.

The chosen series fall mainly within the plus or minus 50 % range, as anyone regularly losing in excess of this figure would probably be better-off giving up altogether; while anyone already averaging over 50 % profit, shouldn't really need any further help.

series	prices									level	prog	prop1	prop2	fixtak
1	W 1/1 L 1/1	L 9/4	L 4/1	L 1/1	W 3/1	L 9/4	L 9/4	L 2/1	L 3/1					
	L 6/4 L 9/4	L 3/1	W 6/4	W 3/1	L 3/1	L 1/1	L 2/1	W 9/4	L 1/1	57.5	13.30	53.92	76.94	60.90
2	L 6/4 L 4/1	L 1/1	W 2/1	W 5/1	L 2/1	L 6/4	L 5/1	L 3/1	L 4/1					
	L 7/1 W 6/4	L 1/1	L 1/1	W 1/1	L 3/1	W 6/4	L 1/1	L 1/1	L 2/1	60	23.13	53.91	77.30	60.83
3	W 2/1 L 9/4	L 6/4	L 5/1	L 1/1	L 6/4	L 5/1	L 9/4	W 1/1	W 9/4					
	L 9/4 L 9/4	W 5/1	L 6/4	L 1/1	W 9/4	L 7/1	L 3/1	L 7/1	L 5/1	75	32.15	61.18	82.78	79.08
4	L 6/4 L 2/1	L 5/1	W 5/1	L 4/1	L 3/1	L 7/1	L 3/1	W 9/4	L 6/4					
	L 4/1 L 7/1	L 5/1	L 6/4	W 5/1	W 6/4	L 4/1	L 7/1	L 4/1	L 7/1	77.5	26.60	58.73	82.24	85.85
5	W 5/1 L 4/1	L 7/1	L 7/1	L 5/1	L 6/4	W 1/1	L 6/4	L 6/4	L 1/1					
	W 1/1 L 5/1	L 1/1	L 7/1	W 6/4	W 6/4	L 5/1	W 2/1	L 3/1	L 7/1	80	43.32	65.89	85.43	101.00
6	W 1/1 W 3/1	L 3/1	L 1/1	L 1/1	L 3/1	L 4/1	W 4/1	L 6/4	L 9/4					
	L 2/1 L 3/1	L 3/1	L 6/4	L 1/1	L 2/1	L 2/1	W 2/1	L 5/1	W 3/1	80	36.26	64.30	84.92	69.85
7	L 1/1 W 4/1	L 9/4	L 3/1	W 2/1	L 6/4	L 3/1	L 6/4	W 1/1	L 3/1					
	L 7/1 L 5/1	L 4/1	L 5/1	L 9/4	W 6/4	L 1/1	W 6/4	W 9/4	L 9/4	82.5	56.35	68.49	86.90	94.55
8	L 9/4 W 6/4	W 2/1	L 6/4	W 2/1	L 4/1	L 5/1	L 1/1	W 2/1	W 1/1					
	L 3/1 L 7/1	L 4/1	L 1/1	L 2/1	L 5/1	L 9/4	L 3/1	L 1/1	W 4/1	85	58.14	70.01	87.92	93.86
9	L 4/1 W 1/1	L 4/1	W 5/1	L 5/1	L 9/4	L 1/1	L 7/1	L 4/1	L 4/1					
	L 4/1 L 7/1	L 7/1	W 4/1	L 9/4	W 3/1	L 1/1	L 1/1	W 1/1	L 9/4	90	47.36	68.01	88.11	88.37
10	L 4/1 L 2/1	W 2/1	L 7/1	W 5/1	W 9/4	W 9/4	L 7/1	W 2/1	L 7/1					
	L 7/1 L 5/1	L 5/1	L 9/4	L 7/1	W 1/1	L 9/4	L 5/1	L 3/1	L 3/1	105	84.17	81.57	95.86	125.55

Staking Systems Series 11 - 20

series	prices										level	prog	prop1	prop2	fixtak
11	W 7/1 L 4/1 L 6/4 L 2/1 L 6/4 W 2/1 L 3/1 L 4/1 L 2/1 W 3/1														
	L 6/4 L 2/1 L 6/4 L 5/1 L 3/1 L 2/1 L 5/1 W 9/4 W 6/4 L 6/4										107.5	72.39	76.92	94.62	80.35
12	L 9/4 L 1/1 L 2/1 L 3/1 W 3/1 L 2/1 L 7/1 L 9/4 W 5/1 W 9/4														
	L 7/1 L 9/4 L 6/4 W 2/1 W 1/1 L 6/4 L 6/4 W 6/4 L 7/1 L 1/1										107.5	97.65	82.95	96.83	92.55
13	W 3/1 L 4/1 L 5/1 L 9/4 L 5/1 L 9/4 L 1/1 W 4/1 W 5/1 W 1/1														
	L 1/1 L 3/1 L 7/1 L 4/1 W 3/1 L 7/1 L 9/4 L 1/1 L 2/1 L 5/1										110	84.76	80.38	96.50	89.54
14	L 6/4 L 9/4 L 5/1 L 1/1 W 2/1 L 9/4 W 1/1 L 4/1 L 5/1 W 3/1														
	L 5/1 W 7/1 L 1/1 L 7/1 L 3/1 L 3/1 L 7/1 W 3/1 L 4/1 L 6/4										110	70.68	78.08	95.54	89.53
15	L 6/4 L 3/1 L 1/1 W 1/1 L 2/1 W 5/1 W 9/4 L 7/1 L 6/4 L 1/1														
	L 4/1 L 5/1 W 6/4 L 6/4 L 5/1 W 4/1 L 3/1 L 2/1 W 6/4 L 1/1										112.5	88.72	85.61	98.75	90.01
16	L 4/1 L 5/1 W 3/1 W 6/4 L 1/1 L 6/4 L 6/4 W 1/1 L 1/1 L 2/1														
	L 5/1 W 3/1 L 5/1 L 5/1 W 6/4 L 7/1 W 9/4 L 4/1 W 9/4 L 2/1										115	124.09	93.78	101.96	118.53
17	W 1/1 L 7/1 L 6/4 L 1/1 L 7/1 L 9/4 W 1/1 W 2/1 L 5/1 L 9/4														
	L 9/4 L 1/1 L 6/4 W 6/4 W 3/1 W 1/1 W 5/1 L 1/1 L 7/1 L 5/1										115	105.78	91.04	101.01	108.37
18	W3/1 L 2/1 L 4/1 L 7/1 L 5/1 L 6/4 L 1/1 W 4/1 L 6/4 L 3/1														
	L 4/1 W 1/1 W 5/1 L 3/1 L 7/1 L 4/1 W 4/1 L 1/1 L 9/4 L 3/1										120	103.28	86.56	100.70	89.51
19	L 2/1 L 7/1 L 1/1 W 2/1 W 4/1 W 1/1 L 7/1 L 2/1 W 6/4 L 3/1														
	L 1/1 W 9/4 W 9/4 L 7/1 L 2/1 L 2/1 L 6/4 L 5/1 W 2/1 L 1/1										120	113.35	97.28	104.13	111.86
20	W 9/4 L 3/1 L 6/4 L 5/1 L 2/1 L 7/1 L 7/1 W 1/1 W 7/1 L 7/1														
	L 7/1 L 9/4 W 3/1 L 3/1 W 4/1 L 2/1 L 5/1 L 1/1 L 3/1 L 7/1										122.5	92.53	85.84	100.82	100.69

series	prices										level	prog	prop1	prop2	fixtak
21	W 4/1	W 3/1	L 3/1	L 5/1	L 6/4	L 5/1	L 6/4	W 5/1	L 7/1	L 3/1					
	W 1/1	L 7/1	L 6/4	L 2/1	L 4/1	W 5/1	L 5/1	L 4/1	L 1/1	L 1/1	130	112.68	92.74	104.89	90.67
22	W 5/1	L 5/1	W 6/4	L 9/4	W 3/1	L 9/4	L 2/1	W 9/4	W 6/4	L 9/4					
	L 6/4	W 4/1	L 2/1	L 3/1	L 1/1	L 4/1	L 4/1	L 1/1	L 7/1	L 5/1	132.5	134.35	101.18	108.15	103.55
23	W 6/4	L 5/1	L 4/1	L 3/1	L 5/1	W 1/1	W 4/1	W 3/1	L 1/1	L 3/1					
	L 2/1	L 2/1	L 7/1	L 4/1	W 3/1	L 5/1	W 2/1	L 5/1	L 3/1	W 2/1	135	154.09	109.55	111.27	132.50
24	W 3/1	L 6/4	L 6/4	L 9/4	W 3/1	L 1/1	L 2/1	L 7/1	L 5/1	L 6/4					
	W 6/4	W 5/1	L 6/4	L 4/1	L 7/1	W 3/1	L 9/4	L 9/4	W 9/4	L 6/4	137.5	150.54	106.21	110.88	100.05
25	L 2/1	W 2/1	W 6/4	L 1/1	W 4/1	L 9/4	L 6/4	L 3/1	L 9/4	L 1/1					
	W 2/1	L 4/1	L 3/1	L 9/4	L 6/4	L 1/1	W 6/4	L 1/1	W 7/1	L 9/4	140	157.01	103.69	110.47	82.88
26	L 9/4	L 7/1	W 1/1	W 6/4	L 2/1	L 5/1	W 6/4	L 3/1	W 4/1	L 1/1					
	W 1/1	L 4/1	W 6/4	W 6/4	L 6/4	W 1/1	L 6/4	W 9/4	L 2/1	L 9/4	142.5	175.05	125.29	117.39	141.37
27	L 4/1	L 5/1	L 2/1	L 3/1	W 1/1	L 2/1	W 4/1	W 1/1	W 7/1	L 2/1					
	L 4/1	L 7/1	L 3/1	W 4/1	L 7/1	W 6/4	L 4/1	L 3/1	L 9/4	L 7/1	145	144.60	106.07	112.36	117.51
28	W 4/1	L 6/4	L 9/4	L 6/4	W 9/4	L 5/1	L 2/1	L 5/1	L 1/1	L 9/4					
	L 2/1	W 9/4	L 5/1	L 1/1	W 9/4	L 4/1	L 4/1	L 6/4	W 5/1	W 3/1	147.5	171.21	114.81	115.83	101.56
29	L 4/1	L 7/1	W 9/4	L 5/1	L 2/1	L 6/4	L 3/1	L 1/1	W 2/1	L 2/1					
	L 3/1	L 6/4	W 3/1	W 4/1	L 3/1	W 3/1	W 1/1	L 4/1	L 7/1	W 5/1	172.5	219.01	145.87	130.85	129.18
30	W 6/4	W 3/1	W 3/1	W 4/1	L 2/1	L 1/1	L 9/4	L 7/1	L 3/1	L 6/4					
	W 5/1	L 6/4	L 2/1	L 5/1	L 3/1	W 1/1	W 6/4	L 3/1	W 1/1	L 7/1	180	241.77	160.40	136.57	137.85

17:Tables I-3

Notes On The Tables

1 Price To Percentage Table - opposite

Gives the equivalent percentage winning chance represented by the price in question.

2 Percentage To Price Table - pages 122,123

Gives the nearest recognisable price to the range of percentages shown.

3 Place Prices And Percentages Table - pages 124 to 127

In addition to giving the win percentage, this also gives the equivalent place price and percentage, when paying 1/4 and 1/5 the odds a place.

Alternative methods of calculating percentages

Besides using the tables, for simpler prices it shouldn't be too difficult to work out a £100 takeout using just mental arithmetic. So that for example, £50 at even money, £40 at 6/4, £33.33 at 2/1, £25 at 3/1, and £20 at 4/1 would all take out £100, and so also represent the equivalent percentage.

Otherwise to convert a price into a chance percentage, add the left and right sides, divide this figure into 100, and multiply the result by the right hand side.

So that for instance (the exact figures are in brackets) -

To convert 5/6 - adding the 5 and the 6 makes 11 - 100 divided by 11 gives 9
- and then multiplying this by the 6 gives 54 percent (54.54).

To convert 7/4 - adding the 7 and the 4 makes 11 - 100 divided by 11 gives 9
- and then multiplying this by the 4 gives 36 percent (36.36).

price	percent	price	percent	price	percent
1 / 28	96.55	4 / 5	55.56	8 / 1	11.11
1 / 25	96.15	5 / 6	54.55	17 / 2	10.53
1 / 16	94.12	10 / 11	52.38	9 / 1	10.00
1 / 14	93.33	20 / 21	51.22	10 / 1	9.09
1 / 12	92.31	1 / 1	50.00	11 / 1	8.33
1 / 11	91.67	21 / 20	48.78	12 / 1	7.69
1 / 10	90.91	11 / 10	47.62	13 / 1	7.14
1 / 9	90.00	6 / 5	45.45	14 / 1	6.67
2 / 17	89.47	5 / 4	44.44	15 / 1	6.25
1 / 8	88.89	11 / 8	42.11	16 / 1	5.88
2 / 15	88.24	7 / 5	41.66	18 / 1	5.26
1 / 7	87.50	6 / 4	40.00	20 / 1	4.76
2 / 13	86.67	13 / 8	38.10	22 / 1	4.35
1 / 6	85.71	7 / 4	36.36	25 / 1	3.85
2 / 11	84.62	15 / 8	34.78	28 / 1	3.45
1 / 5	83.32	2 / 1	33.33	33 / 1	2.94
2 / 9	81.82	85 / 40	32.00	35 / 1	2.78
1 / 4	80.00	9 / 4	30.77	40 / 1	2.44
2 / 7	77.78	95 / 40	29.63	50 / 1	1.96
3 / 10	76.92	5 / 2	28.57	60 / 1	1.64
1 / 3	75.00	11 / 4	26.67	66 / 1	1.49
4 / 11	73.33	3 / 1	25.00	80 / 1	1.23
2 / 5	71.43	100 / 30	23.08	100 / 1	0.99
40 / 95	70.37	7 / 2	22.22	120 / 1	0.82
4 / 9	69.23	4 / 1	20.00	125 / 1	0.79
40 / 85	68.00	9 / 2	18.18	150 / 1	0.66
1 / 2	66.67	5 / 1	16.67	200 / 1	0.50
8 / 15	65.22	11 / 2	15.38	250 / 1	0.40
4 / 7	63.64	6 / 1	14.29	300 / 1	0.33
8 / 13	61.90	13 / 2	13.33	400 / 1	0.25
4 / 6	60.00	7 / 1	12.50	500 / 1	0.20
8 / 11	57.89	15 / 2	11.76	1000 / 1	0.10

Percentages Converted to Prices

percentage range			price	percentage range			price
99.301	-	99.900	1 / 250	70.896	-	72.375	2 / 5
98.751	-	99.300	1 / 100	69.801	-	70.895	40 / 95
98.266	-	98.750	1 / 66	68.616	-	69.800	4 / 9
97.541	-	98.265	1 / 50	67.331	-	68.615	40 / 85
96.801	-	97.540	1 / 33	65.936	-	67.330	1 / 2
96.352	-	96.800	1 / 28	64.421	-	65.935	8 / 15
95.691	-	96.351	1 / 25	62.766	-	64.420	4 / 7
94.671	-	95.690	1 / 20	60.951	-	62.765	8 / 13
93.721	-	94.670	1 / 16	58.946	-	60.950	4 / 6
92.816	-	93.720	1 / 14	56.721	-	58.945	8 / 11
91.981	-	92.815	1 / 12	55.046	-	56.720	4 / 5
91.326	-	91.980	1 / 11	53.461	-	55.045	5 / 6
90.496	-	91.325	1 / 10	51.796	-	53.460	10 / 11
89.736	-	90.495	1 / 9	50.606	-	51.795	20 / 21
89.176	-	89.735	2 / 17	49.391	-	50.605	1 / 1
88.559	-	89.175	1 / 8	48.196	-	49.390	21 / 20
87.864	-	88.558	2 / 15	46.531	-	48.195	11 / 10
87.076	-	87.863	1 / 7	44.946	-	46.530	6 / 5
86.186	-	87.075	2 / 13	43.271	-	44.945	5 / 4
85.161	-	86.185	1 / 6	41.051	-	43.270	11 / 8
83.971	-	85.160	2 / 11	39.046	-	41.050	6 / 4
82.571	-	83.970	1 / 5	37.226	-	39.045	13 / 8
80.906	-	82.570	2 / 9	35.571	-	37.225	7 / 4
78.886	-	80.905	1 / 4	34.056	-	35.570	15 / 8
77.346	-	78.885	2 / 7	32.666	-	34.055	2 / 1
75.961	-	77.345	3 / 10	31.381	-	32.665	85 / 40
74.166	-	75.960	1 / 3	30.195	-	31.380	9 / 4
72.376	-	74.165	4 / 11	29.101	-	30.194	95 / 40

percentage range			price	percentage range			price
27.616	-	29.100	5 / 2	5.571	-	6.065	16 / 1
25.831	-	27.615	11 / 4	5.011	-	5.570	18 / 1
24.036	-	25.830	3 / 1	4.551	-	5.010	20 / 1
22.646	-	24.035	100 / 30	4.091	-	4.550	22 / 1
21.111	-	22.645	7 / 2	3.641	-	4.090	25 / 1
19.091	-	21.110	4 / 1	3.191	-	3.640	28 / 1
17.421	-	19.090	9 / 2	2.859	-	3.190	33 / 1
16.021	-	17.420	5 / 1	2.604	-	2.859	35 / 1
14.831	-	16.020	11 / 2	2.196	-	2.603	40 / 1
13.806	-	14.830	6 / 1	1.796	-	2.195	50 / 1
12.916	-	13.805	13 / 2	1.561	-	1.795	60 / 1
12.131	-	12.915	7 / 1	1.361	-	1.560	66 / 1
11.436	-	12.130	15 / 2	1.111	-	1.360	80 / 1
10.816	-	11.435	8 / 1	0.892	-	1.110	100 / 1
10.261	-	10.815	17 / 2	0.727	-	0.891	125 / 1
9.546	-	10.260	9 / 1	0.576	-	0.726	150 / 1
8.711	-	9.545	10 / 1	0.441	-	0.575	200 / 1
8.011	-	8.710	11 / 1	0.362	-	0.440	250 / 1
7.416	-	8.010	12 / 1	0.291	-	0.361	300 / 1
6.901	-	7.415	13 / 1	0.221	-	0.290	400 / 1
6.456	-	6.900	14 / 1	0.151	-	0.220	500 / 1
6.066	-	6.455	15 / 1	0.081	-	0.150	1000 / 1

Win and Place Prices and Percentages 1/250 to 1/4

win		1/4 the odds		1/5 the odds	
1 / 250	99.60	1 / 1000	99.90	1 / 1250	99.92
1 / 100	99.01	1 / 400	99.75	1 / 500	99.80
1 / 66	98.51	1 / 264	99.62	1 / 330	99.70
1 / 50	98.04	1 / 200	99.50	1 / 250	99.60
1 / 33	97.06	1 / 132	99.25	1 / 165	99.40
1 / 28	96.55	1 / 112	99.12	1 / 140	99.29
1 / 25	96.15	1 / 100	99.01	1 / 125	99.21
1 / 20	95.24	1 / 80	98.77	1 / 100	99.01
1 / 16	94.12	1 / 64	98.46	1 / 80	98.77
1 / 14	93.33	1 / 56	98.25	1 / 70	98.59
1 / 12	92.31	1 / 48	97.96	1 / 60	98.36
1 / 11	91.67	1 / 44	97.78	1 / 55	98.21
1 / 10	90.91	1 / 40	97.56	1 / 50	98.04
1 / 9	90.00	1 / 36	97.30	1 / 45	97.83
2 / 17	89.47	1 / 34	97.14	2 / 85	97.70
1 / 8	88.89	1 / 32	96.97	1 / 40	97.56
2 / 15	88.24	1 / 30	96.77	2 / 75	97.40
1 / 7	87.50	1 / 28	96.55	1 / 35	97.22
2 / 13	86.67	1 / 26	96.30	2 / 65	97.01
1 / 6	85.71	1 / 24	96.00	1 / 30	96.77
2 / 11	84.62	1 / 22	95.65	2 / 55	96.49
1 / 5	83.33	1 / 20	95.24	1 / 25	96.15
2 / 9	81.82	1 / 18	94.74	2 / 45	95.74
1 / 4	80.00	1 / 16	94.12	1 / 20	95.24

win		1/4 the odds		1/5 the odds	
2 / 7	77.78	1 / 14	93.33	2 / 35	94.59
3 / 10	76.92	3 / 40	93.02	3 / 50	94.34
1 / 3	75.00	1 / 12	92.31	1 / 15	93.75
4 / 11	73.33	1 / 11	91.67	4 / 55	93.22
2 / 5	71.43	1 / 10	90.91	2 / 25	92.59
4 / 9	69.23	1 / 9	90.00	4 / 45	91.84
1 / 2	66.67	1 / 8	88.89	1 / 10	90.91
8 / 15	65.22	2 / 15	88.24	8 / 75	90.36
4 / 7	63.64	1 / 7	87.50	4 / 35	89.74
8 / 13	61.90	2 / 13	86.67	8 / 65	89.04
4 / 6	60.00	1 / 6	85.71	2 / 15	88.24
8 / 11	57.89	2 / 11	84.62	8 / 55	87.30
4 / 5	55.56	1 / 5	83.33	4 / 25	86.21
5 / 6	54.55	5 / 24	82.76	1 / 6	85.71
10 / 11	52.38	5 / 22	81.48	2 / 11	84.62
20 / 21	51.22	5 / 21	80.77	4 / 21	84.00
1 / 1	50.00	1 / 4	80.00	1 / 5	83.33
21 / 20	48.78	21 / 80	79.21	21 / 100	82.64
11 / 10	47.62	11 / 40	78.43	11 / 50	81.97
6 / 5	45.45	3 / 10	76.92	6 / 25	80.65
5 / 4	44.44	5 / 16	76.19	1 / 4	80.00
11 / 8	42.11	11 / 32	74.42	11 / 40	78.43
6 / 4	40.00	3 / 8	72.73	3 / 10	76.92
13 / 8	38.10	13 / 32	71.11	13 / 40	75.47

Win and Place Prices and Percentages 7/4 to 13/1

win		1/4 the odds		1/5 the odds	
7 / 4	36.36	7 / 16	69.57	7 / 20	74.07
15 / 8	34.78	15 / 32	68.09	3 / 8	72.73
2 / 1	33.33	1 / 2	66.67	2 / 5	71.43
9 / 4	30.77	9 / 16	64.00	9 / 20	68.97
5 / 2	28.57	5 / 8	61.54	1 / 2	66.67
11 / 4	26.67	11 / 16	59.26	11 / 20	64.52
3 / 1	25.00	3 / 4	57.14	3 / 5	62.50
100 / 30	23.08	5 / 6	54.55	4 / 6	60.00
7 / 2	22.22	7 / 8	53.33	7 / 10	58.82
4 / 1	20.00	1 / 1	50.00	4 / 5	55.56
9 / 2	18.18	9 / 8	47.06	9 / 10	52.63
5 / 1	16.67	5 / 4	44.44	1 / 1	50.00
11 / 2	15.38	11 / 8	42.11	11 / 10	47.62
6 / 1	14.29	6 / 4	40.00	6 / 5	45.45
13 / 2	13.33	13 / 8	38.10	13 / 10	43.48
7 / 1	12.50	7 / 4	36.36	7 / 5	41.67
15 / 2	11.76	15 / 8	34.78	6 / 4	40.00
8 / 1	11.11	2 / 1	33.33	8 / 5	38.46
17 / 2	10.53	17 / 8	32.00	17 / 10	37.04
9 / 1	10.00	9 / 4	30.77	9 / 5	35.71
10 / 1	9.09	5 / 2	28.57	2 / 1	33.33
11 / 1	8.33	11 / 4	26.67	11 / 5	31.25
12 / 1	7.69	3 / 1	25.00	12 / 5	29.41
13 / 1	7.14	13 / 4	23.53	13 / 5	27.78

	win		1/4 the odds			1/5 the odds	
14 / 1	6.67	7 / 2	22.22	14 / 5	26.32
15 / 1	6.25	15 / 4	21.05	3 / 1	25.00
16 / 1	5.88	4 / 1	20.00	16 / 5	23.81
18 / 1	5.26	9 / 2	18.18	18 / 5	21.74
20 / 1	4.76	5 / 1	16.67	4 / 1	20.00
22 / 1	4.35	11 / 2	15.38	22 / 5	18.52
25 / 1	3.85	25 / 4	13.79	5 / 1	16.67
28 / 1	3.45	7 / 1	12.50	28 / 5	15.15
33 / 1	2.94	33 / 4	10.81	33 / 5	13.16
35 / 1	2.78	35 / 4	10.26	7 / 1	12.50
40 / 1	2.44	10 / 1	9.09	8 / 1	11.11
50 / 1	1.96	25 / 2	7.41	10 / 1	9.09
60 / 1	1.64	15 / 1	6.25	12 / 1	7.69
66 / 1	1.49	33 / 2	5.71	66 / 5	7.04
80 / 1	1.23	20 / 1	4.76	16 / 1	5.88
100 / 1	0.99	25 / 1	3.85	20 / 1	4.76
125 / 1	0.79	125 / 4	3.10	25 / 1	3.85
150 / 1	0.66	150 / 4	2.60	30 / 1	3.23
200 / 1	0.50	50 / 1	1.96	40 / 1	2.44
250 / 1	0.40	250 / 4	1.57	50 / 1	1.96
300 / 1	0.33	75 / 1	1.32	60 / 1	1.64
400 / 1	0.25	100 / 1	0.99	80 / 1	1.23
500 / 1	0.20	125 / 1	0.79	100 / 1	0.99
1000/ 1	0.10	250 / 1	0.40	200 / 1	0.50

18:Coupled Prices Table

Notes On The Table

Coupled Prices Table - pages 129 to 141

Coupling a price in bold type from the left hand column with a price in bold type from the row across the top will produce the price where that column and row intersect. So that for example, combining the **9/4** and **8/11** in the table opposite, gives an approximate coupled price of 1/8.

To couple more than two prices -

Couple the first two prices, and then couple the resulting price with the third price, and so on. So that for example to couple 6/4, 4/1, and 6/1 -
Coupling 6/4 with 4/1 gives 4/6, and then coupling that 4/6 with 6/1, gives a final coupled price for all three of 1/3.
To prevent the tables from becoming too unwieldy, some intermediate coupled prices such as 40/95 and 21/20 have been omitted from the columns and rows. And so in these cases it will necessary to use the next available price.

	4/9	1/2	8/15	4/7	8/13	4/6	8/11	4/5
1/10	-	-	-	-	-	-	-	-
1/8	-	-	-	-	-	-	-	-
1/7	-	-	-	-	-	-	-	-
1/6-	-	-	-	-	-	-	-	-
1/5	-	-	-	-	-	-	-	-
1/4	-	-	-	-	-	-	-	-
1/3	-	-	-	-	-	-	-	-
2/5	-	-	-	-	-	-	-	-
4/9	-	-	-	-	-	-	-	-
1/2	-	-	-	-	-	-	-	-
8/15	-	-	-	-	-	-	-	-
4/7	-	-	-	-	-	-	-	-
8/13	-	-	-	-	-	-	-	-
4/6	-	-	-	-	-	-	-	-
8/11	-	-	-	-	-	-	-	-
4/5	-	-	-	-	-	-	-	-
5/6	-	-	-	-	-	-	-	-
10/11	-	-	-	-	-	-	-	-
1/1	-	-	-	-	-	-	-	-
11/10	-	-	-	-	-	-	-	-
6/5	-	-	-	-	-	-	-	-
5/4	-	-	-	-	-	-	-	1/250
11/8	-	-	-	-	-	-	1/250	1/50
6/4	-	-	-	-	-	1/250	1/50	1/20
13/8	-	-	-	-	1/250	1/50	1/25	1/14
7/4	-	-	-	1/250	1/50	1/28	1/16	1/11
15/8	-	-	1/250	1/66	1/28	1/20	1/12	1/9
2/1	-	1/250	1/66	1/33	1/20	1/14	1/10	1/8
9/4	1/250	1/33	1/25	1/16	1/12	1/10	1/8	2/13
5/2	1/50	1/20	1/16	1/12	1/9	1/8	2/13	2/11

Coupled Prices 4/9 to 4/5

	4/9	1/2	8/15	4/7	8/13	4/6	8/11	4/5
11/4	1/25	1/14	1/11	1/9	1/8	2/13	2/11	2/9
3/1	1/16	1/11	1/9	1/8	2/13	2/11	1/5	1/4
100/30	1/12	2/17	2/15	2/13	2/11	1/5	2/9	2/7
7/2	1/11	1/8	1/7	1/6	2/11	2/9	1/4	2/7
4/1	2/17	2/13	1/6	1/5	2/9	1/4	2/7	1/3
9/2	1/7	2/11	1/5	2/9	1/4	2/7	3/10	4/11
5/1	1/6	1/5	2/9	1/4	2/7	3/10	1/3	2/5
11/2	2/11	2/9	1/4	1/4	3/10	1/3	4/11	2/5
6/1	1/5	2/9	1/4	2/7	3/10	1/3	2/5	40/95
13/2	2/9	1/4	2/7	3/10	1/3	4/11	2/5	4/9
7/1	2/9	1/4	2/7	3/10	1/3	4/11	40/95	40/85
15/2	2/9	2/7	3/10	1/3	4/11	2/5	4/9	1/2
8/1	1/4	2/7	3/10	1/3	4/11	2/5	4/9	1/2
17/2	1/4	3/10	1/3	4/11	4/11	40/95	40/85	1/2
9/1	1/4	3/10	1/3	4/11	2/5	40/95	40/85	8/15
10/1	2/7	1/3	1/3	4/11	2/5	4/9	1/2	8/15
11/1	2/7	1/3	4/11	2/5	40/95	40/85	1/2	4/7
12/1	3/10	1/3	4/11	2/5	4/9	40/85	8/15	4/7
13/1	3/10	4/11	2/5	40/95	4/9	1/2	8/15	8/13
14/1	1/3	4/11	2/5	40/95	40/85	1/2	8/15	8/13
15/1	1/3	4/11	2/5	40/95	40/85	1/2	4/7	8/13
16/1	1/3	4/11	2/5	4/9	40/85	8/15	4/7	8/13
18/1	1/3	2/5	40/95	4/9	1/2	8/15	4/7	4/6
20/1	4/11	2/5	40/95	40/85	1/2	8/15	8/13	4/6
25/1	4/11	40/95	4/9	40/85	8/15	4/7	8/13	4/6
33/1	2/5	4/9	40/85	1/2	8/15	4/7	4/6	8/11
50/1	2/5	4/9	1/2	8/15	4/7	8/13	4/6	8/11
66/1	40/95	40/85	1/2	8/15	4/7	8/13	4/6	8/11
100/1	40/95	40/85	1/2	8/15	4/7	8/13	8/11	4/5
250/1	4/9	1/2	8/15	4/7	8/13	4/6	8/11	4/5

	5/6	10/11	1/1	11/10	6/5	5/4	11/8	6/4
1/10	-	-	-	-	-	-	-	-
1/8	-	-	-	-	-	-	-	-
1/7	-	-	-	-	-	-	-	-
1/6	-	-	-	-	-	-	-	-
1/5	-	-	-	-	-	-	-	-
1/4	-	-	-	-	-	-	-	-
1/3	-	-	-	-	-	-	-	-
2/5	-	-	-	-	-	-	-	-
4/9	-	-	-	-	-	-	-	-
1/2	-	-	-	-	-	-	-	-
8/15	-	-	-	-	-	-	-	-
4/7	-	-	-	-	-	-	-	-
8/13	-	-	-	-	-	-	-	-
4/6	-	-	-	-	-	-	-	-
8/11	-	-	-	-	-	-	1/500	1/50
4/5	-	-	-	-	-	1/500	1/50	1/20
5/6	-	-	-	-	-	1/100	1/28	1/16
10/11	-	-	-	-	1/50	1/33	1/16	1/12
1/1	-	-	-	1/50	1/20	1/16	1/12	1/9
11/10	-	-	1/50	1/20	1/14	1/12	2/17	1/7
6/5	-	1/50	1/20	1/14	1/10	1/9	1/7	1/6
5/4	1/100	1/33	1/16	1/12	1/9	1/8	2/13	2/11
11/8	1/28	1/16	1/12	2/17	1/7	2/13	2/11	2/9
6/4	1/16	1/12	1/9	1/7	1/6	2/11	2/9	1/4
13/8	1/12	1/9	2/15	1/6	1/5	2/9	1/4	2/7
7/4	1/10	1/8	2/13	1/5	2/9	1/4	2/7	3/10
15/8	2/17	1/7	2/11	2/9	1/4	1/4	3/10	1/3
2/1	2/15	1/6	1/5	2/9	2/7	2/7	1/3	4/11
9/4	1/6	1/5	1/4	2/7	3/10	1/3	4/11	40/95
5/2	1/5	2/9	2/7	3/10	4/11	4/11	40/95	40/85

Coupled Prices 5/6 to 6/4

	5/6	10/11	1/1	11/10	6/5	5/4	11/8	6/4
11/4	2/9	1/4	3/10	1/3	2/5	2/5	4/9	1/2
3/1	1/4	2/7	1/3	4/11	40/95	4/9	1/2	8/15
100/30	2/7	1/3	4/11	40/95	40/85	40/85	8/15	4/7
7/2	3/10	1/3	2/5	40/95	40/85	1/2	4/7	8/13
4/1	1/3	4/11	40/95	40/85	8/15	8/15	8/13	4/6
9/2	4/11	40/95	40/85	8/15	4/7	8/13	4/6	8/11
5/1	2/5	4/9	1/2	4/7	8/13	8/13	8/11	4/5
11/2	40/95	40/85	8/15	4/7	4/6	4/6	8/11	4/5
6/1	4/9	1/2	4/7	8/13	4/6	8/11	4/5	5/6
13/2	40/85	8/15	4/7	4/6	8/11	8/11	4/5	10/11
7/1	1/2	8/15	8/13	4/6	8/11	8/11	5/6	10/11
15/2	1/2	4/7	8/13	4/6	8/11	4/5	5/6	20/21
8/1	8/15	4/7	8/13	8/11	4/5	4/5	10/11	20/21
17/2	8/15	4/7	4/6	8/11	4/5	5/6	10/11	1/1
9/1	8/15	8/13	4/6	8/11	4/5	5/6	10/11	1/1
10/1	4/7	8/13	4/6	4/5	5/6	5/6	20/21	21/20
11/1	4/7	4/6	8/11	4/5	5/6	10/11	1/1	21/20
12/1	8/13	4/6	8/11	4/5	10/11	10/11	1/1	11/10
13/1	8/13	4/6	8/11	5/6	10/11	20/21	21/20	11/10
4/11	8/13	4/6	4/5	5/6	10/11	20/21	21/20	11/10
15/1	4/6	8/11	4/5	5/6	20/21	20/21	21/20	6/5
16/1	4/6	8/11	4/5	5/6	20/21	1/1	11/10	6/5
18/1	4/6	8/11	4/5	10/11	20/21	1/1	11/10	6/5
20/1	4/6	8/11	5/6	10/11	1/1	21/20	11/10	5/4
25/1	8/11	4/5	5/6	20/21	21/20	21/20	6/5	5/4
33/1	8/11	4/5	10/11	1/1	21/20	11/10	6/5	11/8
50/1	4/5	5/6	10/11	1/1	11/10	6/5	5/4	11/8
66/1	4/5	5/6	20/21	21/20	11/10	6/5	5/4	11/8
100/1	4/5	10/11	20/21	21/20	6/5	6/5	11/8	6/4
250/1	5/6	10/11	1/1	11/10	6/5	5/4	11/8	6/4

	13/8	7/4	15/8	2/1	9/4	5/2	11/4	3/1
1/10	-	-	-	-	-	-	-	-
1/8	-	-	-	-	-	-	-	-
1/7	-	-	-	-	-	-	-	-
1/6	-	-	-	-	-	-	-	-
1/5	-	-	-	-	-	-	-	-
1/4	-	-	-	-	-	-	-	-
1/3	-	-	-	-	-	-	-	1/250
2/5	-	-	-	-	-	1/250	1/50	1/28
4/9	-	-	-	-	1/250	1/50	1/25	1/16
1/2	-	-	-	1/250	1/33	1/20	1/14	1/11
8/15	-	-	1/250	1/66	1/25	1/16	1/11	1/9
4/7	-	1/250	1/66	1/33	1/16	1/12	1/9	1/8
8/13	1/250	1/50	1/28	1/20	1/12	1/9	1/8	2/13
4/6	1/50	1/28	1/20	1/14	1/10	1/8	2/13	2/11
8/11	1/25	1/16	1/12	1/10	1/8	2/13	2/11	1/5
4/5	1/14	1/11	1/9	1/8	2/13	2/11	2/9	1/4
5/6	1/12	1/10	2/17	2/15	1/6	1/5	2/9	1/4
10/11	1/9	1/8	1/7	1/6	1/5	2/9	1/4	2/7
1/1	2/15	2/13	2/11	1/5	1/4	2/7	3/10	1/3
11/10	1/6	1/5	2/9	2/9	2/7	3/10	1/3	4/11
6/5	1/5	2/9	1/4	2/7	3/10	4/11	2/5	40/95
5/4	2/9	1/4	1/4	2/7	1/3	4/11	2/5	4/9
11/8	1/4	2/7	3/10	1/3	4/11	40/95	4/9	1/2
6/4	2/7	3/10	1/3	4/11	40/95	40/85	1/2	8/15
13/8	3/10	1/3	4/11	2/5	4/9	1/2	8/15	4/7
7/4	1/3	4/11	2/5	4/9	1/2	8/15	4/7	8/13
15/8	4/11	2/5	4/9	40/85	8/15	4/7	8/13	4/6
2/1	2/5	4/9	40/85	1/2	4/7	8/13	4/6	8/11
9/4	4/9	1/2	8/15	4/7	8/13	4/6	8/11	4/5
5/2	1/2	8/15	4/7	8/13	4/6	8/11	4/5	5/6

Coupled Prices 13/8 to 3/1

	13/8	7/4	15/8	2/1	9/4	5/2	11/4	3/1
11/4	8/15	4/7	8/13	4/6	8/11	4/5	10/11	20/21
3/1	4/7	8/13	4/6	8/11	4/5	5/6	20/21	1/1
100/30	8/13	4/6	8/11	4/5	5/6	20/21	1/1	11/10
7/2	4/6	8/11	8/11	4/5	10/11	20/21	21/20	11/10
4/1	8/11	4/5	5/6	10/11	20/21	21/20	11/10	6/5
9/2	4/5	5/6	10/11	20/21	21/20	11/10	5/4	11/8
5/1	5/6	10/11	20/21	1/1	11/10	6/5	5/4	11/8
11/2	5/6	20/21	1/1	21/20	6/5	5/4	11/8	6/4
6/1	10/11	20/21	21/20	11/10	6/5	11/8	6/4	6/4
13/2	20/21	1/1	11/10	11/10	5/4	11/8	6/4	13/8
7/1	1/1	21/20	11/10	6/5	11/8	11/8	6/4	13/8
15/2	1/1	11/10	11/10	6/5	11/8	6/4	13/8	7/4
8/1	21/20	11/10	6/5	5/4	11/8	6/4	13/8	7/4
17/2	21/20	11/10	6/5	5/4	11/8	6/4	7/4	15/8
9/1	11/10	6/5	5/4	5/4	6/4	13/8	7/4	15/8
10/1	11/10	6/5	5/4	11/8	6/4	13/8	7/4	15/8
11/1	6/5	5/4	11/8	11/8	6/4	7/4	15/8	2/1
12/1	6/5	5/4	11/8	6/4	13/8	7/4	15/8	2/1
13/1	6/5	5/4	11/8	6/4	13/8	7/4	2/1	85/40
14/1	5/4	11/8	11/8	6/4	13/8	15/8	2/1	85/40
15/1	5/4	11/8	6/4	6/4	7/4	15/8	2/1	9/4
16/1	5/4	11/8	6/4	6/4	7/4	15/8	85/40	9/4
18/1	5/4	11/8	6/4	13/8	7/4	2/1	85/40	9/4
20/1	11/8	11/8	6/4	13/8	15/8	2/1	85/40	95/40
25/1	11/8	6/4	13/8	7/4	15/8	85/40	9/4	5/2
33/1	6/4	6/4	13/8	7/4	2/1	85/40	95/40	5/2
50/1	6/4	13/8	7/4	15/8	2/1	9/4	5/2	11/4
66/1	6/4	13/8	7/4	15/8	85/40	95/40	5/2	11/4
100/1	6/4	13/8	7/4	15/8	85/40	95/40	5/2	11/4
250/1	13/8	7/4	15/8	2/1	9/4	5/2	11/4	3/1

	100/30	7/2	4/1	9/2	5/1	11/2	6/1	13/2
1/10	-	-	-	-	-	-	-	-
1/8	-	-	-	-	-	-	-	-
1/7	-	-	-	-	-	-	-	-
1/6	-	-	-	-	-	-	1/250	1/100
1/5	-	-	-	-	1/250	1/66	1/50	1/28
1/4	-	-	1/250	1/50	1/28	1/20	1/16	1/14
1/3	1/50	1/33	1/20	1/14	1/11	1/9	2/17	2/15
2/5	1/16	1/14	1/11	2/17	2/15	2/13	1/6	2/11
4/9	1/12	1/11	2/17	1/7	1/6	2/11	1/5	2/9
1/2	2/17	1/8	2/13	2/11	1/5	2/9	2/9	1/4
8/15	2/15	1/7	1/6	1/5	2/9	1/4	1/4	2/7
4/7	2/13	1/6	1/5	2/9	1/4	1/4	2/7	3/10
8/13	2/11	2/11	2/9	1/4	2/7	3/10	3/10	1/3
4/6	1/5	2/9	1/4	2/7	3/10	1/3	1/3	4/11
8/11	2/9	1/4	2/7	3/10	1/3	4/11	2/5	2/5
4/5	2/7	2/7	1/3	4/11	2/5	2/5	40/95	4/9
5/6	2/7	3/10	1/3	4/11	2/5	40/95	4/9	40/85
10/11	1/3	1/3	4/11	40/95	4/9	40/85	1/2	8/15
1/1	4/11	2/5	40/95	40/85	1/2	8/15	4/7	4/7
11/10	40/95	40/95	40/85	8/15	4/7	4/7	8/13	4/6
6/5	40/85	40/85	8/15	4/7	8/13	4/6	4/6	8/11
5/4	40/85	1/2	8/15	8/13	8/13	4/6	8/11	8/11
11/8	8/15	4/7	8/13	4/6	8/11	8/11	4/5	4/5
6/4	4/7	8/13	4/6	8/11	4/5	4/5	5/6	10/11
13/8	8/13	4/6	8/11	4/5	5/6	5/6	10/11	20/21
7/4	4/6	8/11	4/5	5/6	10/11	20/21	20/21	1/1
15/8	8/11	8/11	5/6	10/11	20/21	1/1	21/20	11/10
2/1	4/5	4/5	10/11	20/21	1/1	21/20	11/10	11/10
9/4	5/6	10/11	20/21	21/20	11/10	6/5	6/5	5/4
5/2	20/21	20/21	21/20	11/10	6/5	5/4	11/8	11/8

Coupled Prices 100/30 to 13/2

	100/30	7/2	4/1	9/2	5/1	11/2	6/1	13/2
11/4	1/1	21/20	11/10	5/4	5/4	11/8	6/4	6/4
3/1	11/10	11/10	6/5	11/8	11/8	6/4	6/4	13/8
100/30	6/5	6/5	11/8	11/8	6/4	13/8	13/8	7/4
7/2	6/5	5/4	11/8	6/4	13/8	13/8	7/4	15/8
4/1	11/8	11/8	6/4	13/8	7/4	15/8	15/8	2/1
9/2	11/8	6/4	13/8	7/4	15/8	2/1	85/40	85/40
5/1	6/4	13/8	7/4	15/8	2/1	85/40	9/4	95/40
11/2	13/8	13/8	15/8	2/1	85/40	9/4	95/40	5/2
6/1	13/8	7/4	15/8	85/40	9/4	95/40	5/2	11/4
13/2	7/4	15/8	2/1	85/40	95/40	5/2	11/4	11/4
7/1	15/8	15/8	85/40	9/4	95/40	5/2	11/4	3/1
15/2	15/8	2/1	85/40	95/40	5/2	11/4	11/4	3/1
8/1	15/8	2/1	9/4	95/40	5/2	11/4	3/1	3/1
17/2	2/1	2/1	9/4	5/2	11/4	11/4	3/1	100/30
9/1	2/1	85/40	95/40	5/2	11/4	3/1	3/1	100/30
10/1	85/40	9/4	5/2	11/4	3/1	3/1	100/30	7/2
11/1	85/40	9/4	5/2	11/4	3/1	100/30	7/2	7/2
12/1	9/4	95/40	5/2	11/4	3/1	100/30	7/2	4/1
13/1	9/4	95/40	11/4	3/1	100/30	7/2	7/2	4/1
14/1	95/40	5/2	11/4	3/1	100/30	7/2	4/1	4/1
15/1	95/40	5/2	11/4	3/1	100/30	7/2	4/1	4/1
16/1	5/2	5/2	11/4	3/1	7/2	7/2	4/1	4/1
18/1	5/2	11/4	3/1	100/30	7/2	4/1	4/1	9/2
20/1	5/2	11/4	3/1	100/30	7/2	4/1	9/2	9/2
25/1	11/4	11/4	100/30	7/2	4/1	4/1	9/2	5/1
33/1	11/4	3/1	100/30	7/2	4/1	9/2	5/1	5/1
50/1	3/1	3/1	7/2	4/1	9/2	5/1	5/1	11/2
66/1	3/1	100/30	7/2	4/1	9/2	5/1	11/2	6/1
100/1	3/1	100/30	4/1	4/1	9/2	5/1	11/2	6/1
250/1	100/30	7/2	4/1	9/2	5/1	11/2	6/1	13/2

136

	7/1	15/2	8/1	17/2	9/1	10/1	11/1	12/1
1/10	-	-	-	-	-	-	1/250	1/66
1/8	-	-	1/250	1/250	1/100	1/50	1/33	1/28
1/7	1/250	1/100	1/66	1/50	1/33	1/28	1/25	1/20
1/6	1/50	1/33	1/33	1/25	1/25	1/20	1/16	1/14
1/5	1/25	1/20	1/16	1/16	1/14	1/12	1/11	1/10
1/4	1/12	1/11	1/10	1/10	1/9	1/8	2/15	1/7
1/3	1/7	2/13	1/6	1/6	2/11	2/11	1/5	1/5
2/5	1/5	1/5	2/9	2/9	2/9	1/4	1/4	1/4
4/9	2/9	2/9	1/4	1/4	1/4	2/7	2/7	3/10
1/2	1/4	2/7	2/7	3/10	3/10	1/3	1/3	1/3
8/15	2/7	3/10	3/10	1/3	1/3	1/3	4/11	4/11
4/7	3/10	1/3	1/3	4/11	4/11	4/11	2/5	2/5
8/13	1/3	4/11	4/11	4/11	2/5	2/5	40/95	4/9
4/6	4/11	2/5	2/5	40/95	40/95	4/9	40/85	40/85
8/11	40/95	4/9	4/9	40/85	40/85	1/2	1/2	8/15
4/5	40/85	1/2	1/2	1/2	8/15	8/15	4/7	4/7
5/6	1/2	1/2	8/15	8/15	8/15	4/7	4/7	8/13
10/11	8/15	4/7	4/7	4/7	8/13	8/13	4/6	4/6
1/1	8/13	8/13	8/13	4/6	4/6	4/6	8/11	8/11
11/10	4/6	4/6	8/11	8/11	8/11	4/5	4/5	4/5
6/5	8/11	8/11	4/5	4/5	4/5	5/6	5/6	10/11
5/4	8/11	4/5	4/5	5/6	5/6	5/6	10/11	10/11
11/8	5/6	5/6	10/11	10/11	10/11	20/21	1/1	1/1
6/4	10/11	20/21	20/21	1/1	1/1	21/20	21/20	11/10
13/8	1/1	1/1	21/20	21/20	11/10	11/10	6/5	6/5
7/4	21/20	11/10	11/10	11/10	6/5	6/5	5/4	5/4
15/8	11/10	11/10	6/5	6/5	5/4	5/4	11/8	11/8
2/1	6/5	6/5	5/4	5/4	5/4	11/8	11/8	6/4
9/4	11/8	11/8	11/8	11/8	6/4	6/4	6/4	13/8
5/2	11/8	6/4	6/4	6/4	13/8	13/8	7/4	7/4

Coupled Prices 7/1 to 12/1

	7/1	15/2	8/1	17/2	9/1	10/1	11/1	12/1
11/4	6/4	13/8	13/8	7/4	7/4	7/4	15/8	15/8
3/1	13/8	7/4	7/4	15/8	15/8	15/8	2/1	2/1
100/30	15/8	15/8	15/8	2/1	2/1	85/40	85/40	9/4
7/2	15/8	2/1	2/1	2/1	85/40	9/4	9/4	95/40
4/1	85/40	85/40	9/4	9/4	95/40	5/2	5/2	5/2
9/2	9/4	95/40	95/40	5/2	5/2	11/4	11/4	11/4
5/1	95/40	5/2	5/2	11/4	11/4	3/1	3/1	3/1
11/2	5/2	11/4	11/4	11/4	3/1	3/1	100/30	100/30
6/1	11/4	11/4	3/1	3/1	3/1	100/30	7/2	7/2
13/2	3/1	3/1	3/1	100/30	100/30	7/2	7/2	4/1
7/1	3/1	3/1	100/30	100/30	7/2	7/2	4/1	4/1
15/2	3/1	100/30	100/30	7/2	7/2	4/1	4/1	4/1
8/1	100/30	100/30	7/2	7/2	4/1	4/1	4/1	9/2
17/2	100/30	7/2	7/2	4/1	4/1	4/1	9/2	9/2
9/1	7/2	7/2	4/1	4/1	4/1	9/2	9/2	9/2
10/1	7/2	4/1	4/1	4/1	9/2	9/2	5/1	5/1
11/1	4/1	4/1	4/1	9/2	9/2	5/1	5/1	11/2
12/1	4/1	4/1	9/2	9/2	9/2	5/1	11/2	11/2
13/1	4/1	9/2	9/2	9/2	5/1	5/1	11/2	6/1
14/1	4/1	9/2	9/2	5/1	5/1	11/2	11/2	6/1
15/1	9/2	9/2	5/1	5/1	5/1	11/2	6/1	6/1
16/1	9/2	9/2	5/1	5/1	11/2	11/2	6/1	13/2
18/1	9/2	5/1	5/1	11/2	11/2	6/1	13/2	13/2
20/1	5/1	5/1	11/2	11/2	6/1	6/1	13/2	7/1
25/1	5/1	11/2	11/2	6/1	6/1	13/2	7/1	15/2
33/1	11/2	6/1	6/1	13/2	13/2	15/2	8/1	17/2
50/1	6/1	13/2	13/2	7/1	15/2	8/1	17/2	9/1
66/1	13/2	7/1	15/2	15/2	8/1	17/2	9/1	10/1
100/1	13/2	7/1	15/2	15/2	8/1	9/1	10/1	11/1
250/1	7/1	7/1	15/2	8/1	17/2	10/1	10/1	11/1

	13/1	14/1	15/1	16/1	18/1	20/1	25/1	33/1
1/10	1/50	1/50	1/33	1/33	1/25	1/25	1/20	1/16
1/8	1/25	1/20	1/20	1/20	1/16	1/14	1/12	1/11
1/7	1/16	1/16	1/16	1/14	1/12	1/12	1/11	1/9
1/6	1/14	1/12	1/11	1/11	1/10	1/9	2/17	1/8
1/5	1/9	1/9	2/17	2/17	1/8	2/15	1/7	2/13
1/4	1/7	2/13	2/13	1/6	1/6	2/11	1/5	1/5
1/3	2/9	2/9	2/9	1/4	1/4	1/4	2/7	2/7
2/5	2/7	2/7	2/7	3/10	3/10	3/10	1/3	1/3
4/9	3/10	1/3	1/3	1/3	1/3	4/11	4/11	2/5
1/2	4/11	4/11	4/11	4/11	2/5	2/5	40/95	4/9
8/15	2/5	2/5	2/5	2/5	40/95	40/95	4/9	40/85
4/7	40/95	40/95	40/95	4/9	4/9	40/85	40/85	1/2
8/13	4/9	40/85	40/85	40/85	1/2	1/2	8/15	8/15
4/6	1/2	1/2	1/2	8/15	8/15	8/15	4/7	4/7
8/11	8/15	8/15	4/7	4/7	4/7	8/13	8/13	4/6
4/5	8/13	8/13	8/13	8/13	4/6	4/6	4/6	8/11
5/6	8/13	8/13	4/6	4/6	4/6	4/6	8/11	8/11
10/11	4/6	4/6	8/11	8/11	8/11	8/11	4/5	4/5
1/1	8/11	4/5	4/5	4/5	4/5	5/6	5/6	10/11
11/10	5/6	5/6	5/6	5/6	10/11	10/11	20/21	1/1
6/5	10/11	10/11	20/21	20/21	20/21	1/1	21/20	21/20
5/4	20/21	20/21	20/21	1/1	1/1	21/20	21/20	11/10
11/8	21/20	21/20	21/20	11/10	11/10	11/10	6/5	6/5
6/4	11/10	11/10	6/5	6/5	6/5	5/4	5/4	11/8
13/8	6/5	5/4	5/4	5/4	5/4	11/8	11/8	6/4
7/4	5/4	11/8	11/8	11/8	11/8	11/8	6/4	6/4
15/8	11/8	11/8	6/4	6/4	6/4	6/4	13/8	13/8
2/1	6/4	6/4	6/4	6/4	13/8	13/8	7/4	7/4
9/4	13/8	13/8	7/4	7/4	7/4	15/8	15/8	2/1
5/2	7/4	15/8	15/8	15/8	2/1	2/1	85/40	85/40

Coupled Prices 13/1 to 33/1

	13/1	14/1	15/1	16/1	18/1	20/1	25/1	33/1
11/4	2/1	2/1	2/1	85/40	85/40	85/40	9/4	95/40
3/1	85/40	85/40	9/4	9/4	9/4	95/40	5/2	5/2
100/30	9/4	95/40	95/40	5/2	5/2	5/2	11/4	11/4
7/2	95/40	5/2	5/2	5/2	11/4	11/4	11/4	3/1
4/1	11/4	11/4	11/4	11/4	3/1	3/1	100/30	100/30
9/2	3/1	3/1	3/1	3/1	100/30	100/30	7/2	7/2
5/1	100/30	100/30	100/30	7/2	7/2	7/2	4/1	4/1
11/2	7/2	7/2	7/2	7/2	4/1	4/1	4/1	9/2
6/1	7/2	4/1	4/1	4/1	4/1	9/2	9/2	5/1
13/2	4/1	4/1	4/1	4/1	9/2	9/2	5/1	5/1
7/1	4/1	4/1	9/2	9/2	9/2	5/1	5/1	11/2
15/2	9/2	9/2	9/2	9/2	5/1	5/1	11/2	6/1
8/1	9/2	9/2	5/1	5/1	5/1	11/2	11/2	6/1
17/2	9/2	5/1	5/1	5/1	11/2	11/2	6/1	13/2
9/1	5/1	5/1	5/1	11/2	11/2	6/1	6/1	13/2
10/1	5/1	11/2	11/2	11/2	6/1	6/1	13/2	15/2
11/1	11/2	11/2	6/1	6/1	13/2	13/2	7/1	8/1
12/1	6/1	6/1	6/1	13/2	13/2	7/1	15/2	17/2
13/1	6/1	13/2	13/2	13/2	7/1	15/2	8/1	9/1
14/1	13/2	13/2	7/1	7/1	15/2	8/1	17/2	9/1
15/1	13/2	7/1	7/1	15/2	15/2	8/1	9/1	10/1
16/1	13/2	7/1	15/2	15/2	8/1	17/2	9/1	10/1
18/1	7/1	15/2	15/2	8/1	17/2	9/1	10/1	11/1
20/1	15/2	8/1	8/1	17/2	9/1	10/1	11/1	12/1
25/1	8/1	17/2	9/1	9/1	10/1	11/1	12/1	14/1
33/1	9/1	9/1	10/1	10/1	11/1	12/1	14/1	16/1
50/1	10/1	11/1	11/1	12/1	13/1	14/1	16/1	20/1
66/1	11/1	11/1	12/1	13/1	14/1	15/1	18/1	22/1
100/1	11/1	12/1	13/1	14/1	15/1	16/1	20/1	25/1
250/1	12/1	13/1	14/1	15/1	16/1	18/1	22/1	28/1

	50/1	66/1	100/1	250/1		50/1	66/1	100/1	250/1
1/10	1/14	1/12	1/11	1/11	**11/4**	5/2	5/2	5/2	11/4
1/8	1/10	1/9	1/9	2/17	**3/1**	11/4	11/4	11/4	3/1
1/7	2/17	1/8	/15	2/15	**100/30**	3/1	3/1	3/1	100/30
1/6	1/7	1/7	2/13	1/6	**7/2**	3/1	100/30	100/30	7/2
1/5	1/6	2/11	2/11	1/5	**4/1**	7/2	7/2	4/1	4/1
1/4	2/9	2/9	2/9	1/4	**9/2**	4/1	4/1	4/1	9/2
1/3	3/10	3/10	3/10	1/3	**5/1**	9/2	9/2	9/2	5/1
2/5	4/11	4/11	4/11	2/5	**11/2**	5/1	5/1	5/1	11/2
4/9	2/5	40/95	40/95	4/9	**6/1**	5/1	11/2	11/2	6/1
1/2	4/9	40/85	40/85	1/2	**13/2**	11/2	6/1	6/1	13/2
8/15	1/2	1/2	1/2	8/15	**7/1**	6/1	6/1	13/2	7/1
4/7	8/15	8/15	8/15	4/7	**15/2**	13/2	13/2	7/1	7/1
8/13	4/7	4/7	4/7	8/13	**8/1**	13/2	7/1	15/2	15/2
4/6	8/13	8/13	8/13	4/6	**17/2**	7/1	15/2	15/2	8/1
8/11	4/6	4/6	8/11	8/11	**9/1**	15/2	15/2	8/1	17/2
4/5	8/11	8/11	4/5	4/5	**10/1**	8/1	17/2	9/1	10/1
5/6	4/5	4/5	4/5	5/6	**11/1**	17/2	9/1	10/1	10/1
10/11	5/6	5/6	10/11	10/11	**12/1**	9/1	10/1	11/1	11/1
1/1	10/11	20/21	20/21	1/1	**13/1**	10/1	11/1	11/1	12/1
11/10	1/1	21/20	21/20	11/10	**14/1**	11/1	11/1	12/1	13/1
6/5	11/10	11/10	6/5	6/5	**15/1**	11/1	12/1	13/1	14/1
5/4	6/5	6/5	6/5	5/4	**16/1**	12/1	13/1	14/1	15/1
11/8	5/4	5/4	11/8	11/8	**18/1**	13/1	14/1	15/1	16/1
6/4	11/8	11/8	6/4	6/4	**20/1**	14/1	15/1	16/1	18/1
13/8	6/4	6/4	6/4	13/8	**25/1**	16/1	18/1	20/1	22/1
7/4	13/8	13/8	13/8	7/4	**33/1**	20/1	22/1	25/1	28/1
15/8	7/4	7/4	7/4	15/8	**50/1**	25/1	28/1	33/1	40/1
2/1	15/8	15/8	15/8	2/1	**66/1**	28/1	33/1	40/1	50/1
9/4	2/1	85/40	85/40	9/4	**100/1**	33/1	40/1	50/1	66/1
5/2	9/4	95/40	95/40	5/2	**250/1**	40/1	50/1	66/1	125/1

19:Takeout Tables

Takeout Tables - pages 143 to 145

These table are more or less self explanatory. The sum of money at the intersection of any price and takeout is the stake needed to take out that amount at that price.

Takeout Table 1/250 - 4/9

	£25	£50	£100	£200	£500	£1000
1/250	£24.90	£49.80	£99.60	£199.20	£498.00	£996.00
1/100	£24.75	£49.50	£99.00	£198.00	£495.00	£990.00
1/66	£24.62	£49.25	£98.50	£197.00	£492.50	£985.00
1/50	£24.50	£49.01	£98.03	£196.06	£490.15	£980.30
1/33	£24.26	£48.52	£97.05	£194.10	£485.25	£970.50
1/28	£24.13	£48.27	£96.55	£193.10	£482.75	£965.51
1/25	£24.03	£48.07	£96.15	£192.30	£480.75	£961.50
1/20	£23.80	£47.61	£95.23	£190.46	£476.15	£952.30
1/16	£23.52	£47.05	£94.11	£188.22	£470.55	£941.10
1/14	£23.33	£46.66	£93.33	£186.66	£466.65	£933.30
1/12	£23.07	£46.15	£92.30	£184.60	£461.50	£923.00
1/11	£22.91	£45.83	£91.66	£183.32	£458.30	£916.60
1/10	£22.74	£45.49	£90.99	£181.98	£454.95	£909.90
1/9	£22.50	£45.00	£90.00	£180.00	£450.00	£900.00
2/17	£22.36	£44.73	£89.47	£178.94	£447.35	£894.70
1/8	£22.22	£44.44	£88.88	£177.76	£444.40	£888.80
2/15	£22.05	£44.11	£88.23	£176.47	£441.17	£882.35
1/7	£21.87	£43.74	£87.49	£174.98	£437.45	£874.90
2/13	£21.66	£43.33	£86.66	£173.32	£433.30	£866.60
1/6	£21.42	£42.85	£85.71	£171.42	£428.55	£857.10
2/11	£21.15	£42.30	£84.61	£169.22	£423.05	£846.10
1/5	£20.83	£41.66	£83.33	£166.66	£416.65	£833.30
2/9	£20.45	£40.90	£81.81	£163.62	£409.05	£818.10
1/4	£20.00	£40.00	£80.00	£160.00	£400.00	£800.00
2/7	£19.44	£38.88	£77.77	£155.54	£388.85	£777.70
3/10	£19.23	£38.46	£76.92	£153.84	£384.60	£769.20
1/3	£18.75	£37.50	£75.00	£150.00	£375.00	£750.00
4/11	£18.33	£36.66	£73.33	£146.66	£366.65	£733.30
2/5	£17.85	£35.71	£71.42	£142.84	£357.10	£714.20
4/9	£17.30	£34.61	£69.23	£138.46	£346.15	£692.30

	£25	£50	£100	£200	£500	£1000
1/2	£16.66	£33.33	£66.66	£133.32	£333.30	£666.60
8/15	£16.30	£32.60	£65.21	£130.42	£326.05	£652.10
4/7	£15.90	£31.81	£63.63	£127.26	£318.15	£636.30
8/13	£15.47	£30.95	£61.90	£123.80	£309.50	£619.10
4/6	£15.00	£30.00	£60.00	£120.00	£300.00	£600.00
8/11	£14.47	£28.94	£57.89	£115.78	£289.45	£578.90
4/5	£13.88	£27.77	£55.55	£111.10	£277.75	£555.50
5/6	£13.63	£27.27	£54.54	£109.08	£272.70	£545.40
10/11	£13.09	£26.19	£52.38	£104.76	£261.90	£523.80
1/1	£12.50	£25.00	£50.00	£100.00	£250.00	£500.00
11/10	£11.90	£23.80	£47.61	£95.22	£238.05	£476.10
6/5	£11.36	£22.72	£45.45	£90.90	£227.25	£454.50
5/4	£11.11	£22.22	£44.44	£88.88	£222.20	£444.40
11/8	£10.52	£21.05	£42.10	£84.20	£210.50	£421.00
6/4	£10.00	£20.00	£40.00	£80.00	£200.00	£400.00
13/8	£9.52	£19.04	£38.09	£76.18	£190.45	£380.90
7/4	£9.09	£18.18	£36.36	£72.72	£181.80	£363.60
15/8	£8.69	£17.39	£34.78	£69.56	£173.90	£347.80
2/1	£8.33	£16.66	£33.33	£66.66	£166.65	£333.30
9/4	£7.69	£15.38	£30.76	£61.52	£153.80	£307.60
5/2	£7.14	£14.28	£28.57	£57.14	£142.85	£285.70
11/4	£6.66	£13.33	£26.66	£53.32	£133.30	£266.60
3/1	£6.25	£12.50	£25.00	£50.00	£125.00	£250.00
100/30	£5.76	£11.53	£23.07	£46.14	£115.35	£230.70
7/2	£5.55	£11.11	£22.22	£44.44	£111.10	£222.20
4/1	£5.00	£10.00	£20.00	£40.00	£100.00	£200.00
9/2	£4.54	£9.09	£18.18	£36.36	£90.90	£181.80
5/1	£4.16	£8.33	£16.66	£33.32	£83.30	£166.60
11/2	£3.84	£7.69	£15.38	£30.76	£76.90	£153.80
6/1	£3.57	£7.14	£14.28	£28.56	£71.40	£142.80

Takeout Table 13/2 - 500/1

	£25	£50	£100	£200	£500	£1000
13/2	£3.33	£6.66	£13.33	£26.66	£66.65	£133.30
7/1	£3.12	£6.25	£12.50	£25.00	£62.50	£125.00
15/2	£2.94	£5.88	£11.76	£23.52	£58.80	£117.60
8/1	£2.77	£5.55	£11.11	£22.22	£55.55	£111.10
17/2	£2.63	£5.26	£10.52	£21.04	£52.60	£105.20
9/1	£2.50	£5.00	£10.00	£20.00	£50.00	£100.00
10/1	£2.27	£4.54	£9.09	£18.18	£45.45	£90.90
11/1	£2.08	£4.16	£8.33	£16.66	£41.65	£83.30
12/1	£1.92	£3.84	£7.69	£15.38	£38.45	£76.90
13/1	£1.78	£3.57	£7.14	£14.28	£35.70	£71.40
14/1	£1.66	£3.33	£6.66	£13.32	£33.30	£66.60
15/1	£1.56	£3.12	£6.25	£12.50	£31.25	£62.50
16/1	£1.47	£2.94	£5.88	£11.76	£29.40	£58.80
18/1	£1.31	£2.63	£5.26	£10.52	£26.30	£52.60
20/1	£1.19	£2.38	£4.76	£9.52	£23.80	£47.60
22/1	£1.08	£2.17	£4.34	£8.68	£21.70	£43.40
25/1	£0.96	£1.92	£3.84	£7.68	£19.20	£38.40
28/1	£0.86	£1.72	£3.44	£6.88	£17.20	£34.40
33/1	£0.73	£1.47	£2.94	£5.88	£14.70	£29.40
35/1	£0.69	£1.38	£2.77	£5.55	£13.88	£27.77
40/1	£0.60	£1.21	£2.43	£4.86	£12.15	£24.30
50/1	£0.49	£0.98	£1.96	£3.92	£9.80	£19.60
60/1	£0.40	£0.81	£1.63	£3.26	£8.15	£16.30
66/1	£0.37	£0.74	£1.49	£2.98	£7.45	£14.90
80/1	£0.30	£0.61	£1.23	£2.46	£6.15	£12.30
100/1	£0.24	£0.49	£0.99	£1.98	£4.95	£9.90
125/1	£0.19	£0.39	£0.79	£1.58	£3.96	£7.93
150/1	£0.16	£0.33	£0.66	£1.32	£3.30	£6.60
200/1	£0.12	£0.24	£0.49	£0.98	£2.45	£4.90
500/1	£0.04	£0.09	£0.19	£0.38	£0.95	£1.90

20:Tables 6-7 Starting Price Data

Notes On The Tables

6 Starting Price Data pages 147 to 150

This data, which was assembled by hand from a variety of sources, covers two complete seasons of Flat (Turf) and National Hunt racing.

The columns are as follows :-
The price.
The price percentage.
The number of runners.
The number of winners.
The percentage of winners.
The ratio of the percentage of winners to the price percentage.
The outcome to one point staked.
This outcome as a percentage return on the total staked.

Rather than being offered in their own right, some of the prices in the table such as 7/5 and 95/40 are more likely to be averages of the prices which were actually available in the ring at the off, as subsequently agreed on by the Starting Price Reporters.

7 Starting Price Bands Table page 150

This again is the price-bands table derived from the above data, which has already appeared in various forms such as on pages 12 and 98. And again as before, with the exception of the prices, the columns are the same as are used in the full tables.

price	percent	runners	winners	percent	ratio	capital	pc return
1 / 28	96.55	1	1	100.00	1.04	0.04	3.57
1 / 25	96.15	1	1	100.00	1.04	0.04	4.00
1 / 16	94.11	1	1	100.00	1.06	0.06	6.25
1 / 14	93.33	3	2	66.67	0.71	-0.86	-28.57
1 / 12	92.30	1	1	100.00	1.08	0.08	8.33
1 / 11	91.66	2	2	100.00	1.09	0.18	9.09
1 / 10	90.99	2	1	50.00	0.55	-0.90	-45.00
1 / 9	90.00	3	3	100.00	1.11	0.33	0.00
2 / 17	89.47	2	1	50.00	0.56	-0.88	-44.12
1 / 8	88.88	8	8	100.00	1.13	1.00	12.50
2 / 15	88.24	2	1	50.00	0.57	-0.87	-43.33
1 / 7	87.49	12	11	91.67	1.05	0.57	4.76
2 / 13	86.66	2	2	100.00	1.15	0.31	15.38
1 / 6	85.71	15	12	80.00	0.93	-1.00	-6.67
2 / 11	84.61	6	6	100.00	1.18	1.09	18.18
1 / 5	83.33	25	22	88.00	1.06	1.40	5.60
2 / 9	81.81	18	15	83.33	1.02	0.33	1.85
1 / 4	80.00	35	28	80.00	1.00	0.00	0.00
2 / 7	77.77	36	30	83.33	1.07	2.57	7.14
3 / 10	76.92	20	14	70.00	0.91	-1.80	-9.00
1 / 3	75.00	55	40	72.73	0.97	-1.67	-3.03
4 / 11	73.33	52	38	73.08	1.00	-0.18	-0.35
2 / 5	71.42	84	64	76.19	1.07	5.60	6.67
40 / 95	70.37	2	2	100.00	1.42	0.84	42.11
4 / 9	69.23	99	65	65.66	0.95	-5.11	-5.16
40 / 85	68.00	4	4	100.00	1.47	1.88	47.06
1 / 2	66.66	137	88	64.23	0.96	-5.00	-3.65
8 / 15	65.21	53	28	52.83	0.81	-10.07	-18.99
4 / 7	63.63	143	83	58.04	0.91	-12.57	-8.79

Starting Price Data

price	percent	runners	winners	percent	ratio	capital	pc return
8 / 13	61.90	187	114	60.96	0.98	-2.85	-1.52
4 / 6	60.00	252	140	55.56	0.93	-18.67	-7.41
8 / 11	57.89	279	150	53.76	0.93	-19.91	-7.14
4 / 5	55.55	334	165	49.40	0.89	-37.00	-11.08
5 / 6	54.54	160	83	51.88	0.95	-7.83	-4.90
10 / 11	52.38	357	182	50.98	0.97	-9.55	-2.67
20 / 21	51.21	3	3	100.00	1.95	2.86	95.24
1 / 1	50.00	459	201	43.79	0.88	-57.00	-12.42
21 / 20	48.78	11	6	54.55	1.12	1.30	11.82
11 / 10	47.61	377	158	41.91	0.88	-45.20	-11.99
6 / 5	45.45	188	80	42.55	0.94	-12.00	-6.38
5 / 4	44.44	618	259	41.91	0.94	-35.25	-5.70
11 / 8	42.10	606	248	40.92	0.97	-17.00	-2.81
7 / 5	41.67	1	0	0.00	0.00	-1.00	-100.00
6 / 4	40.00	744	259	34.81	0.87	-96.50	-12.97
13 / 8	38.09	637	254	39.87	1.05	29.75	4.67
7 / 4	36.36	1106	359	32.46	0.89	-118.75	-10.74
15 / 8	34.78	500	173	34.60	0.99	-2.63	-0.52
2 / 1	33.33	1448	418	28.87	0.87	-194.00	-13.40
85 / 40	32.00	77	19	24.68	0.77	-17.63	-22.89
9 / 4	30.76	1567	425	27.12	0.88	-185.75	-11.85
95 / 40	29.63	3	2	66.67	2.25	3.75	125.00
5 / 2	28.57	1740	417	23.97	0.84	-280.50	-16.12
11 / 4	26.66	1374	337	24.53	0.92	-110.25	-8.02
3 / 1	25.00	2519	571	22.67	0.91	-235.00	-9.33
10 / 3	23.07	982	241	24.54	1.06	62.33	6.35
7 / 2	22.22	2941	609	20.71	0.93	-200.50	-6.82
4 / 1	20.00	3491	593	16.99	0.85	-526.00	-15.07
9 /2	18.18	3063	496	16.19	0.89	-335.00	-10.94

price	percent	runners	winners	percent	ratio	capital	pc return
5 / 1	16.66	4177	607	14.53	0.87	-535.00	-12.81
11 / 2	15.38	2630	350	13.31	0.87	-355.00	-13.50
6 / 1	14.28	4140	486	11.74	0.82	-738.00	-17.83
13 / 2	13.33	1922	227	11.81	0.89	-219.50	-11.42
7 / 1	12.50	4538	490	10.80	0.86	-618.00	-13.62
15 / 2	11.76	981	105	10.70	0.91	-88.50	-9.02
8 / 1	11.11	5598	492	8.79	0.79	-1170.00	-20.90
17 / 2	10.52	231	19	8.23	0.78	-50.50	-21.86
9 / 1	10.00	3535	291	8.23	0.82	-625.00	-17.68
10 / 1	9.09	6483	508	7.84	0.86	-895.00	-13.81
11 / 1	8.33	2019	120	5.94	0.71	-579.00	-28.68
12 / 1	7.69	6839	405	5.92	0.77	-1574.00	-23.02
13 / 1	7.14	11	1	9.09	1.27	3.00	27.27
14 / 1	6.66	7480	330	4.41	0.66	-2530.00	-33.82
15 / 1	6.25	7	0	0.00	0.00	-7.00	-100.00
16 / 1	5.88	7331	276	3.76	0.64	-2639.00	-36.00
18 / 1	5.26	43	1	2.33	0.44	-24.00	-55.81
20 / 1	4.76	8810	221	2.51	0.53	-4169.00	-47.32
22 / 1	4.34	27	0	0.00	0.00	-27.00	-100.00
25 / 1	3.84	7150	142	1.99	0.52	-3458.00	-48.36
28 / 1	3.44	41	2	4.88	1.42	17.00	41.46
33 / 1	2.94	11141	123	1.10	0.38	-6959.00	-62.46
35 / 1	2.78	1	0	0.00	0.00	-1.00	-100.00
40 / 1	2.43	986	7	0.71	0.29	-699.00	-70.89
50 / 1	1.96	7356	44	0.60	0.31	-5112.00	-69.49
60 / 1	1.63	2	0	0.00	0.00	-2.00	-100.00
66 / 1	1.49	2792	10	0.36	0.24	-2122.00	-76.00
80 / 1	1.23	19	0	0.00	0.00	-19.00	-100.00
100 / 1	0.99	2460	6	0.24	0.25	-1854.00	-75.37

Starting Price Data

price	percent	runners	winners	percent	ratio	capital	pc return
120 / 1	0.83	1	0	0.00	0.00	-1.00	-100.00
125 / 1	0.79	2	0	0.00	0.00	-2.00	-100.00
150 / 1	0.66	132	1	0.76	1.15	19.00	14.39
200 / 1	0.49	385	0	0.00	0.00	-385.00	-100.00
250 / 1	0.39	16	0	0.00	0.00	-16.00	-100.00
300 / 1	0.33	15	0	0.00	0.00	-15.00	-100.00
400 / 1	0.25	4	0	0.00	0.00	-4.00	-100.00
500 / 1	0.19	57	0	0.00	0.00	-57.00	-100.00
		126210	**12800**	**10.14**		**-40000.83**	**-31.69**

7 All 126,210 Runners Sorted Into 8 Price Bands.

Price band			runs	wins	percent	ratio	capital	pcreturn
1 / 28 -	2 /	5	386	304	78.76	1.01	5.46	1.41
40 / 95 -	4 /	5	1490	839	56.31	0.93	-108.45	-7.28
5 / 6 -	6 /	4	3524	1479	41.97	0.92	-277.17	-7.87
13 / 8 -	3 /	1	10971	2975	27.12	0.90	-1111.00	-10.13
100 / 30 -	15 /	2	28865	4204	14.56	0.88	-3553.17	-12.31
8 / 1 -	16 /	1	39534	2442	6.18	0.75	-10066.50	-25.46
18 / 1 -	60 /	1	35557	540	1.52	0.43	-20434.00	-57.47
66 / 1 - 500 /	1		5883	17	0.29	0.24	-4456.00	-75.74
			126210	**12800**	**10.14**		**-40000.83**	**-31.69**

21:Race Profiles

Notes On The Profiles

All the profiles are based on actual races, selected from among those originally used in the compilation of the starting price data.

Profile Order

To prevent profiles from running over onto the next page, and to make the best use of the available space, they have been arranged as follows -

runners	pages		runners	pages		runners	pages
5	152 - 154		13	165 - 167		21	179 - 180
6	155 - 157		14	161 - 163		22	181 - 182
7	158 - 160		15	158 - 160		23	183 - 184
8	161 - 164		16	155 - 157		24	185
9	165 - 167		17	152 - 154		25	186
10	168 - 170		18	173 - 174		26	187
11	171 - 172		19	175 - 176			
12	168 - 170		20	177 - 178			

The column headings used in the profiles are as follows -

s.p.	The returned starting price.
s.p. win %	The starting price as a percentage.
s.p. place %	The equivalent place price as a percentage.
nearest fair odds	The nearest equivalent fair price.
fair win %	The horse's fair win chance.
fair place %	The horse's fair place chance.
win return	The percentage return on win only bets.
each way return	The percentage return on each-way bets.
place return	Shows the place contribution to each-way returns.

Race Profiles 5 and 17 Runners

Race no. 1   5 Runners   2 Places at 1/4 odds

s.p.	s.p win%	s.p place%	nearest fair odds	fair win%	fair place%	win	returns e/w	place
2 /17	89.47	97.14	1 / 8	88.96	99.66	-0.58	1.01	2.59
13 / 2	13.33	38.10	10 / 1	9.41	85.36	-29.43	47.31	124.06
40 / 1	2.44	9.09	150 / 1	0.58	5.34	-76.10	-58.66	-41.21
40 / 1	2.44	9.09	150 / 1	0.58	5.34	-76.10	-58.66	-41.21
50 / 1	1.96	7.41	200 / 1	0.47	4.30	-76.10	-59.04	-41.99
	109.65	160.83		100.00	200.00			

Race no. 2   17 Runners   4 Places at 1/4 odds

s.p.	s.p win%	s.p place%	nearest fair odds	fair win%	fair place%	win	returns e/w	place
8 /11	57.89	84.62	21 / 20	49.33	96.71	-14.79	-0.25	14.29
9 / 2	18.18	47.06	6 / 1	14.64	71.50	-19.46	16.24	51.95
7 / 1	12.50	36.36	9 / 1	10.05	57.89	-19.62	19.79	59.19
7 / 1	12.50	36.36	9 / 1	10.05	57.89	-19.62	19.79	59.19
14 / 1	6.67	22.22	22 / 1	4.10	28.31	-38.56	-5.58	27.39
25 / 1	3.85	13.79	60 / 1	1.74	12.74	-54.71	-31.16	-7.61
25 / 1	3.85	13.79	60 / 1	1.74	12.74	-54.71	-31.16	-7.61
33 / 1	2.94	10.81	100 / 1	1.04	7.69	-64.80	-46.81	-28.83
33 / 1	2.94	10.81	100 / 1	1.04	7.69	-64.80	-46.81	-28.83
33 / 1	2.94	10.81	100 / 1	1.04	7.69	-64.80	-46.81	-28.83
33 / 1	2.94	10.81	100 / 1	1.04	7.69	-64.80	-46.81	-28.83
33 / 1	2.94	10.81	100 / 1	1.04	7.69	-64.80	-46.81	-28.83
33 / 1	2.94	10.81	100 / 1	1.04	7.69	-64.80	-46.81	-28.83
50 / 1	1.96	7.41	200 / 1	0.53	4.01	-72.75	-59.29	-45.82
50 / 1	1.96	7.41	200 / 1	0.53	4.01	-72.75	-59.29	-45.82
50 / 1	1.96	7.41	200 / 1	0.53	4.01	-72.75	-59.29	-45.82
50 / 1	1.96	7.41	200 / 1	0.53	4.01	-72.75	-59.29	-45.82
	140.93	348.70		100.00	400.00			

Race no. 3   5 Runners   2 Places at 1/4 odds

s.p.	s.p win%	s.p place%	nearest fair odds	fair win%	fair place%	returns win	e/w	place
11 / 8	42.11	74.42	6 / 4	39.80	70.99	-5.47	-5.04	-4.61
2 / 1	33.33	66.67	9 / 4	30.87	61.69	-7.38	-7.42	-7.47
9 / 2	18.18	47.06	5 / 1	16.71	37.49	-8.12	-14.23	-20.33
9 / 1	10.00	30.77	10 / 1	8.87	20.83	-11.26	-21.74	-32.30
16 / 1	5.88	20.00	25 / 1	3.74	9.00	-36.39	-45.69	-54.99
	109.50	**238.91**		**100.00**	**200.00**			

Race no. 4   17 Runners   4 Places at 1/4 odds

s.p.	s.p win%	s.p place%	nearest fair odds	fair win%	fair place%	returns win	e/w	place
5/ 2	28.57	61.54	11 / 4	26.54	78.43	-7.11	10.17	27.46
5 / 1	16.67	44.44	11 / 2	15.43	59.58	-7.43	13.32	34.06
6 / 1	14.29	40.00	13 / 2	13.22	53.85	-7.46	13.58	34.63
7 / 1	12.50	36.36	15 / 2	11.55	48.95	-7.57	13.51	34.60
7 / 1	12.50	36.36	15 / 2	11.55	48.95	-7.57	13.51	34.60
16 / 1	5.88	20.00	25 / 1	3.77	18.80	-35.89	-20.94	-5.99
16 / 1	5.88	20.00	25 / 1	3.77	18.80	-35.89	-20.94	-5.99
16 / 1	5.88	20.00	25 / 1	3.77	18.80	-35.89	-20.94	-5.99
20 / 1	4.76	16.67	35 / 1	2.74	13.90	-42.53	-29.56	-16.58
25 / 1	3.85	13.79	50 / 1	2.00	10.31	-47.93	-36.60	-25.26
33 / 1	2.94	10.81	80 / 1	1.19	6.21	-59.52	-51.02	-42.51
33 / 1	2.94	10.81	80 / 1	1.19	6.21	-59.52	-51.02	-42.51
33 / 1	2.94	10.81	80 / 1	1.19	6.21	-59.52	-51.02	-42.51
50 / 1	1.96	7.41	150 / 1	0.61	3.24	-68.67	-62.48	-56.28
50 / 1	1.96	7.41	150 / 1	0.61	3.24	-68.67	-62.48	-56.28
66 / 1	1.49	5.71	250 / 1	0.43	2.25	-71.49	-66.05	-60.62
66 / 1	1.49	5.71	250 / 1	0.43	2.25	-71.49	-66.05	-60.62
	126.51	**367.85**		**100.00**	**400.00**			

Race Profiles 5 and 17 Runners

Race no. 5   5 Runners   2 Places at 1/4 odds

s.p.	s.p win%	s.p place%	nearest fair odds	fair win%	fair place%	returns win	returns e/w	place
2 / 1	33.33	66.67	9 / 4	30.93	58.21	-7.21	-9.95	-12.69
11 / 4	26.67	59.26	3 / 1	24.62	49.32	-7.68	-12.23	-16.78
100 /30	23.08	54.55	7 / 2	21.27	43.81	-7.83	-13.76	-19.69
7 / 2	22.22	53.33	4 / 1	20.46	42.41	-7.92	-14.21	-20.49
20 / 1	4.76	16.67	35 / 1	2.72	6.26	-42.88	-52.66	-62.44
	110.06	250.47		100.00	200.00			

Race no. 6   17 Runners   4 Places at 1/4 odds

s.p.	s.p win%	s.p place%	nearest fair odds	fair win%	fair place%	returns win	returns e/w	place
9 / 2	18.18	47.06	5 / 1	16.99	59.16	-6.54	9.58	25.71
9 / 2	18.18	47.06	5 / 1	16.99	59.16	-6.54	9.58	25.71
7 / 1	12.50	36.36	15 / 2	11.66	45.60	-6.73	9.34	25.40
8 / 1	11.11	33.33	9 / 1	10.19	41.11	-8.26	7.54	23.33
9 / 1	10.00	30.77	10 / 1	9.03	37.28	-9.74	5.71	21.17
10 / 1	9.09	28.57	11 / 1	8.01	33.77	-11.87	3.16	18.19
12 / 1	7.69	25.00	16 / 1	6.02	26.37	-21.73	-8.13	5.48
14 / 1	6.67	22.22	20 / 1	4.75	21.31	-28.71	-16.41	-4.11
16 / 1	5.88	20.00	25 / 1	3.81	17.36	-35.30	-24.26	-13.22
20 / 1	4.76	16.67	35 / 1	2.76	12.83	-42.01	-32.53	-23.04
20 / 1	4.76	16.67	35 / 1	2.76	12.83	-42.01	-32.53	-23.04
20 / 1	4.76	16.67	35 / 1	2.76	12.83	-42.01	-32.53	-23.04
33 / 1	2.94	10.81	80 / 1	1.20	5.73	-59.15	-53.08	-47.01
33 / 1	2.94	10.81	80 / 1	1.20	5.73	-59.15	-53.08	-47.01
50 / 1	1.96	7.41	150 / 1	0.62	2.98	-68.38	-64.05	-59.71
50 / 1	1.96	7.41	150 / 1	0.62	2.98	-68.38	-64.05	-59.71
50 / 1	1.96	7.41	150 / 1	0.62	2.98	-68.38	-64.05	-59.71
	125.36	384.22		100.00	400.00			

Race no. 7   6 Runners   2 Places at 1/4 odds

s.p.	s.p win%	s.p place%	nearest fair odds	fair win%	fair place%	win	return s e/w	place
1 / 5	83.33	95.24	2 / 11	84.28	98.63	1.14	2.35	3.57
6 / 1	14.29	40.00	17 / 2	10.27	65.89	-28.14	18.29	64.72
16 / 1	5.88	20.00	33 / 1	2.93	19.04	-50.21	-27.50	-4.78
20 / 1	4.76	16.67	50 / 1	2.13	13.84	-55.37	-36.18	-16.98
100 / 1	0.99	3.85	500 / 1	0.20	1.30	-79.92	-73.08	-66.25
100 / 1	0.99	3.85	500 / 1	0.20	1.30	-79.92	-73.08	-66.25
	110.24	179.60		100.00	200.00			

Race no. 8   16 Runners   4 Places at 1/4 odds

s.p.	s.p win%	s.p place%	nearest fair odds	fair win%	fair place%	win	returns e/w	place
8 /13	61.90	86.67	4 / 5	55.70	98.53	-10.03	1.83	13.69
5 / 1	16.67	44.44	6 / 1	13.98	76.90	-16.13	28.45	73.03
13 / 2	13.33	38.10	8 / 1	11.18	69.52	-16.17	33.16	82.49
9 / 1	10.00	30.77	11 / 1	8.10	57.74	-18.95	34.36	87.67
20 / 1	4.76	16.67	40 / 1	2.48	21.31	-47.93	-10.04	27.86
25 / 1	3.85	13.79	50 / 1	1.81	15.87	-52.82	-18.88	15.07
25 / 1	3.85	13.79	50 / 1	1.81	15.87	-52.82	-18.88	15.07
33 / 1	2.94	10.81	100 / 1	1.08	9.61	-63.32	-37.21	-11.10
33 / 1	2.94	10.81	100 / 1	1.08	9.61	-63.32	-37.21	-11.10
33 / 1	2.94	10.81	100 / 1	1.08	9.61	-63.32	-37.21	-11.10
66 / 1	1.49	5.71	250 / 1	0.39	3.49	-74.17	-56.52	-38.88
66 / 1	1.49	5.71	250 / 1	0.39	3.49	-74.17	-56.52	-38.88
100 / 1	0.99	3.85	400 / 1	0.23	2.11	-76.57	-60.88	-45.18
100 / 1	0.99	3.85	400 / 1	0.23	2.11	-76.57	-60.88	-45.18
100 / 1	0.99	3.85	400 / 1	0.23	2.11	-76.57	-60.88	-45.18
100 / 1	0.99	3.85	400 / 1	0.23	2.11	-76.57	-60.88	-45.18
	130.13	303.47		100.00	400.00			

Race Profiles 6 and 16 Runners

Race no. 9   6 Runners   2 Places at 1/4 odds

s.p.	s.p win%	s.p place%	nearest fair odds	fair win%	fair place%	win	returns e/w	place
5 / 4	44.44	76.19	6 / 4	40.39	73.91	-9.12	-6.05	-2.99
6 / 4	40.00	72.73	7 / 4	35.98	70.00	-10.05	-6.90	-3.75
5 / 1	16.67	44.44	6 / 1	14.69	34.31	-11.86	-17.34	-22.81
10 / 1	9.09	28.57	12 / 1	7.56	18.34	-16.85	-26.33	-35.82
33 / 1	2.94	10.81	80 / 1	1.13	2.83	-61.46	-67.64	-73.83
100 / 1	0.99	3.85	400 / 1	0.24	0.61	-75.38	-79.75	-84.13
	114.13	**236.59**		**100.00**	**200.00**			

Race no. 10   16 Runners   4 Places at 1/4 odds

s.p.	s.p win%	s.p place%	nearest fair odds	fair win%	fair place%	win	returns e/w	place
9 / 4	30.77	64.00	3 / 1	25.21	79.14	-18.05	2.80	23.66
7 / 2	22.22	53.33	9 / 2	18.13	68.12	-18.41	4.66	27.72
7 / 2	22.22	53.33	9 / 2	18.13	68.12	-18.41	4.66	27.72
13 / 2	13.33	38.10	8 / 1	10.86	49.01	-18.52	5.06	28.64
7 / 1	12.50	36.36	9 / 1	10.17	46.64	-18.60	4.83	28.25
8 / 1	11.11	33.33	10 / 1	8.90	41.97	-19.93	2.99	25.91
25 / 1	3.85	13.79	60 / 1	1.76	9.58	-54.14	-42.35	-30.56
25 / 1	3.85	13.79	60 / 1	1.76	9.58	-54.14	-42.35	-30.56
25 / 1	3.85	13.79	60 / 1	1.76	9.58	-54.14	-42.35	-30.56
33 / 1	2.94	10.81	100 / 1	1.05	5.76	-64.35	-55.51	-46.68
66 / 1	1.49	5.71	250 / 1	0.37	2.08	-74.89	-69.21	-63.53
66 / 1	1.49	5.71	250 / 1	0.37	2.08	-74.89	-69.21	-63.53
66 / 1	1.49	5.71	250 / 1	0.37	2.08	-74.89	-69.21	-63.53
66 / 1	1.49	5.71	250 / 1	0.37	2.08	-74.89	-69.21	-63.53
66 / 1	1.49	5.71	250 / 1	0.37	2.08	-74.89	-69.21	-63.53
66 / 1	1.49	5.71	250 / 1	0.37	2.08	-74.89	-69.21	-63.53
	135.59	**364.93**		**100.00**	**400.00**			

Race no. 11   6 Runners   2 Places at 1/4 odds

s.p.	s.p win%	s.p place%	nearest fair odds	fair win%	fair place%	returns win	returns e/w	place
2 / 1	33.33	66.67	9 / 4	30.76	57.84	-7.71	-10.47	-13.24
5 / 2	28.57	61.54	11 / 4	26.24	51.66	-8.17	-12.12	-16.06
7 / 2	22.22	53.33	4 / 1	20.35	42.11	-8.42	-14.73	-21.05
4 / 1	20.00	50.00	9 / 2	18.31	38.46	-8.43	-15.75	-23.07
16 / 1	5.88	20.00	25 / 1	3.73	8.52	-36.62	-47.01	-57.39
50 / 1	1.96	7.41	150 / 1	0.61	1.41	-69.03	-75.01	-80.99
	111.97	**258.95**		**100.00**	**200.00**			

Race no. 12   16 Runners   4 Places at 1/4 odds

s.p.	s.p win%	s.p place%	nearest fair odds	fair win%	fair place%	returns win	returns e/w	place
4 / 1	20.00	50.00	9 / 2	18.81	65.81	-5.97	12.82	31.61
4 / 1	20.00	50.00	9 / 2	18.81	65.81	-5.97	12.82	31.61
9 / 2	18.18	47.06	5 / 1	17.09	62.30	-5.98	13.20	32.38
8 / 1	11.11	33.33	9 / 1	10.25	43.73	-7.71	11.74	31.20
9 / 1	10.00	30.77	10 / 1	9.08	39.71	-9.20	9.93	29.05
10 / 1	9.09	28.57	11 / 1	8.06	36.00	-11.34	7.33	26.01
12 / 1	7.69	25.00	16 / 1	6.06	28.16	-21.26	-4.31	12.64
14 / 1	6.67	22.22	20 / 1	4.78	22.78	-28.28	-12.90	2.49
25 / 1	3.85	13.79	50 / 1	2.03	10.17	-47.14	-36.69	-26.24
25 / 1	3.85	13.79	50 / 1	2.03	10.17	-47.14	-36.69	-26.24
50 / 1	1.96	7.41	150 / 1	0.62	3.20	-68.19	-62.53	-56.86
50 / 1	1.96	7.41	150 / 1	0.62	3.20	68.19	-62.53	-56.86
50 / 1	1.96	7.41	150 / 1	0.62	3.20	-68.19	-62.53	-56.86
66 / 1	1.49	5.71	250 / 1	0.43	2.22	-71.06	-66.10	-61.14
66 / 1	1.49	5.71	250 / 1	0.43	2.22	-71.06	-66.10	-61.14
100 / 1	0.99	3.85	400 / 1	0.26	1.34	-73.75	-69.46	-65.17
	120.29	**352.04**		**100.00**	**400.00**			

Race Profiles 7 and 15 Runners

Race no. 13   7 Runners   2 Places at 1/4 odds

s.p.	s.p win%	s.p place%	nearest fair odds	fair win%	fair place%	win	returns e/w	place
2 / 9	81.82	94.74	2 / 9	82.30	98.33	0.59	2.19	3.79
5 / 1	16.67	44.44	15 / 2	11.92	68.05	-28.50	12.31	53.12
14 / 1	6.67	22.22	28 / 1	3.64	21.13	-45.43	-25.17	-4.91
25 / 1	3.85	13.79	66 / 1	1.55	9.02	-59.78	-47.19	-34.61
100 / 1	0.99	3.85	500 / 1	0.20	1.16	-80.03	-74.99	-69.96
100 / 1	0.99	3.85	500 / 1	0.20	1.16	-80.03	-74.99	-69.96
100 / 1	0.99	3.85	500 / 1	0.20	1.16	-80.03	-74.99	-69.96
	111.97	186.74		100.00	200.00			

Race no. 14   15 Runners   3 Places at 1/4 odds

s.p.	s.p win%	s.p place%	nearest fair odds	fair win%	fair place%	win	returns e/w	place
4 / 5	55.56	83.33	21 / 20	48.28	93.51	-13.10	-0.44	12.22
7 / 4	36.36	69.57	9 / 4	30.24	85.46	-16.84	3.00	22.85
14 / 1	6.67	22.22	22 / 1	4.18	23.22	-37.29	-16.41	4.47
14 / 1	6.67	22.22	22 / 1	4.18	23.22	-37.29	-16.41	4.47
16 / 1	5.88	20.00	28 / 1	3.35	18.75	-43.09	-24.66	-6.23
20 / 1	4.76	16.67	40 / 1	2.43	13.74	-48.98	-33.28	-17.58
33 / 1	2.94	10.81	100 / 1	1.06	6.06	-64.07	-54.02	-43.98
33 / 1	2.94	10.81	100 / 1	1.06	6.06	-64.07	-54.02	-43.98
33 / 1	2.94	10.81	100 / 1	1.06	6.06	64.07	-54.02	-43.98
33 / 1	2.94	10.81	100 / 1	1.06	6.06	-64.07	-54.02	-43.98
33 / 1	2.94	10.81	100 / 1	1.06	6.06	-64.07	-54.02	-43.98
33 / 1	2.94	10.81	100 / 1	1.06	6.06	-64.07	-54.02	-43.98
50 / 1	1.96	7.41	200 / 1	0.55	3.14	-72.19	-64.90	-57.61
100 / 1	0.99	3.85	400 / 1	0.23	1.31	-77.05	-71.46	-65.88
100 / 1	0.99	3.85	400 / 1	0.23	1.31	-77.05	-71.46	-65.88
	137.48	313.97		100.00	300.00			

Race no. 15   7 Runners 2 Places at 1/4 odds

s.p.	s.p win%	s.p place%	nearest fair odds	fair win%	fair place%	win	returns e/w	place
11 /10	47.62	78.43	11 / 10	46.58	75.75	-2.19	-2.80	-3.41
4 / 1	20.00	50.00	9 / 2	18.59	42.20	-7.04	-11.32	-15.60
9 / 2	18.18	47.06	5 / 1	16.90	38.78	-7.06	-12.33	-17.59
8 / 1	11.11	33.33	9 / 1	10.14	24.18	-8.77	-18.11	-27.45
12 / 1	7.69	25.00	16 / 1	5.99	14.58	-22.16	-31.93	-41.69
33 / 1	2.94	10.81	80 / 1	1.19	2.97	-59.38	-65.95	-72.52
50 / 1	1.96	7.41	150 / 1	0.62	1.54	-68.56	-73.91	-79.26
	109.51	**252.04**		**100.00**	**200.00**			

Race no. 16   15 Runners 3 Places at 1/4 odds

s.p.	s.p win%	s.p place%	nearest fair odds	fair win%	fair place%	win	returns e/w	place
15 / 8	34.78	68.09	5 / 2	28.58	67.21	-17.84	-9.56	-1.29
11 / 2	15.38	42.11	7 / 1	12.51	38.13	-18.69	-14.07	-9.44
13 / 2	13.33	38.10	8 / 1	10.84	33.82	-18.72	-14.97	-11.22
8 / 1	11.11	33.33	10 / 1	8.87	28.43	-20.13	-17.42	-14.71
10 / 1	9.09	28.57	13 / 1	6.97	22.89	-23.28	-21.58	-19.89
10 / 1	9.09	28.57	13 / 1	6.97	22.89	-23.28	-21.58	-19.89
14 / 1	6.67	22.22	22 / 1	4.14	14.04	-37.94	-37.38	-36.82
14 / 1	6.67	22.22	22 / 1	4.14	14.04	-37.94	-37.38	-36.82
16 / 1	5.88	20.00	28 / 1	3.31	11.35	-43.68	-43.47	-43.27
16 / 1	5.88	20.00	28 / 1	3.31	11.35	-43.68	-43.47	-43.27
16 / 1	5.88	20.00	28 / 1	3.31	11.35	-43.68	-43.47	-43.27
25 / 1	3.85	13.79	60 / 1	1.76	6.13	-54.25	-54.91	-55.57
25 / 1	3.85	13.79	60 / 1	1.76	6.13	-54.25	-54.91	-55.57
25 / 1	3.85	13.79	60 / 1	1.76	6.13	54.25	-54.91	-55.57
25 / 1	3.85	13.79	60 / 1	1.76	6.13	-54.25	-54.91	-55.57
	139.16	**398.38**		**100.00**	**300.00**			

Race Profiles 7 and 15 Runners

Race no. 17   7 Runners 2 Places at 1/4 odds

s.p.	s.p win%	s.p place%	nearest fair odds	fair win%	fair place%	win	returns e/w	place
7 / 4	36.36	69.57	15 / 8	34.12	61.31	-6.18	-9.02	-11.87
7 / 2	22.22	53.33	4 / 1	20.62	42.37	-7.21	-13.88	-20.55
7 / 2	22.22	53.33	4 / 1	20.62	42.37	-7.21	-13.88	-20.55
11 / 2	15.38	42.11	6 / 1	14.26	30.64	-7.31	-17.27	-27.23
10 / 1	9.09	28.57	12 / 1	7.95	17.72	-12.53	-25.26	-37.98
25 / 1	3.85	13.79	50 / 1	2.01	4.60	-47.85	-57.24	-66.63
66 / 1	1.49	5.71	250 / 1	0.43	0.98	-71.44	-77.10	-82.77
	110.62	266.42		100.00	200.00			

Race no. 18   15 Runners 3 Places at 1/4 odds

s.p.	s.p win%	s.p place%	nearest fair odds	fair win%	fair place%	win	returns e/w	place
6 / 1	14.29	40.00	13 / 2	13.19	37.23	-7.68	-7.30	-6.92
6 / 1	14.29	40.00	13 / 2	13.19	37.23	-7.68	-7.30	-6.92
8 / 1	11.11	33.33	9 / 1	10.08	29.65	-9.30	-10.17	-11.05
9 / 1	10.00	30.77	10 / 1	8.92	26.64	-10.76	-12.09	-13.42
10 / 1	9.09	28.57	12 / 1	7.92	23.94	-12.87	-14.54	-16.20
10 / 1	9.09	28.57	12 / 1	7.92	23.94	-12.87	-14.54	-16.20
10 / 1	9.09	28.57	12 / 1	7.92	23.94	-12.87	-14.54	-16.20
12 / 1	7.69	25.00	16 / 1	5.95	18.42	-22.62	-24.47	-26.32
14 / 1	6.67	22.22	20 / 1	4.70	14.75	-29.52	-31.57	-33.63
15 / 1	6.25	21.05	22 / 1	4.19	13.23	-32.94	-35.04	-37.15
16 / 1	5.88	20.00	25 / 1	3.76	11.93	-36.04	-38.18	-40.33
16 / 1	5.88	20.00	25 / 1	3.76	11.93	-36.04	-38.18	-40.33
16 / 1	5.88	20.00	25 / 1	3.76	11.93	-36.04	-38.18	-40.33
20 / 1	4.76	16.67	35 / 1	2.73	8.76	-42.67	-45.06	-47.45
25 / 1	3.85	13.79	50 / 1	2.00	6.46	-48.05	-50.61	-53.17
	123.82	388.51		100.00	300.00			

Race no. 19   8 Runners   3 Places at 1/5 odds

s.p.	s.p win%	s.p place%	nearest fair odds	fair win%	fair place%	win	returns e/w	place
1 / 7	87.50	97.22	1 / 6	85.43	99.82	-2.37	0.15	2.67
12 / 1	7.69	29.41	22 / 1	4.47	54.84	-41.89	22.29	86.47
20 / 1	4.76	20.00	50 / 1	2.05	29.09	-56.94	-5.76	45.43
20 / 1	4.76	20.00	50 / 1	2.05	29.09	-56.94	-5.76	45.43
25 / 1	3.85	16.67	66 / 1	1.50	21.79	-60.98	-15.12	30.75
25 / 1	3.85	16.67	66 / 1	1.50	21.79	-60.98	-15.12	30.75
25 / 1	3.85	16.67	66 / 1	1.50	21.79	-60.98	-15.12	30.75
25 / 1	3.85	16.67	66 / 1	1.50	21.79	60.98	-15.12	30.75
	120.10	233.30		100.00	300.00			

Race no. 20   14 Runners   3 Places at 1/4 odds

s.p.	s.p win%	s.p place%	nearest fair odds	fair win%	fair place%	win	returns e/w	place
4 / 7	63.64	87.50	4 / 5	55.23	92.84	-13.20	-3.55	6.10
9 / 1	10.00	30.77	12 / 1	7.81	34.65	-21.88	-4.64	12.60
10 / 1	9.09	28.57	13 / 1	6.93	31.24	-23.73	-7.20	9.33
12 / 1	7.69	25.00	18 / 1	5.21	24.15	-32.26	-17.83	-3.39
12 / 1	7.69	25.00	18 / 1	5.21	24.15	-32.26	-17.83	-3.39
12 / 1	7.69	25.00	18 / 1	5.21	24.15	-32.26	-17.83	-3.39
12 / 1	7.69	25.00	18 / 1	5.21	24.15	-32.26	-17.83	-3.39
20 / 1	4.76	16.67	40 / 1	2.39	11.54	-49.81	-40.28	-30.75
20 / 1	4.76	16.67	40 / 1	2.39	11.54	-49.81	-40.28	-30.75
25 / 1	3.85	13.79	60 / 1	1.75	8.52	-54.52	-46.38	-38.24
33 / 1	2.94	10.81	100 / 1	1.04	5.11	-64.65	-58.69	-52.73
50 / 1	1.96	7.41	200 / 1	0.54	2.65	-72.64	-68.41	-64.18
50 / 1	1.96	7.41	200 / 1	0.54	2.65	-72.64	-68.41	-64.18
50 / 1	1.96	7.41	200 / 1	0.54	2.65	-72.64	-68.41	-64.18
	135.69	327.00		100.00	300.00			

Race Profiles 8 and 14 Runners

Race no. 21   8 Runners   3 Places at 1/5 odds

s.p.	s.p win%	s.p place%	nearest fair odds	fair win%	fair place%	win	returns e/w	place
6 / 4	40.00	76.92	15 / 8	34.75	78.06	-13.13	-5.83	1.47
9 / 2	18.18	52.63	11 / 2	15.48	49.34	-14.84	-10.55	-6.26
11 / 2	15.38	47.62	13 / 2	13.09	43.35	-14.90	-11.93	-8.96
6 / 1	14.29	45.45	7 / 1	12.15	40.83	-14.92	-12.55	-10.18
17 / 2	10.53	37.04	10 / 1	8.73	30.77	-17.09	-17.00	-16.92
11 / 1	8.33	31.25	14 / 1	6.64	24.05	-20.33	-21.69	-23.05
11 / 1	8.33	31.25	14 / 1	6.64	24.05	-20.33	-21.69	-23.05
20 / 1	4.76	20.00	40 / 1	2.52	9.56	-47.16	-49.68	-52.20
	119.81	**342.17**		**100.00**	**300.00**			

Race no. 22   14 Runners   3 Places at 1/4 odds

s.p.	s.p win%	s.p place%	nearest fair odds	fair win%	fair place%	win	returns e/w	place
9 / 4	30.77	64.00	5 / 2	29.01	68.32	-5.73	0.51	6.75
9 / 2	18.18	47.06	5 / 1	17.06	49.11	-6.17	-0.91	4.36
10 / 1	9.09	28.57	11 / 1	8.04	26.39	-11.52	-9.58	-7.65
10 / 1	9.09	28.57	11 / 1	8.04	26.39	-11.52	-9.58	-7.65
12 / 1	7.69	25.00	16 / 1	6.04	20.32	-21.42	-20.06	-18.70
12 / 1	7.69	25.00	16 / 1	6.04	20.32	-21.42	-20.06	-18.70
14 / 1	6.67	22.22	20 / 1	4.77	16.29	-28.43	-27.57	-26.71
16 / 1	5.88	20.00	25 / 1	3.82	13.18	-35.05	-34.57	-34.09
16 / 1	5.88	20.00	25 / 1	3.82	13.18	-35.05	-34.57	-34.09
16 / 1	5.88	20.00	25 / 1	3.82	13.18	-35.05	-34.57	-34.09
20 / 1	4.76	16.67	35 / 1	2.77	9.68	-41.78	-41.86	-41.94
20 / 1	4.76	16.67	35 / 1	2.77	9.68	-41.78	-41.86	-41.94
20 / 1	4.76	16.67	35 / 1	2.77	9.68	-41.78	-41.86	-41.94
33 / 1	2.94	10.81	80 / 1	1.21	4.28	--58.99	-59.69	-60.40
	124.06	**361.23**		**100.00**	**300.00**			

Race no. 23   8 Runners   3 Places at 1/5 odds

s.p.	s.p win%	s.p place%	nearest fair odds	fair win%	fair place%	win	returns e/w	place
3 / 1	25.00	62.50	7 / 2	21.82	59.25	-12.71	-8.95	-5.19
4 / 1	20.00	55.56	9 / 2	17.42	50.85	-12.89	-10.68	-8.47
4 / 1	20.00	55.56	9 / 2	17.42	50.85	-12.89	-10.68	-8.47
5 / 1	16.67	50.00	6 / 1	14.51	44.29	-12.95	-12.19	-11.43
7 / 1	12.50	41.67	8 / 1	10.87	34.92	-13.08	-14.64	-16.19
7 / 1	12.50	41.67	8 / 1	10.87	34.92	-13.08	-14.64	-16.19
16 / 1	5.88	23.81	28 / 1	3.55	12.46	-39.71	-43.69	-47.67
16 / 1	5.88	23.81	28 / 1	3.55	12.46	-39.71	-43.69	-47.67
	118.43	354.56		100.00	300.00			

Race no. 24   14 Runners   3 Places at 1/4 odds

s.p.	s.p win%	s.p place%	nearest fair odds	fair win%	fair place%	win	returns e/w	place
9 / 2	18.18	47.06	5 / 1	16.10	44.26	-11.44	-8.70	-5.95
6 / 1	14.29	40.00	7 / 1	12.64	36.49	-11.51	-10.15	-8.78
8 / 1	11.11	33.33	9 / 1	9.66	29.00	-13.07	-13.03	-12.99
8 / 1	11.11	33.33	9 / 1	9.66	29.00	-13.07	-13.03	-12.99
8 / 1	11.11	33.33	9 / 1	9.66	29.00	-13.07	-13.03	-12.99
9 / 1	10.00	30.77	11 / 1	8.55	26.04	-14.47	-14.91	-15.36
9 / 1	10.00	30.77	11 / 1	8.55	26.04	-14.47	-14.91	-15.36
10 / 1	9.09	28.57	12 / 1	7.59	23.39	-16.49	-17.31	-18.13
14 / 1	6.67	22.22	22 / 1	4.50	14.39	-32.45	-33.86	-35.26
14 / 1	6.67	22.22	22 / 1	4.50	14.39	32.45	-33.86	-35.26
16 / 1	5.88	20.00	28 / 1	3.61	11.63	-38.69	-40.26	-41.83
25 / 1	3.85	13.79	50 / 1	1.92	6.29	-50.21	-52.30	-54.39
25 / 1	3.85	13.79	50 / 1	1.92	6.29	-50.21	-52.30	-54.39
33 / 1	2.94	10.81	80 / 1	1.14	3.77	-61.29	-63.21	-65.12
	124.74	380.01		100.00	300.00			

Race Profiles 8 Runners

Race no. 25   8 Runners   3 Places at 1/5 odds

s.p.	s.p win%	s.p place%	nearest fair odds	fair win%	fair place%	win	returns e/w	place
100 /30	23.08	60.00	4 / 1	20.23	55.89	-12.35	-9.60	-6.85
4 / 1	20.00	55.56	9 / 2	17.51	50.54	-12.45	-10.74	-9.03
5 / 1	16.67	50.00	6 / 1	14.58	44.01	-12.51	-12.24	-11.98
5 / 1	16.67	50.00	6 / 1	14.58	44.01	-12.51	-12.24	-11.98
11 / 2	15.38	47.62	13 / 2	13.46	41.29	-12.52	-12.91	-13.29
7 / 1	12.50	41.67	8 / 1	10.92	34.71	-12.64	-14.67	-16.71
11 / 1	8.33	31.25	14 / 1	6.83	22.85	-18.10	-22.49	-26.88
25 / 1	3.85	16.67	50 / 1	1.89	6.70	-50.78	-55.30	-59.82
	116.47	352.77		100.00	300.00			

Race no. 26   8 Runners   3 Places at 1/5 odds

s.p.	s.p win%	s.p place%	nearest fair odds	fair win%	fair place%	win	returns e/w	place
7 / 2	22.22	58.82	4 / 1	19.49	54.76	-12.31	-9.61	-6.91
7 / 2	22.22	58.82	4 / 1	19.49	54.76	-12.31	-9.61	-6.91
7 / 2	22.22	58.82	4 / 1	19.49	54.76	-12.31	-9.61	-6.91
7 / 1	12.50	41.67	8 / 1	10.94	34.94	-12.51	-14.32	-16.13
7 / 1	12.50	41.67	8 / 1	10.94	34.94	-12.51	-14.32	-16.13
8 / 1	11.11	38.46	9 / 1	9.56	31.11	-13.95	-16.53	-19.10
12 / 1	7.69	29.42	16 / 1	5.65	19.28	-26.58	-30.51	-34.44
14 / 1	6.67	26.32	22 / 1	4.46	15.43	-33.13	-37.25	-41.37
	117.14	354.00		100.00	300.00			

Race no. 27   9   Runners   3   Places at 1/5 odds

s.p.	s.p win%	s.p place%	nearest fair odds	fair win%	fair place%	win	returns e/w	place
1 / 3	75.00	93.75	3 / 10	76.74	99.48	2.31	4.22	6.12
6 / 1	14.29	45.45	17 / 2	10.39	74.83	-27.28	18.68	64.63
10 / 1	9.09	33.33	15 / 1	6.24	56.80	-31.37	19.52	70.40
20 / 1	4.76	20.00	50 / 1	2.15	22.06	-54.84	-22.27	10.29
25 / 1	3.85	16.67	60 / 1	1.57	16.35	-59.08	-30.50	-1.93
25 / 1	3.85	16.67	60 / 1	1.57	16.35	-59.08	-30.50	-1.93
33 / 1	2.94	13.16	100 / 1	0.94	9.84	-68.19	-46.69	-25.19
100 / 1	0.99	4.76	500 / 1	0.20	2.15	-79.68	-67.31	-54.94
100 / 1	0.99	4.76	500 / 1	0.20	2.15	-79.68	-67.31	-54.94
	115.75	**248.55**		**100.00**	**300.00**			

Race no. 28   13   Runners   3   Places at 1/4 odds

s.p.	s.p win%	s.p place%	nearest fair odds	fair win%	fair place%	win	returns e/w	place
1 / 1	50.00	80.00	6 / 5	45.64	89.27	-8.73	1.43	11.59
3 / 1	25.00	57.14	7 / 2	21.71	69.02	-13.16	3.81	20.79
8 / 1	11.11	33.33	10 / 1	9.45	38.92	-14.94	0.91	16.76
10 / 1	9.09	28.57	12 / 1	7.43	31.50	-18.29	-4.03	10.24
16 / 1	5.88	20.00	28 / 1	3.53	15.72	-40.01	-30.71	-21.40
20 / 1	4.76	16.67	40 / 1	2.56	11.53	-46.23	-38.51	-30.79
20 / 1	4.76	16.67	40 / 1	2.56	11.53	-46.23	-38.51	-30.79
25 / 1	3.85	13.79	50 / 1	1.87	8.51	-51.28	-44.80	-38.33
25 / 1	3.85	13.79	50 / 1	1.87	8.51	-51.28	-44.80	-38.33
33 / 1	2.94	10.81	80 / 1	1.11	5.10	-62.13	-57.48	-52.84
33 / 1	2.94	10.81	80 / 1	1.11	5.10	-62.13	-57.48	-52.84
50 / 1	1.96	7.41	200 / 1	0.57	2.65	-70.69	-67.48	-64.28
50 / 1	1.96	7.41	200 / 1	0.57	2.65	70.69	-67.48	-64.28
	128.10	**316.40**		**100.00**	**300.00**			

Race Profiles 9 and 13 Runners

Race no. 29   9 Runners 3 Places at 1/5 odds

s.p.	s.p win%	s.p place%	nearest fair odds	fair win%	fair place%	win	returns e/w	place
11 /10	47.62	81.97	5 / 4	44.63	93.30	-6.27	3.78	13.83
11 / 4	26.67	64.52	100 / 30	23.82	81.22	-10.67	7.61	25.89
3 / 1	25.00	62.50	7 / 2	22.31	79.45	-10.74	8.18	27.11
16 / 1	5.88	23.81	28 / 1	3.63	17.82	-38.35	-31.74	-25.14
25 / 1	3.85	16.67	50 / 1	1.93	9.64	-49.92	-46.05	-42.18
33 / 1	2.94	13.16	80 / 1	1.14	5.77	-61.07	-58.60	-56.12
33 / 1	2.94	13.16	80 / 1	1.14	5.77	-61.07	-58.60	-56.12
33 / 1	2.94	13.16	80 / 1	1.14	5.77	-61.07	-58.60	-56.12
100 / 1	0.99	4.76	400 / 1	0.25	1.25	-75.14	-74.42	-73.70
	118.83	**293.70**		**100.00**	**300.00**			

Race no. 30   13 Runners 3 Places at 1/4 odds

s.p.	s.p win%	s.p place%	nearest fair odds	fair win%	fair place%	win	returns e/w	place
5 / 2	28.57	61.54	100 / 30	23.16	59.20	-18.94	-11.37	-3.81
5 / 1	16.67	44.44	13 / 2	13.46	40.02	-19.22	-14.59	-9.95
11 / 2	15.38	42.11	7 / 1	12.43	37.48	-19.23	-15.11	-10.98
11 / 2	15.38	42.11	7 / 1	12.43	37.48	-19.23	-15.11	-10.98
6 / 1	14.29	40.00	15 / 2	11.54	35.23	-19.25	-15.59	-11.93
12 / 1	7.69	25.00	18 / 1	5.21	17.22	-32.31	-31.72	-31.13
12 / 1	7.69	25.00	18 / 1	5.21	17.22	-32.31	-31.72	-31.13
14 / 1	6.67	22.22	22 / 1	4.11	13.76	-38.35	-38.21	-38.08
16 / 1	5.88	20.00	28 / 1	3.29	11.12	-44.05	-44.23	-44.40
16 / 1	5.88	20.00	28 / 1	3.29	11.12	-44.05	-44.23	-44.40
20 / 1	4.76	16.67	40 / 1	2.39	8.15	49.85	-50.48	-51.12
25 / 1	3.85	13.79	60 / 1	1.75	6.00	-54.56	-55.52	-56.48
25 / 1	3.85	13.79	60 / 1	1.75	6.00	-54.56	-55.52	-56.48
	136.56	**386.67**		**100.00**	**300.00**			

Race no. 31 9 Runners 3 Places at 1/5 odds

s.p.	s.p win%	s.p place%	nearest fair odds	fair win%	fair place%	win	returns e/w	place
2 / 1	33.33	71.43	5 / 2	28.25	70.25	-15.25	-8.45	-1.66
3 / 1	25.00	62.50	4 / 1	21.06	59.57	-15.74	-10.21	-4.69
9 / 2	18.18	52.63	11 / 2	15.29	47.65	-15.92	-12.69	-9.46
6 / 1	14.29	45.45	15 / 2	12.00	39.29	-15.99	-14.78	-13.56
10 / 1	9.09	33.33	13 / 1	7.21	25.15	-20.72	-22.64	-24.56
12 / 1	7.69	29.41	18 / 1	5.42	19.31	-29.59	-31.97	-34.36
12 / 1	7.69	29.41	18 / 1	5.42	19.31	-29.59	-31.97	-34.36
14 / 1	6.67	26.32	22 / 1	4.28	15.44	-35.87	-38.60	-41.33
33 / 1	2.94	13.16	100 / 1	1.08	4.04	-63.25	-66.28	-69.30
	124.88	**363.65**		**100.00**	**300.00**			

Race no. 32 13 Runners 3 Places at 1/4 odds

s.p.	s.p win%	s.p place%	nearest fair odds	fair win%	fair place%	win	returns e/w	place
7 / 2	22.22	53.33	9 / 2	19.01	50.89	-14.47	-9.53	-4.59
6 / 1	14.29	40.00	7 / 1	12.20	36.09	-14.57	-12.17	-9.76
7 / 1	12.50	36.36	17 / 2	10.67	32.20	-14.67	-13.06	-11.44
7 / 1	12.50	36.36	17 / 2	10.67	32.20	-14.67	-13.06	-11.44
7 / 1	12.50	36.36	17 / 2	10.67	32.20	-14.67	-13.06	-11.44
7 / 1	12.50	36.36	17 / 2	10.67	32.20	-14.67	-13.06	-11.44
9 / 1	10.00	30.77	11 / 1	8.26	25.71	-17.43	-16.93	-16.43
11 / 1	8.33	26.67	14 / 1	6.67	21.16	-20.01	-20.32	-20.64
20 / 1	4.76	16.67	40 / 1	2.53	8.40	-46.95	-48.26	-49.58
20 / 1	4.76	16.67	40 / 1	2.53	8.40	-46.95	-48.26	-49.58
20 / 1	4.76	16.67	40 / 1	2.53	8.40	-46.95	-48.26	-49.58
20 / 1	4.76	16.67	40 / 1	2.53	8.40	-46.95	-48.26	-49.58
33 / 1	2.94	10.81	100 / 1	1.10	3.71	-62.63	-64.15	-65.67
	126.83	**373.70**		**100.00**	**300.00**			

Race Profiles 10 and 12 Runners

Race no. 33   10 Runners 3 Places at 1/5 odds

s.p.	s.p win%	s.p place%	nearest fair odds	fair win%	fair place%	win	returns e/w	place
4 / 9	69.23	91.84	1 / 2	66.69	98.02	-3.68	1.53	6.73
6 / 1	14.29	45.45	7 / 1	12.77	66.65	-10.64	18.00	46.64
11 / 1	8.33	31.25	13 / 1	6.97	44.03	-16.32	12.29	40.90
12 / 1	7.69	29.41	16 / 1	5.76	37.38	-25.10	1.01	27.11
16 / 1	5.88	23.81	25 / 1	3.64	24.63	-38.09	-17.33	3.43
25 / 1	3.85	16.67	50 / 1	1.93	13.46	-49.71	-34.49	-19.27
33 / 1	2.94	13.16	80 / 1	1.15	8.09	-60.91	-49.69	-38.48
50 / 1	1.96	9.09	150 / 1	0.59	4.21	-69.74	-61.71	-53.68
100 / 1	0.99	4.76	400 / 1	0.25	1.76	-75.03	-69.00	-62.98
100 / 1	0.99	4.76	400 / 1	0.25	1.76	75.03	-69.00	-62.98
	116.15	**270.20**		**100.00**	**300.00**			

Race no. 34   12 Runners 3 Places at 1/4 odds

s.p.	s.p win%	s.p place%	nearest fair odds	fair win%	fair place%	win	returns e/w	place
7 / 2	22.22	53.33	7 / 2	21.37	57.12	-3.82	1.64	7.09
4 / 1	20.00	50.00	4 / 1	19.23	53.23	-3.84	1.31	6.45
9 / 2	18.18	47.06	9 / 2	17.48	49.75	-3.85	0.93	5.72
10 / 1	9.09	28.57	11 / 1	8.24	26.74	-9.34	-7.88	-6.42
11 / 1	8.33	26.67	12 / 1	7.50	24.54	-10.04	-9.00	-7.96
12 / 1	7.69	25.00	15 / 1	6.19	20.60	-19.48	-18.54	-17.60
14 / 1	6.67	22.22	20 / 1	4.89	16.51	-26.66	-26.18	-25.71
14 / 1	6.67	22.22	20 / 1	4.89	16.51	-26.66	-26.18	-25.71
14 / 1	6.67	22.22	20 / 1	4.89	16.51	-26.66	-26.18	-25.71
20 / 1	4.76	16.67	35 / 1	2.84	9.81	-40.34	-40.73	-41.12
33 / 1	2.94	10.81	80 / 1	1.24	4.34	-57.98	-58.91	-59.84
33 / 1	2.94	10.81	80 / 1	1.24	4.34	-57.98	-58.91	-59.84
	116.16	**335.59**		**100.00**	**300.00**			

Race no. 35   10 Runners   3 Places at 1/5 odds

s.p.	s.p win%	s.p place%	nearest fair odds	fair win%	fair place%	returns win	returns e/w	place
7 / 4	36.36	74.07	15 / 8	34.49	78.44	-5.15	0.37	5.90
4 / 1	20.00	55.56	9 / 2	18.76	57.20	-6.22	-1.63	2.95
11 / 2	15.38	47.62	6 / 1	14.42	47.39	-6.29	-3.39	-0.48
7 / 1	12.50	41.67	15 / 2	11.70	40.09	-6.42	-5.10	-3.77
10 / 1	9.09	33.33	11 / 1	8.04	28.98	-11.58	-12.32	-13.07
14 / 1	6.67	26.32	20 / 1	4.77	17.89	-28.47	-30.24	-32.00
16 / 1	5.88	23.81	25 / 1	3.82	14.48	-35.09	-37.13	-39.16
20 / 1	4.76	20.00	35 / 1	2.77	10.63	-41.81	-44.32	-46.83
50 / 1	1.96	9.09	150 / 1	0.62	2.44	-68.28	-70.71	-73.14
50 / 1	1.96	9.09	150 / 1	0.62	2.44	-68.28	-70.71	-73.14
	114.57	**340.56**		**100.00**	**300.00**			

Race no. 36   12 Runners   3 Places at 1/4 odds

s.p.	s.p win%	s.p place%	nearest fair odds	fair win%	fair place%	returns win	returns e/w	place
9 / 4	30.77	64.00	85 / 40	31.58	72.59	2.64	8.03	13.42
8 / 1	11.11	33.33	8 / 1	11.14	36.03	0.28	4.18	8.08
8 / 1	11.11	33.33	8 / 1	11.14	36.03	0.28	4.18	8.08
10 / 1	9.09	28.57	10 / 1	8.76	29.25	-3.67	-0.65	2.38
10 / 1	9.09	28.57	10 / 1	8.76	29.25	-3.67	-0.65	2.38
10 / 1	9.09	28.57	10 / 1	8.76	29.25	-3.67	-0.65	2.38
10 / 1	9.09	28.57	10 / 1	8.76	29.25	-3.67	-0.65	2.38
11 / 1	8.33	26.67	12 / 1	7.97	26.88	-4.42	-1.81	0.79
33 / 1	2.94	10.81	80 / 1	1.31	4.79	-55.35	-55.54	-55.72
50 / 1	1.96	7.41	150 / 1	0.68	2.49	-65.44	-65.94	-66.43
50 / 1	1.96	7.41	150 / 1	0.68	2.49	-65.44	-65.94	-66.43
66 / 1	1.49	5.71	200 / 1	0.47	1.73	-68.55	-69.17	-69.79
	106.04	**302.96**		**100.00**	**300.00**			

Race Profiles 10 and 12 Runners

Race no. 37   10 Runners 3 Places at 1/5 odds

s.p.	s.p win%	s.p place%	nearest fair odds	fair win%	fair place%	win	returns e/w	place
3 / 1	25.00	62.50	3 / 1	24.45	62.44	-2.19	-1.14	-0.10
6 / 1	14.29	45.45	6 / 1	13.93	42.11	-2.48	-4.92	-7.36
6 / 1	14.29	45.45	6 / 1	13.93	42.11	-2.48	-4.92	-7.36
13 / 2	13.33	43.48	13 / 2	13.00	39.83	-2.50	-5.45	-8.40
8 / 1	11.11	38.46	17 / 2	10.65	33.69	-4.19	-8.30	-12.40
10 / 1	9.09	33.33	11 / 1	8.37	27.28	-7.97	-13.07	-18.17
10 / 1	9.09	33.33	11 / 1	8.37	27.28	-7.97	-13.07	-18.17
16 / 1	5.88	23.81	25 / 1	3.97	13.65	-32.44	-37.55	-42.67
20 / 1	4.76	20.00	33 / 1	2.88	10.02	-39.44	-44.66	-49.88
66 / 1	1.49	7.04	200 / 1	0.45	1.60	-69.95	-73.62	-77.30
	108.33	**352.87**		**100.00**	**300.00**			

Race no. 38   12 Runners 3 Places at 1/4 odds

s.p.	s.p win%	s.p place%	nearest fair odds	fair win%	fair place%	win	returns e/w	place
4 / 5	55.56	83.33	11 / 10	46.54	89.08	-16.24	-4.67	6.89
4 / 1	20.00	50.00	11 / 2	15.85	56.32	-20.74	-4.05	12.63
5 / 1	16.67	44.44	13 / 2	13.20	49.50	-20.79	-4.70	11.39
12 / 1	7.69	25.00	18 / 1	5.11	21.73	-33.63	-23.35	-13.08
12 / 1	7.69	25.00	18 / 1	5.11	21.73	-33.63	-23.35	-13.08
12 / 1	7.69	25.00	18 / 1	5.11	21.73	-33.63	-23.35	-13.08
14 / 1	6.67	22.22	25 / 1	4.03	17.39	-39.55	-30.65	-21.75
20 / 1	4.76	16.67	40 / 1	2.34	10.31	-50.83	-44.48	-38.14
33 / 1	2.94	10.81	100 / 1	1.02	4.55	-65.36	-61.63	-57.89
40 / 1	2.44	9.09	150 / 1	0.65	2.93	-73.19	-70.46	-67.73
50 / 1	1.96	7.41	200 / 1	0.53	2.36	-73.19	-70.65	-68.12
50 / 1	1.96	7.41	200 / 1	0.53	2.36	-73.19	-70.65	-68.12
	136.03	**326.38**		**100.00**	**300.00**			

Race no. 39   11 Runners   3 Places at 1/5 odds

s.p.	s.p win%	s.p place%	nearest fair odds	fair win%	fair place%	win	returns e/w	place
4 / 6	60.00	88.24	10 / 11	51.89	91.43	-13.51	-4.95	3.62
9 / 1	10.00	35.71	12 / 1	7.89	33.56	-21.12	-13.57	-6.02
9 / 1	10.00	35.71	12 / 1	7.89	33.56	-21.12	-13.57	-6.02
9 / 1	10.00	35.71	12 / 1	7.89	33.56	-21.12	-13.57	-6.02
10 / 1	9.09	33.33	13 / 1	7.00	30.23	-22.98	-16.15	-9.32
10 / 1	9.09	33.33	13 / 1	7.00	30.23	-22.98	-16.15	-9.32
14 / 1	6.67	26.32	22 / 1	4.15	18.70	-37.70	-33.32	-28.93
14 / 1	6.67	26.32	22 / 1	4.15	18.70	-37.70	-33.32	-28.93
33 / 1	2.94	13.16	100 / 1	1.05	4.92	-64.30	-63.46	-62.62
50 / 1	1.96	9.09	200 / 1	0.54	2.55	-72.37	-72.14	-71.91
50 / 1	1.96	9.09	200 / 1	0.54	2.55	-72.37	-72.14	-71.91
	128.38	**346.02**		**100.00**	**300.00**			

Race no. 40   11 Runners   3 Places at 1/5 odds

s.p.	s.p win%	s.p place%	nearest fair odds	fair win%	fair place%	win	return e/w	place
9 / 4	30.77	68.97	11 / 4	26.96	68.12	-12.37	-6.79	-1.22
3 / 1	25.00	62.50	7 / 2	21.85	60.46	-12.59	-7.93	-3.26
9 / 2	18.18	52.63	11 / 2	15.86	48.56	-12.78	-10.25	-7.73
8 / 1	11.11	38.46	10 / 1	9.51	31.93	-14.38	-15.68	-16.97
8 / 1	11.11	38.46	10 / 1	9.51	31.93	-14.38	-15.68	-16.97
14 / 1	6.67	26.32	22 / 1	4.44	15.84	-33.47	-36.64	-39.81
16 / 1	5.88	23.81	28 / 1	3.55	12.81	-39.62	-42.91	-46.20
20 / 1	4.76	20.00	40 / 1	2.58	9.39	-45.88	-49.45	-53.03
20 / 1	4.76	20.00	40 / 1	2.58	9.39	-45.88	-49.45	-53.03
20 / 1	4.76	20.00	40 / 1	2.58	9.39	-45.88	-49.45	-53.03
50 / 1	1.96	9.09	150 / 1	0.58	2.15	-70.49	-73.40	-76.32
	124.97	**380.24**		**100.00**	**300.00**			

Race Profiles 11 Runners

Race no. 41   11 Runners 3 Places at 1/5 odds

s.p.	s.p win%	s.p place%	nearest fair odds	fair win%	fair place%	win	returns e/w	place
3 / 1	25.00	62.50	100 / 30	22.80	59.00	--8.82	-7.21	-5.60
5 / 1	16.67	50.00	11 / 2	15.16	44.26	-9.06	-10.27	-11.48
7 / 1	12.50	41.67	8 / 1	11.35	34.99	-9.20	-12.61	-16.02
7 / 1	12.50	41.67	8 / 1	11.35	34.99	-9.20	-12.61	-16.02
15 / 2	11.76	40.00	17 / 2	10.59	33.00	-9.95	-13.73	-17.51
9 / 1	10.00	35.71	10 / 1	8.79	28.02	-12.13	-16.84	-21.55
10 / 1	9.09	33.33	12 / 1	7.80	25.18	-14.20	-19.33	-24.46
11 / 1	8.33	31.25	13 / 1	7.09	23.10	-14.87	-20.48	-26.08
20 / 1	4.76	20.00	35 / 1	2.69	9.21	-43.54	-48.76	-53.97
25 / 1	3.85	16.67	50 / 1	1.97	6.79	-48.84	-54.06	-59.27
66 / 1	1.49	7.04	250 / 1	0.42	1.47	-71.99	-75.59	-79.19
	115.96	**379.84**		**100.00**	**300.00**			

Race no. 42   11 Runners 3 Places at 1/5 odds

s.p.	s.p win%	s.p place%	nearest fair odds	fair win%	fair place%	win	return e/w	place
9 / 2	18.18	52.63	5 / 1	16.44	40.08	-9.58	-10.87	-12.16
9 / 2	18.18	52.63	5 / 1	16.44	40.08	-9.58	-10.87	-12.16
5 / 1	16.67	50.00	11 / 2	15.06	38.08	-9.63	-11.58	-13.54
7 / 1	12.50	41.67	8 / 1	11.28	31.74	-9.76	-13.91	-18.07
9 / 1	10.00	35.71	10 / 1	8.73	27.20	-12.67	-18.09	-23.51
9 / 1	10.00	35.71	10 / 1	8.73	27.20	-12.67	-18.09	-23.51
10 / 1	9.09	33.33	12 / 1	7.75	25.38	-14.73	-20.55	-26.36
12 / 1	7.69	29.41	16 / 1	5.83	22.41	-24.27	-30.05	-35.82
12 / 1	7.69	29.41	16 / 1	5.83	22.41	-24.27	-30.05	-35.82
25 / 1	3.85	16.67	50 / 1	1.96	12.71	-49.16	-54.74	-60.32
25 / 1	3.85	16.67	50 / 1	1.96	12.71	-49.16	-54.74	-60.32
	117.70	**393.84**		**100.00**	**300.00**			

Race no. 43   18 Runners   4 Places at 1/4 odds

s.p.	s.p win%	s.p place%	nearest fair odds	fair win%	fair place%	win	returns e/w	place
10 /11	52.38	81.48	5 / 4	44.18	93.38	-15.66	-0.53	14.61
5 / 1	16.67	44.44	13 / 2	13.31	60.67	-20.11	8.20	36.52
9 / 1	10.00	30.77	12 / 1	7.72	41.30	22.81	5.71	34.23
9 / 1	10.00	30.77	12 / 1	7.72	41.30	-22.81	5.71	34.23
12 / 1	7.69	25.00	18 / 1	5.15	29.41	-33.06	-7.71	17.65
16 / 1	5.88	20.00	28 / 1	3.25	19.42	-44.67	-23.78	-2.88
16 / 1	5.88	20.00	28 / 1	3.25	19.42	-44.67	-23.78	-2.88
20 / 1	4.76	16.67	40 / 1	2.36	14.37	-50.40	-32.09	-13.78
20 / 1	4.76	16.67	40 / 1	2.36	14.37	-50.40	-32.09	-13.78
25 / 1	3.85	13.79	60 / 1	1.73	10.66	-55.06	-38.90	-22.73
25 / 1	3.85	13.79	60 / 1	1.73	10.66	-55.06	-38.90	-22.73
25 / 1	3.85	13.79	60 / 1	1.73	10.66	-55.06	-38.90	-22.73
25 / 1	3.85	13.79	60 / 1	1.73	10.66	-55.06	-38.90	-22.73
33 / 1	2.94	10.81	100 / 1	1.03	6.43	-65.07	-52.81	-40.55
33 / 1	2.94	10.81	100 / 1	1.03	6.43	-65.07	-52.81	-40.55
40 / 1	2.44	9.09	150 / 1	0.66	4.16	-72.96	-63.63	-54.29
50 / 1	1.96	7.41	200 / 1	0.53	3.35	-72.96	-63.87	-54.79
50 / 1	1.96	7.41	200 / 1	0.53	3.35	-72.96	-63.87	-54.79
	145.66	**386.50**		**100.00**	**400.00**			

Race Profile 18 Runners

Race no. 44   18 Runners   4 Places at 1/4 odds

s.p.	s.p win%	s.p place%	nearest fair odds	fair win%	fair place%	win	returns e/w	place
11 / 2	15.38	42.11	7 / 1	12.91	47.27	-16.12	-1.92	12.28
11 / 2	15.38	42.11	7 / 1	12.91	47.27	-16.12	-1.92	12.28
7 / 1	12.50	36.36	17 / 2	10.47	40.30	-16.23	-2.70	10.84
7 / 1	12.50	36.36	17 / 2	10.47	40.30	-16.23	-2.70	10.84
9 / 1	10.00	30.77	11 / 1	8.11	32.68	-18.93	-6.36	6.22
9 / 1	10.00	30.77	11 / 1	8.11	32.68	-18.93	-6.36	6.22
10 / 1	9.09	28.57	13 / 1	7.20	29.51	-20.85	-8.77	3.30
12 / 1	7.69	25.00	18 / 1	5.41	22.92	-29.70	-19.01	-8.31
12 / 1	7.69	25.00	18 / 1	5.41	22.92	-29.70	-19.01	-8.31
12 / 1	7.69	25.00	18 / 1	5.41	22.92	-29.70	-19.01	-8.31
20 / 1	4.76	16.67	40 / 1	2.48	11.06	-47.91	-40.77	-33.62
20 / 1	4.76	16.67	40 / 1	2.48	11.06	-47.91	-40.77	-33.62
20 / 1	4.76	16.67	40 / 1	2.48	11.06	-47.91	-40.77	-33.62
25 / 1	3.85	13.79	50 / 1	1.82	8.19	-52.81	-46.73	-40.65
25 / 1	3.85	13.79	50 / 1	1.82	8.19	-52.81	-46.73	-40.65
33 / 1	2.94	10.81	100 / 1	1.08	4.93	-63.31	-58.88	-54.44
33 / 1	2.94	10.81	100 / 1	1.08	4.93	-63.31	-58.88	-54.44
66 / 1	1.49	5.71	250 / 1	0.39	1.78	-74.16	-71.50	-68.85
	137.29	426.97		100.00	400.00			

Race no. 45   19 Runners   4 Places at 1/4 odds

s.p.	s.p win%	s.p place%	nearest fair odds	fair win%	fair place%	win	returns e/w	place
6 / 4	40.00	72.73	15 / 8	35.16	88.21	-12.11	4.59	21.29
7 / 2	22.22	53.33	4 / 1	19.15	71.06	-13.82	9.72	33.25
8 / 1	11.11	33.33	10 / 1	9.40	45.34	-15.43	10.30	36.03
9 / 1	10.00	30.77	11 / 1	8.32	41.23	-16.79	8.61	34.00
10 / 1	9.09	28.57	13 / 1	7.39	37.42	-18.76	6.11	30.98
16 / 1	5.88	20.00	28 / 1	3.51	19.34	-40.36	-21.84	-3.31
20 / 1	4.76	16.67	40 / 1	2.55	14.30	-46.54	-30.37	-14.20
20 / 1	4.76	16.67	40 / 1	2.55	14.30	-46.54	-30.37	-14.20
25 / 1	3.85	13.79	50 / 1	1.86	10.60	-51.56	-37.34	-23.13
25 / 1	3.85	13.79	50 / 1	1.86	10.60	-51.56	-37.34	-23.13
25 / 1	3.85	13.79	50 / 1	1.86	10.60	-51.56	-37.34	-23.13
25 / 1	3.85	13.79	50 / 1	1.86	10.60	-51.56	-37.34	-23.13
33 / 1	2.94	10.81	100 / 1	1.11	6.39	-62.34	-51.61	-40.88
50 / 1	1.96	7.41	200 / 1	0.57	3.33	-70.85	-62.95	-55.04
50 / 1	1.96	7.41	200 / 1	0.57	3.33	-70.85	-62.95	-55.04
50 / 1	1.96	7.41	200 / 1	0.57	3.33	-70.85	-62.95	-55.04
50 / 1	1.96	7.41	200 / 1	0.57	3.33	-70.85	-62.95	-55.04
50 / 1	1.96	7.41	200 / 1	0.57	3.33	-70.85	-62.95	-55.04
50 / 1	1.96	7.41	200 / 1	0.57	3.33	-70.85	-62.95	-55.04
	137.92	**382.50**		**100.00**	**400.00**			

Race Profile 19 Runners

Race no. 46   19 Runners   4 Places at 1/4 odds

s.p.	s.p win%	s.p place%	nearest fair odds	fair win%	fair place%	win	returns e/w	place
4 / 1	20.00	50.00	6 / 1	14.30	51.43	-28.49	-12.82	2.85
9 / 2	18.18	47.06	13 / 2	13.00	48.04	-28.50	-13.20	2.09
5 / 1	16.67	44.44	15 / 2	11.91	45.03	-28.54	-13.61	1.31
5 / 1	16.67	44.44	15 / 2	11.91	45.03	-28.54	-13.61	1.31
6 / 1	14.29	40.00	9 / 1	10.21	39.95	-28.56	-14.35	-0.14
10 / 1	9.09	28.57	15 / 1	6.13	25.96	-32.58	-20.86	-9.15
12 / 1	7.69	25.00	20 / 1	4.61	20.05	40.12	-29.95	-19.78
12 / 1	7.69	25.00	20 / 1	4.61	20.05	-40.12	-29.95	-19.78
12 / 1	7.69	25.00	20 / 1	4.61	20.05	-40.12	-29.95	-19.78
14 / 1	6.67	22.22	28 / 1	3.64	16.10	-45.46	-36.50	-27.54
16 / 1	5.88	20.00	33 / 1	2.91	13.06	-50.50	-42.61	-34.72
16 / 1	5.88	20.00	33 / 1	2.91	13.06	-50.50	-42.61	-34.72
16 / 1	5.88	20.00	33 / 1	2.91	13.06	-50.50	-42.61	-34.72
20 / 1	4.76	16.67	50 / 1	2.11	9.60	-55.63	-49.01	-42.38
25 / 1	3.85	13.79	66 / 1	1.55	7.09	-59.80	-54.18	-48.57
25 / 1	3.85	13.79	66 / 1	1.55	7.09	-59.80	-54.18	-48.57
50 / 1	1.96	7.41	200 / 1	0.47	2.21	-75.81	-72.96	-70.11
50 / 1	1.96	7.41	200 / 1	0.47	2.21	-75.81	-72.96	-70.11
100 / 1	0.99	3.85	500 / 1	0.20	0.93	-80.04	-77.97	-75.91
	159.65	474.66		100.00	400.00			

Race no. 47   20 Runners 4 Places at 1/4 odds

s.p.	s.p win%	s.p place%	nearest fair odds	fair win%	fair place%	win	returns e/w	place
13 / 8	38.10	71.11	95 / 40	29.64	81.24	-22.19	-3.97	14.25
5 / 1	16.67	44.44	7 / 1	12.79	52.26	-23.24	-2.83	17.59
11 / 2	15.38	42.11	15 / 2	11.81	49.37	-23.26	-3.00	17.25
13 / 2	13.33	38.10	9 / 1	10.23	44.36	-23.28	-3.42	16.45
7 / 1	12.50	36.36	9 / 1	9.58	42.16	-23.36	-3.71	15.93
14 / 1	6.67	22.22	25 / 1	3.91	19.32	-41.42	-27.23	-13.04
14 / 1	6.67	22.22	25 / 1	3.91	19.32	-41.42	-27.23	-13.04
14 / 1	6.67	22.22	25 / 1	3.91	19.32	-41.42	-27.23	-13.04
14 / 1	6.67	22.22	25 / 1	3.91	19.32	-41.42	-27.23	-13.04
16 / 1	5.88	20.00	33 / 1	3.13	15.70	-46.84	-34.17	-21.50
25 / 1	3.85	13.79	60 / 1	1.66	8.56	-56.82	-47.38	-37.94
33 / 1	2.94	10.81	100 / 1	0.99	5.15	-66.43	-59.40	-52.37
33 / 1	2.94	10.81	100 / 1	0.99	5.15	-66.43	-59.40	-52.37
50 / 1	1.96	7.41	200 / 1	0.51	2.68	-74.02	-68.93	-63.84
50 / 1	1.96	7.41	200 / 1	0.51	2.68	-74.02	-68.93	-63.84
50 / 1	1.96	7.41	200 / 1	0.51	2.68	-74.02	-68.93	-63.84
50 / 1	1.96	7.41	200 / 1	0.51	2.68	-74.02	-68.93	-63.84
50 / 1	1.96	7.41	200 / 1	0.51	2.68	-74.02	-68.93	-63.84
50 / 1	1.96	7.41	200 / 1	0.51	2.68	-74.02	-68.93	-63.84
50 / 1	1.96	7.41	200 / 1	0.51	2.68	-74.02	-68.93	-63.84
	151.98	428.28		100.00	400.00			

Race Profile 20 Runners

Race no. 48   20 Runners 4 Places at 1/4 odds

s.p.	s.p win%	s.p place%	nearest fair odds	fair win%	fair place%	returns win	returns e/w	place
5 / 2	28.57	61.54	7 / 2	22.49	70.94	-21.28	-3.00	15.28
3 / 1	25.00	57.14	4 / 1	19.66	66.21	-21.34	-2.73	15.87
5 / 1	16.67	44.44	13 / 2	13.07	51.31	-21.55	-3.05	15.45
17 / 2	10.53	32.00	11 / 1	8.04	35.23	-23.58	-6.74	10.10
12 / 1	7.69	25.00	18 / 1	5.06	23.49	-34.27	-20.15	-6.02
12 / 1	7.69	25.00	18 / 1	5.06	23.49	-34.27	-20.15	-6.02
12 / 1	7.69	25.00	18 / 1	5.06	23.49	-34.27	-20.15	-6.02
16 / 1	5.88	20.00	28 / 1	3.20	15.37	-45.67	-34.41	-23.16
16 / 1	5.88	20.00	28 / 1	3.20	15.37	-45.67	-34.41	-23.16
20 / 1	4.76	16.67	40 / 1	2.32	11.33	-51.30	-41.67	-32.04
25 / 1	3.85	13.79	60 / 1	1.70	8.38	-55.87	-47.56	-39.25
25 / 1	3.85	13.79	60 / 1	1.70	8.38	-55.87	-47.56	-39.25
25 / 1	3.85	13.79	60 / 1	1.70	8.38	-55.87	-47.56	-39.25
25 / 1	3.85	13.79	60 / 1	1.70	8.38	-55.87	-47.56	-39.25
33 / 1	2.94	10.81	100 / 1	1.01	5.04	-65.69	-59.54	-53.39
33 / 1	2.94	10.81	100 / 1	1.01	5.04	-65.69	-59.54	-53.39
33 / 1	2.94	10.81	100 / 1	1.01	5.04	-65.69	-59.54	-53.39
33 / 1	2.94	10.81	100 / 1	1.01	5.04	-65.69	-59.54	-53.39
33 / 1	2.94	10.81	100 / 1	1.01	5.04	-65.69	-59.54	-53.39
33 / 1	2.94	10.81	100 / 1	1.01	5.04	-65.69	-59.54	-53.39
	153.40	446.83		100.00	400.00			

Race no. 49   21 Runners   4 Places at 1/4 odds

s.p.	s.p win%	s.p place%	nearest fair odds	fair win%	fair place%	win	returns e/w	place
6 / 4	40.00	72.73	85 / 40	32.20	85.07	-19.51	-1.27	16.97
100 /30	23.08	54.55	9 / 2	18.23	67.54	-20.99	1.42	23.82
13 / 2	13.33	38.10	17 / 2	10.51	47.45	-21.18	1.69	24.56
8 / 1	11.11	33.33	11 / 1	8.61	40.66	-22.55	-0.29	21.97
10 / 1	9.09	28.57	14 / 1	6.76	33.30	-25.60	-4.52	16.56
12 / 1	7.69	25.00	18 / 1	5.08	25.93	-33.92	-15.10	3.72
12 / 1	7.69	25.00	18 / 1	5.08	25.93	-33.92	-15.10	3.72
20 / 1	4.76	16.67	40 / 1	2.33	12.55	-51.04	-37.88	-24.71
20 / 1	4.76	16.67	40 / 1	2.33	12.55	-51.04	-37.88	-24.71
33 / 1	2.94	10.81	100 / 1	1.01	5.59	-65.51	-56.90	-48.28
33 / 1	2.94	10.81	100 / 1	1.01	5.59	-65.51	-56.90	-48.28
33 / 1	2.94	10.81	100 / 1	1.01	5.59	-65.51	-56.90	-48.28
33 / 1	2.94	10.81	100 / 1	1.01	5.59	-65.51	-56.90	-48.28
33 / 1	2.94	10.81	100 / 1	1.01	5.59	-65.51	-56.90	-48.28
40 / 1	2.44	9.09	150 / 1	0.65	3.61	-73.31	-66.79	-60.27
50 / 1	1.96	7.41	200 / 1	0.52	2.91	-73.31	-67.01	-60.72
50 / 1	1.96	7.41	200 / 1	0.52	2.91	-73.31	-67.01	-60.72
50 / 1	1.96	7.41	200 / 1	0.52	2.91	-73.31	-67.01	-60.72
50 / 1	1.96	7.41	200 / 1	0.52	2.91	-73.31	-67.01	-60.72
50 / 1	1.96	7.41	200 / 1	0.52	2.91	-73.31	-67.01	-60.72
50 / 1	1.96	7.41	200 / 1	0.52	2.91	-73.31	-67.01	-60.72
	150.43	**418.20**		**100.00**	**400.00**			

Race Profile 21 Runners

Race no. 50   21 Runners   4 Places at 1/4 odds

s.p.	s.p win%	s.p place%	nearest fair odds	fair win%	fair place%	win	returns e/w	place
9 / 2	18.18	47.06	5 / 1	17.40	57.22	-4.27	8.66	21.59
9 / 1	10.00	30.77	10 / 1	9.25	35.89	-7.55	4.55	16.65
10 / 1	9.09	28.57	11 / 1	8.21	32.50	-9.73	2.01	13.76
10 / 1	9.09	28.57	11 / 1	8.21	32.50	-9.73	2.01	13.76
10 / 1	9.09	28.57	11 / 1	8.21	32.50	-9.73	2.01	13.76
12 / 1	7.69	25.00	15 / 1	6.17	25.37	-19.83	-9.17	1.49
14 / 1	6.67	22.22	20 / 1	4.87	20.50	-26.98	-17.36	-7.74
14 / 1	6.67	22.22	20 / 1	4.87	20.50	-26.98	-17.36	-7.74
16 / 1	5.88	20.00	25 / 1	3.90	16.70	-33.73	-25.12	-16.50
16 / 1	5.88	20.00	25 / 1	3.90	16.70	-33.73	-25.12	-16.50
16 / 1	5.88	20.00	25 / 1	3.90	16.70	-33.73	-25.12	-16.50
20 / 1	4.76	16.67	35 / 1	2.83	12.34	-40.60	-33.28	-25.95
20 / 1	4.76	16.67	35 / 1	2.83	12.34	-40.60	-33.28	-25.95
20 / 1	4.76	16.67	35 / 1	2.83	12.34	-40.60	-33.28	-25.95
20 / 1	4.76	16.67	35 / 1	2.83	12.34	-40.60	-33.28	-25.95
20 / 1	4.76	16.67	35 / 1	2.83	12.34	-40.60	-33.28	-25.95
25 / 1	3.85	13.79	50 / 1	2.07	9.15	-46.18	-39.93	-33.68
33 / 1	2.94	10.81	80 / 1	1.23	5.51	-58.16	-53.58	-49.00
33 / 1	2.94	10.81	80 / 1	1.23	5.51	-58.16	-53.58	-49.00
33 / 1	2.94	10.81	80 / 1	1.23	5.51	-58.16	-53.58	-49.00
33 / 1	2.94	10.81	80 / 1	1.23	5.51	-58.16	-53.58	-49.00
	133.55	433.36		100.00	400.00			

Race no. 51   22 Runners   4 Places at 1/4 odds

s.p.	s.p win%	s.p place%	nearest fair odds	fair win%	fair place%	win	returns e/w	place
2 / 1	33.33	66.67	3 / 1	25.33	75.15	-24.02	-5.65	12.72
3 / 1	25.00	57.14	9 / 2	18.88	65.02	-24.47	-5.34	13.78
7 / 1	12.50	36.36	10 / 1	9.40	40.28	-24.78	-7.00	10.77
17 / 2	10.53	32.00	12 / 1	7.72	34.29	-26.61	-9.73	7.15
17 / 2	10.53	32.00	12 / 1	7.72	34.29	-26.61	-9.73	7.15
12 / 1	7.69	25.00	20 / 1	4.86	22.82	-36.88	-22.80	-8.73
14 / 1	6.67	22.22	25 / 1	3.83	18.36	-42.51	-29.94	-17.38
14 / 1	6.67	22.22	25 / 1	3.83	18.36	-42.51	-29.94	-17.38
16 / 1	5.88	20.00	33 / 1	3.07	14.91	-47.82	-36.64	-25.46
20 / 1	4.76	16.67	40 / 1	2.23	10.98	-53.23	-43.67	-34.11
20 / 1	4.76	16.67	40 / 1	2.23	10.98	-53.23	-43.67	-34.11
20 / 1	4.76	16.67	40 / 1	2.23	10.98	-53.23	-43.67	-34.11
25 / 1	3.85	13.79	60 / 1	1.63	8.12	-57.62	-49.37	-41.12
25 / 1	3.85	13.79	60 / 1	1.63	8.12	-57.62	-49.37	-41.12
33 / 1	2.94	10.81	100 / 1	0.97	4.88	-67.06	-60.95	-54.84
33 / 1	2.94	10.81	100 / 1	0.97	4.88	-67.06	-60.95	-54.84
33 / 1	2.94	10.81	100 / 1	0.97	4.88	-67.06	-60.95	-54.84
50 / 1	1.96	7.41	200 / 1	0.50	2.54	-74.50	-70.11	-65.72
50 / 1	1.96	7.41	200 / 1	0.50	2.54	-74.50	-70.11	-65.72
50 / 1	1.96	7.41	200 / 1	0.50	2.54	-74.50	-70.11	-65.72
50 / 1	1.96	7.41	200 / 1	0.50	2.54	-74.50	-70.11	-65.72
50 / 1	1.96	7.41	200 / 1	0.50	2.54	-74.50	-70.11	-65.72
	159.40	460.67		100.00	400.00			

Race Profile 22 Runners

Race no. 52   22 Runners   4 Places at 1/4 odds

s.p.	s.p win%	s.p place%	nearest fair odds	fair win%	fair place%	win	returns e/w	place
7 / 2	22.22	53.33	4 / 1	19.68	62.74	-11.45	3.09	17.64
7 / 1	12.50	36.36	8 / 1	11.04	42.27	-11.66	2.29	16.24
8 / 1	11.11	33.33	9 / 1	9.65	38.01	-13.11	0.46	14.02
9 / 1	10.00	30.77	11 / 1	8.55	34.40	-14.51	-1.36	11.80
10 / 1	9.09	28.57	12 / 1	7.59	31.11	-16.53	-3.83	8.87
11 / 1	8.33	26.67	13 / 1	6.90	28.66	-17.18	-4.85	7.49
12 / 1	7.69	25.00	16 / 1	5.70	24.22	-25.87	-14.50	-3.12
14 / 1	6.67	22.22	22 / 1	4.50	19.54	-32.48	-22.28	-12.08
20 / 1	4.76	16.67	35 / 1	2.62	11.73	-45.07	-37.34	-29.61
20 / 1	4.76	16.67	35 / 1	2.62	11.73	-45.07	-37.34	-29.61
20 / 1	4.76	16.67	35 / 1	2.62	11.73	-45.07	-37.34	-29.61
20 / 1	4.76	16.67	35 / 1	2.62	11.73	-45.07	-37.34	-29.61
20 / 1	4.76	16.67	35 / 1	2.62	11.73	-45.07	-37.34	-29.61
20 / 1	4.76	16.67	35 / 1	2.62	11.73	-45.07	-37.34	-29.61
20 / 1	4.76	16.67	35 / 1	2.62	11.73	-45.07	-37.34	-29.61
25 / 1	3.85	13.79	50 / 1	1.91	8.69	-50.23	-43.62	-37.01
25 / 1	3.85	13.79	50 / 1	1.91	8.69	-50.23	-43.62	-37.01
33 / 1	2.94	10.81	80 / 1	1.14	5.23	-61.31	-56.46	-51.61
33 / 1	2.94	10.81	80 / 1	1.14	5.23	-61.31	-56.46	-51.61
33 / 1	2.94	10.81	80 / 1	1.14	5.23	-61.31	-56.46	-51.61
50 / 1	1.96	7.41	150 / 1	0.59	2.72	-70.05	-66.64	-63.23
100 / 1	0.99	3.85	400 / 1	0.24	1.14	-75.29	-72.81	-70.33
	140.42	444.20		100.00	400.00			

Race no. 53 23 Runners 4 Places at 1/4 odds

s.p.	s.p win%	s.p place%	nearest fair odds	fair win%	fair place%	win	returns e/w	place
2 / 1	33.33	66.67	100 / 30	23.15	70.61	-30.56	-12.33	5.91
9 / 2	18.18	47.06	7 / 1	12.52	48.43	-31.12	-14.10	2.92
5 / 1	16.67	44.44	15 / 2	11.47	45.39	-31.15	-14.51	2.14
6 / 1	14.29	40.00	9 / 1	9.83	40.27	-31.18	-15.25	0.69
8 / 1	11.11	33.33	12 / 1	7.51	32.26	-32.38	-17.80	-3.21
9 / 1	10.00	30.77	14 / 1	6.65	29.05	-33.47	-19.52	-5.57
10 / 1	9.09	28.57	16 / 1	5.90	26.16	-35.05	-21.74	-8.43
10 / 1	9.09	28.57	16 / 1	5.90	26.16	-35.05	-21.74	-8.43
14 / 1	6.67	22.22	28 / 1	3.50	16.22	-47.46	-37.23	-27.00
20 / 1	4.76	16.67	50 / 1	2.04	9.67	-57.26	-49.62	-41.98
33 / 1	2.94	10.81	125 / 1	0.89	4.29	-69.89	-65.11	-60.33
33 / 1	2.94	10.81	125 / 1	0.89	4.29	-69.89	-65.11	-60.33
33 / 1	2.94	10.81	125 / 1	0.89	4.29	-69.89	-65.11	-60.33
33 / 1	2.94	10.81	125 / 1	0.89	4.29	-69.89	-65.11	-60.33
33 / 1	2.94	10.81	125 / 1	0.89	4.29	-69.89	-65.11	-60.33
33 / 1	2.94	10.81	125 / 1	0.89	4.29	-69.89	-65.11	-60.33
33 / 1	2.94	10.81	125 / 1	0.89	4.29	-69.89	-65.11	-60.33
33 / 1	2.94	10.81	125 / 1	0.89	4.29	-69.89	-65.11	-60.33
33 / 1	2.94	10.81	125 / 1	0.89	4.29	-69.89	-65.11	-60.33
33 / 1	2.94	10.81	125 / 1	0.89	4.29	-69.89	-65.11	-60.33
33 / 1	2.94	10.81	125 / 1	0.89	4.29	-69.89	-65.11	-60.33
33 / 1	2.94	10.81	125 / 1	0.89	4.29	-69.89	-65.11	-60.33
33 / 1	2.94	10.81	125 / 1	0.89	4.29	-69.89	-65.11	-60.33
	171.42	498.84		100.00	400.00			

Race Profile 23 Runners

Race no. 54   23 Runners 4 Places at 1/4 odds

s.p.	s.p win%	s.p place%	nearest fair odds	fair win%	fair place%	win	returns e/w	place
8 / 1	11.11	33.33	10 / 1	9.29	34.91	-16.39	-5.84	4.72
8 / 1	11.11	33.33	10 / 1	9.29	34.91	-16.39	-5.84	4.72
8 / 1	11.11	33.33	10 / 1	9.29	34.91	-16.39	-5.84	4.72
10 / 1	9.09	28.57	13 / 1	7.30	28.47	-19.68	-10.02	-0.37
10 / 1	9.09	28.57	13 / 1	7.30	28.47	-19.68	-10.02	-0.37
11 / 1	8.33	26.67	14 / 1	6.64	26.20	20.31	-11.02	-1.74
12 / 1	7.69	25.00	18 / 1	5.49	22.10	-28.67	-20.13	-11.60
12 / 1	7.69	25.00	18 / 1	5.49	22.10	-28.67	-20.13	-11.60
14 / 1	6.67	22.22	22 / 1	4.33	17.80	-35.03	-27.47	-19.90
14 / 1	6.67	22.22	22 / 1	4.33	17.80	-35.03	-27.47	-19.90
16 / 1	5.88	20.00	28 / 1	3.47	14.46	-41.04	-34.36	-27.68
16 / 1	5.88	20.00	28 / 1	3.47	14.46	-41.04	-34.36	-27.68
20 / 1	4.76	16.67	40 / 1	2.52	10.66	-47.15	-41.59	-36.03
20 / 1	4.76	16.67	40 / 1	2.52	10.66	-47.15	-41.59	-36.03
20 / 1	4.76	16.67	40 / 1	2.52	10.66	-47.15	-41.59	-36.03
20 / 1	4.76	16.67	40 / 1	2.52	10.66	-47.15	-41.59	-36.03
20 / 1	4.76	16.67	40 / 1	2.52	10.66	-47.15	-41.59	-36.03
20 / 1	4.76	16.67	40 / 1	2.52	10.66	-47.15	-41.59	-36.03
25 / 1	3.85	13.79	50 / 1	1.84	7.89	-52.11	-47.45	-42.80
25 / 1	3.85	13.79	50 / 1	1.84	7.89	-52.11	-47.45	-42.80
25 / 1	3.85	13.79	50 / 1	1.84	7.89	-52.11	-47.45	-42.80
25 / 1	3.85	13.79	50 / 1	1.84	7.89	-52.11	-47.45	-42.80
25 / 1	3.85	13.79	50 / 1	1.84	7.89	-52.11	-47.45	-42.80
	148.13	487.22		100.00	400.00			

Race no. 55   24 Runners   4 Places at 1/4 odds

s.p.	s.p win%	s.p place%	nearest fair odds	fair win%	fair place%	win	returns e/w	place
6 / 4	40.00	72.73	7 / 4	35.96	88.29	-10.11	5.64	21.40
5 / 1	16.67	44.44	6 / 1	14.68	60.75	-11.93	12.38	36.70
8 / 1	11.11	33.33	9 / 1	9.61	45.37	-13.50	11.30	36.11
8 / 1	11.11	33.33	9 / 1	9.61	45.37	13.50	11.30	36.11
10 / 1	9.09	28.57	12 / 1	7.55	37.46	-16.91	7.10	31.10
12 / 1	7.69	25.00	16 / 1	5.68	29.36	-26.20	-4.39	17.42
14 / 1	6.67	22.22	22 / 1	4.48	23.77	-32.78	-12.92	6.95
16 / 1	5.88	20.00	28 / 1	3.59	19.38	-39.00	-21.05	-3.10
25 / 1	3.85	13.79	50 / 1	1.91	10.63	-50.46	-36.68	-22.91
33 / 1	2.94	10.81	80 / 1	1.13	6.41	-61.49	-51.09	-40.69
33 / 1	2.94	10.81	80 / 1	1.13	6.41	-61.49	-51.09	-40.69
50 / 1	1.96	7.41	150 / 1	0.58	3.34	-70.19	-62.54	-54.89
50 / 1	1.96	7.41	150 / 1	0.58	3.34	-70.19	-62.54	-54.89
50 / 1	1.96	7.41	150 / 1	0.58	3.34	-70.19	-62.54	-54.89
66 / 1	1.49	5.71	250 / 1	0.40	2.32	-72.87	-66.12	-59.37
66 / 1	1.49	5.71	250 / 1	0.40	2.32	-72.87	-66.12	-59.37
66 / 1	1.49	5.71	250 / 1	0.40	2.32	-72.87	-66.12	-59.37
100 / 1	0.99	3.85	400 / 1	0.24	1.40	-75.40	-69.49	-63.58
100 / 1	0.99	3.85	400 / 1	0.24	1.40	-75.40	-69.49	-63.58
100 / 1	0.99	3.85	400 / 1	0.24	1.40	-75.40	-69.49	-63.58
100 / 1	0.99	3.85	400 / 1	0.24	1.40	-75.40	-69.49	-63.58
100 / 1	0.99	3.85	400 / 1	0.24	1.40	-75.40	-69.49	-63.58
100 / 1	0.99	3.85	400 / 1	0.24	1.40	-75.40	-69.49	-63.58
100 / 1	0.99	3.85	400 / 1	0.24	1.40	-75.40	-69.49	-63.58
	135.24	381.33		100.00	400.00			

Race Profile 25 Runners

Race no. 56   25 Runners   4 Places at 1/4 odds

s.p. s.p.	s.p win%	nearest place%	fair fair odds	fair win%	returns place%	win	e/w	place
13 / 2	13.33	38.10	7 / 1	12.40	43.65	-7.02	3.78	14.58
11 / 1	8.33	26.67	13 / 1	7.26	28.16	-12.92	-3.65	5.61
12 / 1	7.69	25.00	16 / 1	6.00	23.80	-22.05	-13.42	-4.79
12 / 1	7.69	25.00	16 / 1	6.00	23.80	-22.05	-13.42	-4.79
12 / 1	7.69	25.00	16 / 1	6.00	23.80	-22.05	-13.42	-4.79
12 / 1	7.69	25.00	16 / 1	6.00	23.80	-22.05	-13.42	-4.79
12 / 1	7.69	25.00	16 / 1	6.00	23.80	-22.05	-13.42	-4.79
14 / 1	6.67	22.22	20 / 1	4.73	19.21	-29.00	-21.28	-13.56
14 / 1	6.67	22.22	20 / 1	4.73	19.21	-29.00	-21.28	-13.56
14 / 1	6.67	22.22	20 / 1	4.73	19.21	-29.00	-21.28	-13.56
16 / 1	5.88	20.00	25 / 1	3.79	15.63	-35.57	-28.71	-21.84
16 / 1	5.88	20.00	25 / 1	3.79	15.63	-35.57	-28.71	-21.84
16 / 1	5.88	20.00	25 / 1	3.79	15.63	-35.57	-28.71	-21.84
16 / 1	5.88	20.00	25 / 1	3.79	15.63	-35.57	-28.71	-21.84
20 / 1	4.76	16.67	35 / 1	2.75	11.54	-42.25	-36.50	-30.75
20 / 1	4.76	16.67	35 / 1	2.75	11.54	-42.25	-36.50	-30.75
20 / 1	4.76	16.67	35 / 1	2.75	11.54	-42.25	-36.50	-30.75
20 / 1	4.76	16.67	35 / 1	2.75	11.54	-42.25	-36.50	-30.75
25 / 1	3.85	13.79	50 / 1	2.01	8.55	-47.67	-42.84	-38.01
25 / 1	3.85	13.79	50 / 1	2.01	8.55	-47.67	-42.84	-38.01
33 / 1	2.94	10.81	80 / 1	1.20	5.15	-59.32	-55.84	-52.37
33 / 1	2.94	10.81	80 / 1	1.20	5.15	-59.32	-55.84	-52.37
33 / 1	2.94	10.81	80 / 1	1.20	5.15	-59.32	-55.84	-52.37
33 / 1	2.94	10.81	80 / 1	1.20	5.15	-59.32	-55.84	-52.37
33 / 1	2.94	10.81	80 / 1	1.20	5.15	-59.32	-55.84	-52.37
	145.10	**484.74**		**100.00**	**400.00**			

Race no. 57   26 Runners   4 Places at 1/4 odds

s.p.	s.p win%	s.p place%	nearest fair odds	fair win%	fair place%	win	returns e/w	place
10 / 1	9.09	28.57	10 / 1	8.99	34.12	-1.11	9.16	19.43
10 / 1	9.09	28.57	10 / 1	8.99	34.12	-1.11	9.16	19.43
10 / 1	9.09	28.57	10 / 1	8.99	34.12	-1.11	9.16	19.43
11 / 1	8.33	26.67	11 / 1	8.18	31.51	-1.89	8.14	18.16
12 / 1	7.69	25.00	14 / 1	6.76	26.72	-12.18	-2.64	6.89
12 / 1	7.69	25.00	14 / 1	6.76	26.72	-12.18	-2.64	6.89
12 / 1	7.69	25.00	14 / 1	6.76	26.72	-12.18	-2.64	6.89
12 / 1	7.69	25.00	14 / 1	6.76	26.72	-12.18	-2.64	6.89
14 / 1	6.67	22.22	18 / 1	5.33	21.64	-20.01	-11.32	-2.63
16 / 1	5.88	20.00	22 / 1	4.27	17.65	-27.41	-19.58	-11.76
16 / 1	5.88	20.00	22 / 1	4.27	17.65	-27.41	-19.58	-11.76
20 / 1	4.76	16.67	33 / 1	3.10	13.06	-34.93	-28.28	-21.62
20 / 1	4.76	16.67	33 / 1	3.10	13.06	-34.93	-28.28	-21.62
20 / 1	4.76	16.67	33 / 1	3.10	13.06	-34.93	-28.28	-21.62
20 / 1	4.76	16.67	33 / 1	3.10	13.06	-34.93	-28.28	-21.62
25 / 1	3.85	13.79	40 / 1	2.27	9.69	-41.04	-35.38	-29.73
25 / 1	3.85	13.79	40 / 1	2.27	9.69	-41.04	-35.38	-29.73
33 / 1	2.94	10.81	80 / 1	1.35	5.85	-54.17	-50.03	-45.90
33 / 1	2.94	10.81	80 / 1	1.35	5.85	-54.17	-50.03	-45.90
33 / 1	2.94	10.81	80 / 1	1.35	5.85	-54.17	-50.03	-45.90
50 / 1	1.96	7.41	150 / 1	0.70	3.05	-64.52	-61.68	-58.83
50 / 1	1.96	7.41	150 / 1	0.70	3.05	-64.52	-61.68	-58.83
50 / 1	1.96	7.41	150 / 1	0.70	3.05	-64.52	-61.68	-58.83
66 / 1	1.49	5.71	200 / 1	0.48	2.12	-67.72	-65.31	-62.91
100 / 1	0.99	3.85	400 / 1	0.29	1.28	-70.73	-68.74	-66.75
200 / 1	0.50	1.96	1000 / 1	0.13	0.57	-74.32	-72.75	-71.18
	129.23	435.03		100.00	400.00			

22:Useful Addresses

Once you start winning regularly, or even before you do, you might consider occasionally donating a small percentage of any winnings to -

The Injured Jockeys' Fund
PO BOX 9 Newmarket,
SUFFOLK CB8 7SH
Tel. 01638 662 246
Which aims to help jockeys who have been forced by injury to give up riding, by way of rehabilitation, retraining, and general welfare.

And also to -

The International League For The Protection Of Horses
Anne Colvin House,
Snetterton,
NORFOLK NR16 2LR
Tel 01953 498 682
Which is concerned with the welfare of horses of all kinds including thoroughbreds both in the U.K. and internationally.

Both these organisations are represented at most major race meetings.

Those thinking of going racing on a regular basis might wish to contact -

The Racegoers' Club,
Winkfield Road,
Ascot,
BERKS SL5 7HX
Tel 01344 625912
which among other things organises members evenings, stable visits, discounts and the like.

While for details of Racing Clubs covering specific areas contact -

The Federation Of British Racing Clubs
4 Boseley Crescent
Wallingford
OXON

23:Further Reading

All the following books can be recommended to readers wanting more information on the topics in question. While some of these titles may have been reprinted since the dates given here, it's more likely that many of them will have to be sought out - either in second-hand bookshops or in a well stocked public library.

**Better Betting With A Decent Feller
Bookmakers, Betting And The British
Working Class 1750 - 1990**
Carl Chinn
Harvester Wheatsheaf 1991
Index

A comprehensive history of bookmaking, written by a social historian from a bookmaking family. The book covers the history of both on and off-course bookmaking between 1750 and 1990 in painstaking detail,

is fully documented with references and sources, and can be thoroughly recommended to anyone looking for a more serious treatment of the subject.

The Art Of Legging
Charles Sidney
Maxline International 1976
Illustrated Index

Written by a former on-course bookmaker, the first half of the book comprises a history of bookmaking from the early days, and includes numerous first-hand anecdotes concerning bookmaking characters of the 1930's, 40's, and 50's. The second half meanwhile, is concerned with the mathematics of bookmaking and settling, and gives a good idea of the fractional methods which were in use before the advent of electronic calculators.

A Licence To Print Money
Jamie Reid
Macmillan 1992 Hbk
Mainstream 1995 Pbk
Index

A highly readable, informative and at times humorous account of bookmakers and backers both past and present, written by a playwright, novelist and journalist who has written for among others "The Guardian", "The Independent" and "Private Eye".

Emperors Of The Turf
Jamie Reid
Macmillan 1989
Illustrated Index

A previous publication by the same author, this is an equally readable and irreverent account of thoroughbred breeders, owners and trainers on both sides of the Atlantic.

High Rollers Of The Turf
Raymond Smith
Sporting Books Publishers Dublin 1992
Illustrated. No Index

Written by an Irish racing journalist, in a similarly readable though less irreverent style to Jamie Reid, this book deals mainly with Irish personalities, and includes extensive interviews with Barney Curley, J.P.McManus, and the late Terry Rogers, among others. The Gay Future Affair, and the careers of both Phil Bull and Alex Bird are also covered.

The Racegoers' Encyclopaedia
John White
Collins Willow 1992
Index. Illustrated throughout both in colour and b/w. Bibliography

Written by a former Magazine Sports Writer of the Year, the backbone of the book consists of descriptions of all 85 racecourses in the British Isles, written up in a personalised style which offers a refreshing change from the standardised approach of most racecourse directories. While interspersed with these are numerous entries, many of them illustrated, covering topics as diverse as racing colours, racecourse slang, and the more exotic types of speciality bet. A well-researched and well-produced book with something of interest to offer all racegoers, whether actual or aspiring.

Scarne's New Complete Guide To Gambling
John Scarne
1974 Simon and Schuster (New York)
Illustrated with Index

Anyone familiar with such standard works as "Scarne On Cards", and "Scarne On Dice", won't be disappointed with this book in which the late author provides a comprehensive account of betting and gambling in all its forms; from horse-racing and casinos around the world to national lotteries, fruit machines, and fairground games. 871 pages of well presented and thoroughly researched information and practical advice for anyone with an interest in any form of gambling; and still streets ahead of anything which has appeared since.

The Guinness Guide To Steeplechasing
Gerry Cranham, John Oaksey, and Richard Pitman
Guinness Superlatives 1979
Large Format, Illustrated Throughout, Index

This book features numerous photographs of National Hunt Racing both in colour and black-and-white by Gerry Cranham, and chapters on the history of steeplechasing and the (then) contemporary scene by John (Lord) Oaksey. But what also makes it especially useful, are chapters on the technical side of steeplechasing written by Richard Pitman, covering such topics as horses, jockeys, training, and jumping.

While for reference only -

The Royal Commission On Gambling 1978
a.k.a. The Rothschild Report
2 vols H.M.S.O 1978

Volume1 includes chapters on the Finance and Organisation of Horseracing, Bookmakers' profit margins, and the possible effect of the dominance of the (then) Big Three; and it clearly sets out and effectively lays to rest many of the arguments which are still generating so much hot air more than 20 years later. So it would still make useful reading for anyone with an interest in racing politics.

Volume 2 includes a detailed account of the likely returns from various forms of gambling, including an explanation of bookmakers' odds and the overround, and the likely returns to backers both on and off-course, in theory and in practice.

Information about Phil Bull and Timeform can be found in -

Bull The Biography
Howard Wright
Portway Press 1995
Illustrated Index

While information about Alex Bird can be found in -

Alex Bird The Life And Secrets Of A Professional Punter
Alex Bird with Terry Manners
Macdonald Queen Anne Press 1985
Illustrated Index

Unfortunately neither book is very helpful in terms of betting advice, if only because they contradict one another more than once. What is clear from both books however, is that both Bird and Bull often seemed to display all the characteristic charm of self-made-men who were determined not to let anyone forget the fact.

Calling The Horses
A Racing Autobiography
Peter O'Sullevan
Stanley Paul 1989
Illustrated Index

By way of contrast, Sir Peter O'Sullevan's tendency to self-effacement and understatement generally, are among the things that make his autobiography such a pleasure to read, and a richly deserved best-seller. The book combines an account of the author's life in racing, told with a dry wit and replete with numerous anecdotes, with more measured discussions both of the controversies of the day, and of more perennial topics in racing, many of which touch on the author's long-term concern for animal welfare.

While finally, again for reference purposes - anyone whose appetite for incomprehensible mathematics has been whetted by the equations in second part of the "Art of Legging", could do worse than consult -

The Theory Of Gambling & Statistical Logic
Richard A.Epstein
Academic Press. New York and London 1967
Index

This book covers every type of speculative activity from casino games to the stock market and betting on the horses, from a strictly mathematical perspective. And it includes what appears to be a complete "explanation" of the **Kelly System**.

Biographical Details

Robert Lynd
Born in Belfast, Robert Lynd (1879-1949) was a literary critic, a Fleet Street journalist, and also a racing-man for over 40 years. His lightness of touch was most evident in the weekly columns he wrote for the "New Statesman" under the pen-name of "YY", many of which also regularly appeared in book form; and it's from the following two of these, that the extracts, all of which can be found listed in the index, have been taken. One or two words and phrases have been altered slightly from the original, in order to better preserve the overall sense.

The Pleasures Of Ignorance
Grant Richards London 1921

The Sporting Life
Grant Richards London 1922

A.B. "Banjo" Paterson
Andrew Barton Paterson (1864-1941), who wrote "The Riders in The Stand" on page 107, was an Australian solicitor, turned war-correspondent and journalist. He is now probably best remembered for the lyrics of "Waltzing Matilda", his treatment of one of a number of traditional "bush ballads" which he regularly contributed to a Sydney newspaper, "The Bulletin". "The Riders in the Stand" first appeared in book form in **Saltbush Bill, J.P., and Other Verses,** in 1917. The pen-name "Banjo" by the way, was from a racehorse once owned by his father.

Rock Roi 1967 ch.c.
The real irony in all of this, (see page i) is that amidst much regret, the unfortunate Rock Roi did subsequently lose the race on a technicality, but with all concerned being totally exonerated and fined the statutory minimum. All of which took place long after I'd already drawn a moral from the situation and both Bert and myself had collected. Rock Roi went on to win the Goodwood and Doncaster Cups, plus the John Porter and the Prix Du Cadran the following year, only to again be disqualified in what turned out to be his final race, the '72 running of the Ascot Gold Cup; this time for interfering with the second, Erimo Hawk. After which he was finally retired to stud in France.

Index

Entries in **bold type** refer either to technical terms, or words with a specific meaning in the context of form and betting - and to where they're defined in the text.

Index